EMT EXAM
POWER PRACTICE

LEARNINGEXPRESS®

NEW YORK

Library of Congress Cataloging-in-Publication Data On File

Printed in the United States of America

ISBN 978-1-61103-028-0

For more information or to place an order, contact LearningExpress at:
    80 Broad Street
    4th Floor
    New York, NY 10004

CONTENTS

CONTRIBUTORS — v

CHAPTER 1 The EMT Exam — 1

CHAPTER 2 The LearningExpress Test Preparation System — 5

CHAPTER 3 EMT Practice Exam 1 — 23

CHAPTER 4 EMT Practice Exam 2 — 53

CHAPTER 5 EMT Practice Exam 3 — 79

CHAPTER 6 EMT Practice Exam 4 — 109

CHAPTER 7 EMT Practice Exam 5 — 137

CHAPTER 8 EMT Practice Exam 6 — 159

CHAPTER 9 EMT Practice Exam 7 — 179

CHAPTER 10 EMT Practice Exam 8 — 201

CHAPTER 11 EMT Practice Exam 9 — 223

CHAPTER 12 EMT Practice Exam 10 — 245

CONTENTS

CHAPTER 13   EMT Practical Skills Exam Resources   275

CHAPTER 14   State Certification Requirements   291

ADDITIONAL ONLINE PRACTICE   295

CONTRIBUTORS

Mike Clumpner is a co-founder and senior partner with Nimshi International, a Charlotte, North Carolina consulting firm. Mike is also a full-time fire captain and paramedic for the Charlotte Fire Department where he is currently assigned to the Special Operations Division. Mike is a decorated 18-year veteran of the fire service, with 16 years of experience as a firefighter and paramedic serving on busy inner-city fire companies. He is a Federal Emergency Management Agency (FEMA) Medical Task Force Leader assigned to North Carolina Urban Search and Rescue Task Force 3 (NCTF-3) and has worked since 2004 as a helicopter flight paramedic with Regional One Air Medical Service in Spartanburg, South Carolina. Mike is also clinical faculty at the University of Maryland at Baltimore County where he teaches a variety of classes and assists with program development and is also a sworn civilian law enforcement officer with a large metropolitan law enforcement agency where he is currently assigned to the Special Response Team as a SWAT officer and tactical paramedic.

Clumpner has three undergraduate degrees, an MBA, and is now completing a PhD in homeland security policy. He has published numerous articles in peer-reviewed journals and has authored and co-authored multiple books on a variety of subjects. Clumpner has lectured extensively throughout North America, Latin America, Europe, Australia, New Zealand, and the Caribbean presenting at more than 250 major congresses and symposiums on a variety of subjects.

Meredith C. White, CCEMT-P, EMT-P, CCT has been working in health care and EMS for 12 years, including working as a helicopter flight paramedic for the last four years. She obtained her paramedic certificate in 1998 and received her critical care training at the Medical College of Georgia in Augusta, Georgia. In addition to her EMS career, she has also been employed with Southeastern Tissue Alliance as a tissue procurement technician and is also a certified cardiographic technician (CCT) with a nuclear medicine lab in Atlanta, Georgia. White lives in New Orleans, Louisiana and is employed as a consultant at Nimshi International, where she is actively involved in the development of various critical care education programs.

Malcolm D. Devine, NREMT-Paramedic worked as a paramedic in the New York City 911 system following graduation from the State University of New York (SUNY) at Stony Brook EMT-Paramedic Program. Devine currently holds the position of clinical coordinator–paramedic instructor at SUNY Stony Brook and is an active paramedic with the Setauket fire district in Setauket, New York.

Gregory R. Sharpe MPA, Paramedic is a Battalion Chief with the Charlotte, North Carolina Fire Department. He has been with the fire department for 18 years and has been a paramedic for 17 of those years. He began his EMS career as a volunteer for the St. Michael's College Fire and Rescue Department in February 1986. Sharpe has served with various law enforcement agencies as a law enforcement officer, for the Mecklenburg EMS Agency as a Paramedic Crew Chief, and has been an EMS Instructor for the past 14 years. He earned his MPA from the University of North Carolina at Charlotte in December 2009.

1 ▶ THE EMT EXAM

CHAPTER SUMMARY

This chapter tells you how to become certified as an Emergency Medical Technician (EMT). It outlines the certification requirements of the National Registry of Emergency Medical Technicians and tells you how to use this book to study for the written exam.

The National Registry of Emergency Medical Technicians (NREMT) was established in 1970 in response to a suggestion of the U.S. Committee on Highway Safety. Today, the NREMT is an independent, not-for-profit agency that certifies that EMTs have the knowledge and skills to do their job—to save lives and preserve health. By setting uniform national standards for training, testing, and continuing education, the NREMT helps ensure patient safety throughout the United States.

In some states, the NREMT certification process is the only licensure process for EMTs. Other states have their own testing procedures. (A list of specific certification requirements for all 50 states, Washington, D.C., Puerto Rico, and the U.S. Virgin Islands appears in Chapter 14.) Nearly all states and U.S. territories base their curriculums and tests on the National EMS Educational Standards. The NREMT exam uses the same curriculum to guide the construction of exam questions. Therefore, whether you will be taking a state test or the NREMT test, you will be learning and studying similar material. This book is based on the NREMT cognitive examination.

Minimum Requirements

To apply for national registration as an EMT with the NREMT, you must:

- be at least 18 years old.
- have successfully completed a state-approved National Standard EMT training program within the last two years.
- provide documentation of 24 hours of state-approved EMT continuing education within the past two years if you currently hold a valid EMT certification.
- obtain official documentation of your current state EMT certification if your state does not require national EMT registration.
- have successfully completed all sections of a state-approved EMT practical exam within the past 12 months. This exam must meet or exceed all the criteria established by the National Registry.
- complete the felony statement on the application and submit the required documentation.
- submit current cardiopulmonary resuscitation (CPR) credentials from either the American Heart Association or the American Red Cross.
- submit an acceptable application attesting to the satisfaction of the previous requirements.
- send a $70 nonrefundable/nontransferable application fee (money order only). All fees must be made payable to the National Registry of Emergency Medical Technicians and submitted with the application to cover processing of the application.
- successfully complete the National Registry EMT cognitive and state-approved psychomotor examinations.

How to Apply

When you have met all the requirements and are ready to take the exam, visit the NREMT website at www.nremt.org. From there, you will click on the link "Apply for your NREMT Exam" to create an account, fill out your application, pay your $70 fee, and ensure you are approved to take the exam. After you finish these introductory steps, you will be able to apply for the computerized exam by calling your state testing center.

The EMT Cognitive Exam

The National Registry's EMT cognitive examination ranges from 70 to 120 items, and the maximum time allotted to take the exam is two hours from the time it begins. The exam is administered using a computer adaptive test (CAT). With the CAT method, each question is modified to fit your abilities. For example, if you answer a question correctly, the following question will be somewhat more challenging. If you answer a question incorrectly, the following question will be a bit easier. The more questions you answer correctly, the more likely you are to end the exam early. Once you complete each section of questions, the CAT will reevaluate your ability, and as the exam continues, the program will adapt to match your skill level.

The purpose of the CAT-administered cognitive exam is to find your highest ability level. The exam is pass/fail, and in order to pass, you must meet entry-level competency. Entry-level competency is the NREMT's criteria for an EMT candidate, which includes being able to practice carefully and capably.

The exam consists of five content areas:

CATEGORY	PERCENT OF OVERALL TEST
Airway, Respiration and Ventilations	19.0%
Medical, Obstetrics and Gynecology	29.0%
Cardiology and Resuscitation	18.0%
EMS Operations	14.0%
Trauma	20.0%
TOTAL	**100%**

For more information on the EMT cognitive exam, visit http://www.nremt.org.

The EMT Practical Exam

When you apply for National Registry EMT registration, you will fill out an application that consists of several sections. The application requires verification of your credentials. The verification may be in the form of your program director's electronic signature attesting to competency in the following skills:

1. Patient Assessment/Management—Trauma
2. Patient Assessment/Management—Medical
3. Bag-Valve-Mask Ventilation of an Apneic Adult Patient
4. Oxygen Administration by Non-rebreather Mask
5. Cardiac Arrest Management/AED
6. Spinal Immobilization—Supine Patient
7. Spinal Immobilization—Seated Patient
8. Bleeding Control/Shock Management
9. Long Bone Immobilization
10. Joint Immobilization

The National Registry EMT application also requires proof that you have successfully completed a state-approved practical examination within a 12-month period. At a minimum, the exam must evaluate your performance in the following skills. To pass the practical exam, you must meet or exceed the NREMT's criteria in the following six areas:

- **Station #1:** Patient Assessment/Management—Trauma
- **Station #2:** Patient Assessment/Management—Medical
- **Station #3:** Bag-Valve-Mask Ventilation of an Apneic Adult Patient
- **Station #4:** Oxygen Administration by Non-rebreather Mask
- **Station #5:** Cardiac Arrest Management/AED
- **Station #6:** Spinal Immobilization—Supine Patient
- **Station #7:** Random Skill
  - Spinal Immobilization—Seated Patient
  - Bleeding Control/Shock Management
  - Long Bone Immobilization
  - Joint Immobilization

Chapter 13 contains more detailed information about the NREMT practical exam.

Using This Book to Prepare

The bulk of this book consists of ten practice tests, each containing 120 to 150 questions similar to those on the National Registry's EMT cognitive examination. All practice tests represent content from the NREMT examination.

The first step in using this book to prepare for the EMT cognitive examination is to read Chapter 2, which presents the nine-step LearningExpress Test Preparation System. Chapter 2 introduces essential test-taking strategies that you can practice as you take the exams in this book.

Next, take one complete practice test and score your answers using the answer key. Complete explanations for the answers are included. Even though the EMT cognitive exam is pass/fail, LearningExpress recommends scoring at least a 70% on the practice tests in order to achieve the best results on your final EMT exam.

If you score more than 70% on your first practice exam, congratulations! However, even if you do very well on the practice test, don't become overconfident and simply assume that you'll pass the actual test easily—the items on that test will be different from those on the practice test. You'll still need to do some test preparation. No matter what your initial score, follow the suggestions in the next paragraphs.

If you score less than 70% on your first practice test, don't panic, but do put in some concentrated study time. Begin your studying by determinining your major areas of weakness. For example, perhaps you answered 40 items on the practice test incorrectly, giving you a score of 80, or approximately 67%. Upon rereading the questions you missed, try to determine the content area in which they belong: Airway, Respirations & Ventilations, Medical, Obstetrics and Gynecology, Cardiology and Resuscitation, EMS Operations, or Trauma.

This analysis tells you where you need to concentrate your studying. Try putting in one or two concentrated evenings of study on each area. Review all the material on these topics in the textbook and printed materials from your EMS course. Then take a second practice test and check your total score and content area breakdown again. Chances are that your total will have improved.

In the time leading up to the EMT cognitive exam, use the remaining practice tests to further pinpoint areas of weakness and to find areas to review. For example, suppose that after additional study sessions, you take the third practice test. You now do well on all the questions about circulation *except* the ones that ask you to recognize signs and symptoms of shock. This information tells you which specific pages of your textbook you should review.

Once you have worked on and improved your areas of weakness, use the final days before the test to do some general reviewing. Devote a short period of time each day to reviewing one or two chapters of your textbook. Then use the fourth and tenth practice tests to rehearse free-response testing. Although this method is not included on the official exam, it provides an alternative form of evaluation, and the challenge will help you achieve greater understanding of the concepts.

After reading and studying this book, you'll be well on your way to obtaining certification as an EMT. Good luck as you enter this rewarding and worthwhile career!

THE LEARNINGEXPRESS TEST PREPARATION SYSTEM

CHAPTER SUMMARY

Taking the EMT exam can be tough. It demands a lot of preparation if you want to achieve a top score. Your career in emergency medical services depends on your passing the exam. The LearningExpress Test Preparation System, developed exclusively for LearningExpress by leading test experts, gives you the discipline and attitude you need to be a winner.

First, the bad news: Taking the EMT exam is no picnic, and neither is getting ready for it. Your future career as an EMT depends on passing, but there are all sorts of pitfalls that can keep you from doing your best on this all-important exam. Here are some of the obstacles that can stand in the way of your success:

- being unfamiliar with the format of the exam
- being paralyzed by test anxiety
- leaving your preparation to the last minute
- not preparing at all!
- not knowing vital test-taking skills: how to pace yourself through the exam, how to use the process of elimination, and when to guess
- not being in tip-top mental and physical shape
- arriving late at the test site, working on an empty stomach, or shivering through the exam because the room is cold

What's the common denominator in all these test-taking pitfalls? One thing: *control*. Who's in control, you or the exam?

Now the good news: The LearningExpress Test Preparation System puts *you* in control. In just nine easy-to-follow steps, you will learn everything you need to know to ensure that you are in charge of your preparation and your performance on the exam. Other test takers may let the test get the better of them; other test takers may be unprepared or out of shape, but not you. You will have taken all the steps you need to get a high score on the EMT exam.

Here's how the LearningExpress Test Preparation System works: Nine easy steps lead you through everything you need to know and do to get ready to master your exam. Each of the following steps includes both reading about the step and one or more activities. It's important that you do the activities along with the reading, or you won't get the full benefits of the system. Each step tells you approximately how much time that step will take you to complete.

Step 1. Get Information	50 minutes
Step 2. Conquer Test Anxiety	20 minutes
Step 3. Make a Plan	30 minutes
Step 4. Learn to Manage Your Time	10 minutes
Step 5. Learn to Use the Process of Elimination	20 minutes
Step 6. Know When to Guess	20 minutes
Step 7. Reach Your Peak Performance Zone	10 minutes
Step 8. Get Your Act Together	10 minutes
Step 9. Do It!	10 minutes
Total	**3 hours**

We estimate that working through the entire system will take you approximately three hours, though it's perfectly okay if you work more quickly or slowly than the time estimates assume. If you have a whole afternoon or evening free, you can work through the whole LearningExpress Test Preparation System in one sitting. Otherwise, you can break it up and do just one or two steps a day for the next several days. It's up to you—remember, *you're* in control.

Step 1: Get Information

Time to complete: 50 minutes
Activities: Read Chapter 1, "The EMT Exam" and Chapter 14, "State Certification Requirements"

Knowledge is power. The first step in the LearningExpress Test Preparation System is finding out everything you can about the EMT exam. Once you have your information, the next steps in the LearningExpress Test Preparation System will show you what to do about it.

Part A: Straight Talk about the EMT Exam

Why do you have to take this exam anyway? Simply put, because lives depend on your performance in the field. The EMT cognitive exam is just one part of a whole series of evaluations you have to go through to show that you can be trusted with the health and safety of the people you serve. The cognitive exam attempts to measure your knowledge of your trade. The practical skills exam attempts to measure your ability to apply what you know.

It's important for you to remember that your score on the EMT cognitive exam does not determine how smart you are or even whether you will make a good EMT. There are all kinds of things an exam like this can't test: whether you are likely to frequently show up late or call in sick, whether you can keep your cool under the stress of trying to revive a victim of cardiac arrest, whether you can be trusted with confidential information about people's health, etc. Those kinds of things are hard to evaluate, while whether you can click on the right answer on a computer is easy to evaluate.

This is not to say that clicking on the right answer is not important. The knowledge tested on the cognitive exam is knowledge you will need to do your job. Furthermore, your ability to enter the profession you've trained for depends on your passing this exam. And that's why you're here—using the LearningExpress Test Preparation System to achieve control over the exam.

Part B: What's on the Test
If you haven't already done so, stop here and read Chapter 1 of this book, which gives you an overview of EMT cognitive exams in general and the National Registry of Emergency Medical Technicians (NREMT) exam in particular.

Many states use the NREMT exam, but others do not. If you haven't already received the full rundown on certification procedures and requirements as part of your training program, you can contact your state's EMS office. State EMS office information can be found at the NREMT website (www.nremt.org) by clicking on "State EMS Agency Information" on the NREMT home page.

Step 2: Conquer Test Anxiety

Time to complete: 20 minutes
Activity: Take the Test Stress Exam

Having complete information about the exam is the first step in getting control of it. Next, you have to overcome one of the biggest obstacles to test success: anxiety. Test anxiety can not only impair your performance on the exam itself, it can even keep you from preparing! In Step 2, you'll learn stress-management techniques that will help you succeed on your exam. Learn these strategies now, and practice them as you work through the exams in this book so they'll be second nature to you by exam day.

Combating Test Anxiety
The first thing you need to know is that a little test anxiety is a good thing. Everyone gets nervous before a big exam—and if that nervousness motivates you to prepare thoroughly, so much the better. It's said that Sir Laurence Olivier, one of the foremost British actors of the twentieth century, felt sick before every performance. His stage fright didn't impair his performance; in fact, it probably gave him a little extra edge—just the kind of edge you need to do well, whether on a stage or in an examination room.

The Test Stress Exam is on page 9. Stop here and answer the questions on that page to find out whether your level of test anxiety is cause for worry.

Stress Management before the Test
If you feel your level of anxiety is getting the best of you in the weeks before the test, here is what you need to do to bring the level down again:

- **Get prepared.** There's nothing like knowing what to expect and being prepared for it to put you in control of test anxiety. That's why you're reading this book. Use it faithfully, and remind yourself that you're better prepared than most of the people taking the test.
- **Practice self-confidence.** A positive attitude is a great way to combat test anxiety. This is no time to be humble or shy. Stand in front of the mirror and say to your reflection, "I'm prepared. I'm full of self-confidence. I'm going to ace this test. I know I can do it." Record it and play it back once a day. If you hear it often enough, you'll believe it.
- **Fight negative messages.** Every time someone starts telling you how hard the exam is or how it's almost impossible to get a high score, start telling them your self-confidence messages. If that

someone with the negative messages is *you* telling yourself *you don't do well on exams, you just can't do this,* don't listen. Turn on your recording and listen to your self-confidence messages.

- **Visualize.** Imagine yourself reporting for duty on your first day as an EMT. Think of yourself responding to calls, interacting with patients, preserving health, and saving lives. Visualizing success can help make it happen—and it reminds you of why you're doing all this work preparing for the exam.
- **Exercise.** Physical activity helps calm your body and focus your mind. Besides, being in good physical shape can actually help you do well on the exam. Go for a run, lift weights, go swimming—and do it regularly.

Stress Management on Test Day

There are several ways you can lower your anxiety on test day. They'll work best if you practice them in the weeks before the test, so you know which ones work best for you.

- **Deep breathing.** Take a deep breath while you count to five. Hold it for a count of one, then let it out for a count of five. Repeat several times.
- **Move your body.** Try rolling your head in a circle. Rotate your shoulders. Shake your hands from the wrist. Many people find these movements very relaxing.
- **Visualize again.** Think of the place where you are most relaxed: lying on the beach in the sun, walk-

ing through the park, or wherever. Now close your eyes and imagine you're actually there. If you practice in advance, you'll find that you need only a few seconds of this exercise to experience a significant increase in your sense of well-being.

When anxiety threatens to overwhelm you right there during the exam, there are still things you can do to manage the stress level.

- **Repeat your self-confidence messages.** You should have them memorized by now. Say them quietly to yourself, and believe them!
- **Visualize one more time.** This time, visualize yourself moving smoothly and quickly through the test, answering every question correctly and finishing just before time is up. Like most visualization techniques, this one works best if you've practiced it ahead of time.
- **Take a mental break.** Everyone loses concentration once in a while during a long test. It's normal, so you shouldn't worry about it. Instead, accept what has happened. Say to yourself, "Hey, I lost it there for a minute. My brain is taking a break." Close your eyes and do some deep breathing for a few seconds. Then, you'll be ready to go back to work.

Try these techniques ahead of time and watch them work for you!

You need to worry about test anxiety only if it is extreme enough to impair your performance. The following questionnaire will diagnose your level of test anxiety. In the blank before each statement, write the number that most accurately describes your experience preparing for or taking a test or exam.

0 = Never   1 = Once or twice   2 = Sometimes   3 = Often

_____ I have gotten so nervous before an exam that I simply put down the books and didn't study for it.

_____ I have experienced disabling physical symptoms such as vomiting and severe headaches because I was nervous about an exam.

_____ I have simply not shown up for an exam because I was scared to take it.

_____ I have experienced dizziness and disorientation while taking an exam.

_____ I have had trouble filling in the little circles because my hands were shaking too hard.

_____ I have failed an exam because I was too nervous to complete it.

_____ **Total: Add up the numbers in the blanks above.**

Your Test Stress Score

Here are the steps you should take, depending on your score. If you scored:

- **Below 3,** your level of test anxiety is nothing to worry about; it's probably just enough to give you that little extra edge.
- **Between 3 and 6,** your test anxiety may be enough to impair your performance, and you should practice the stress-management techniques listed in this section to try to bring your test anxiety down to manageable levels.
- **Above 6,** your level of test anxiety is a serious concern. In addition to practicing the stress-management techniques listed in this section, you may want to seek additional personal help. Call your local high school or community college and ask for the academic counselor. Tell the counselor that you have a level of test anxiety that sometimes keeps you from being able to take the exam. The counselor may be willing to help you or may suggest someone else with whom you should talk.

Step 3: Make a Plan

Time to complete: 30 minutes
Activity: Construct a study plan

Maybe the most important thing you can do to get control of yourself and your exam is to make a study plan. Too many people fail to prepare simply because they fail to plan. Spending hours the day before the exam poring over sample test questions not only raises your level of test anxiety, it also is simply no substitute for careful preparation and practice over time.

Don't fall into the cram trap. Take control of your preparation time by mapping out a study schedule. On the following pages are two sample schedules based on the amount of time you have before you take the EMT cognitive exam. If you're the kind of person who needs deadlines and assignments to motivate you for a project, here they are. If you're the kind of person who doesn't like to follow other people's plans, you can use the following suggested schedules to construct your own.

Even more important than making a plan is making a commitment. You can't review everything you learned in your EMT course in one night. You have to set aside some time every day for study and practice. Try for at least 20 minutes a day. Twenty minutes daily will do you much more good than two hours on Saturday.

Don't put off your studying until the day before the exam. Start now. A few minutes a day, with half an hour or more on weekends, can make a big difference in your score.

Schedule A: The 30-Day Plan

If you have at least a month before you take the EMT exam, you have plenty of time to prepare—as long as you don't waste it! If you have less than a month, turn to Schedule B.

TIME	PREPARATION
Days 1–3	Skim over the written materials from your training program, particularly noting 1) areas you expect to be emphasized on the exam and 2) areas you don't remember well. On Day 3, concentrate on those areas.
Day 4	Take the first and second practice exams in Chapters 3 and 4.
Day 5	Score the practice exams. Use the outline of skills in Chapter 1 to reveal your strongest and weakest areas. Identify two areas that you will concentrate on before you take the next practice exams.
Days 6–9	Study the two areas you identified as your weak points. Don't worry about the other areas.
Day 10	Take the third and fourth practice exams in Chapters 5 and 6.
Day 11	Score the practice exams. Identify one area to concentrate on before you take the next practice exams.
Days 12–17	Study the one area you identified for review. In addition, review the practice exams you've already taken, with special attention to the answer explanations.
Day 18	Take the fifth and sixth practice exams in Chapters 7 and 8.
Day 19	Once again, identify one area to review, based on your score on the practice exams.
Day 20	Study the one area you identified for review.
Days 21–23	Take an overview of all your training materials, consolidating your strengths and improving on your weaknesses.
Days 24–25	Review all the areas that have given you the most trouble in the practice exams you've already taken.
Day 26	Take the seventh and eighth practice exams in Chapters 9 and 10 and score them. See how much you've improved!
Day 27	Take the ninth and tenth practice exams in Chapters 11 and 12. Score and take note of any remaining areas that need improvement.
Days 28–29	Review one or two weak areas.
Day before the exam	Relax. Do something unrelated to the exam, and go to bed at a reasonable hour.

Schedule B: The 10-Day Plan

If you have two weeks or less before you take the exam, you have your work cut out for you. Use this 10-day schedule to help you make the most of your time.

TIME	PREPARATION
Day 1	Take the first and second practice exams in Chapters 3 and 4 and score them using the answer keys at the end. Turn to the list of subject areas on the exam in Chapter 1 and find out which areas need the most work based on your exam score.
Day 2	Review one area that gave you trouble on the first two practice exams.
Day 3	Review another area that gave you trouble on the first two practice exams.
Day 4	Take the third, fourth, and fifth practice exams and score them.
Day 5	If your scores on these practice exams do not show improvement in the two areas you studied, review them. If you did improve in those areas, choose a new weak area to study.
Day 6	Take the sixth, seventh, and eighth practice exams and score them.
Day 7	Choose your weakest area from these exams to review.
Day 8	Review any areas that you have not yet reviewed in this schedule.
Day 9	Take the final practice exams in Chapters 11 and 12 and score them. Brush up on any remaining trouble areas.
Day before the exam	Relax. Do something unrelated to the exam, and go to bed at a reasonable hour.

Step 4: Learn to Manage Your Time

Time to complete: ten minutes to read, many hours of practice!

Activities: Practice these strategies as you take the sample tests in this book

Steps 4, 5, and 6 of the LearningExpress Test Preparation System put you in charge of your exam by showing you test-taking strategies that work. Practice these strategies as you take the sample tests in this book, and then you'll be ready to use them on test day.

First, you'll take control of your time on the exam. Many state EMT exams are still paper and pencil, much like these practice exams, and have a three-

hour time limit. Three hours may be plenty of time to complete a 150 question exam—or it may not. Also, remember the computer-based NREMT exam only allots two hours for completion. It is a terrible feeling to hear the test examiner say, "Five minutes left," or to see the computer timer winding down and you're only three-quarters through the test. Here are some tips to avoid that feeling of panic.

- **Follow directions.** If the directions are given orally, listen to them. If they're written on-screen, read them carefully. Ask questions *before* the exam begins if there's anything you don't understand. If you're allowed to take notes, write down the beginning and ending time of the exam.

- **Pace yourself.** Glance at your watch every few minutes, and compare the time to how far you've gotten in the test. When one-quarter of the time has elapsed, you should be one-quarter through the test, and so on. If you're falling behind, pick up the pace a bit.
- **Don't rush.** Though you should keep moving, rushing won't help. Try to keep calm and work methodically and quickly.

Step 5: Learn to Use the Process of Elimination

Time to complete: 20 minutes
Activity: Complete worksheet on Using the Process of Elimination

After time management, the next most important tool for taking control of your exam is using the process of elimination wisely. It's standard test-taking wisdom that you should always read all the answer choices before choosing your answer. This helps you find the right answer by eliminating wrong answer choices. And, sure enough, that standard wisdom applies to your exam, too.

Let's say you're facing a question that goes like this:

13. Which of the following lists of signs and symptoms indicates cardiac compromise?
    a. headache, dizziness, nausea, confusion
    b. dull chest pain, sudden sweating, difficulty breathing
    c. wheezing, labored breathing, chest pain
    d. difficulty breathing, high fever, rapid pulse

You should always use the process of elimination on a question like this, even if the right answer jumps out at you. Sometimes the answer that jumps out isn't right after all. Let's assume, for the purpose of this exercise, that you're a little rusty on your signs and symptoms of cardiac compromise, so you need to use a little intuition to make up for what you don't remember. Proceed through the answer choices in order.

Start with answer **a**. This one is pretty easy to eliminate; none of these signs and symptoms is consistent with cardiac compromise. On a piece of scrap paper, mark an **X** next to choice **a** so you never have to look at it again.

On to the next. "Dull chest pain" looks good, though if you're not up on your cardiac signs and symptoms you might wonder if it should be "acute chest pain" instead. "Sudden sweating" and "difficulty breathing"? Check. And that's what you write next to answer **b** on your scrap paper—a check mark, meaning, "Good answer, I might use this one."

Choice **c** is a possibility. Maybe you don't really expect wheezing in cardiac compromise, but you know "chest pain" is right, and let's say you're not sure whether "labored breathing" is a sign of cardiac compromise. Put a question mark next to **c**, meaning, "Well, maybe."

Choice **d** strikes you about the same; "difficulty breathing" is a good sign of cardiac compromise. But wait a minute. "High fever"? Not really. "Rapid pulse"? Well, maybe. This doesn't really sound like cardiac compromise, and you've already got a better answer picked out in choice **b**. If you're feeling sure of yourself, put an X next to this one. If you want to be careful, put a question mark.

Now your notes on the question look like this:

13. Which of the following lists of signs and symptoms indicates cardiac compromise?
    X a. headache, dizziness, nausea, confusion
    ✔ b. dull chest pain, sudden sweating, difficulty breathing
    ? c. wheezing, labored breathing, chest pain
    ? d. difficulty breathing, high fever, rapid pulse

You've got just one check mark for a good answer. It's good to have a system for marking good, bad, and maybe answers. We're recommending this one:

X = bad
✔ = good
? = maybe

If you don't like these marks, devise your own system. Just make sure you do it long before test day (while you're working through the practice exams in this book) so you won't have to worry about it during the test.

Even when you think you're absolutely clueless about a question, you can often use the process of elimination to get rid of one answer choice. If so, you're better prepared to make an educated guess, as you'll see in Step 6. More often, the process of elimination helps you get down to only *two* possibly right answers. Then you're in a strong position to guess. And sometimes, even though you don't know the right answer, you find it simply by getting rid of the wrong ones, as you did in the previous example.

Try using your powers of elimination on the questions in the worksheet Using the Process of Elimination beginning on the next page. The questions aren't about EMT work; they're just designed to show you how the process of elimination works. The answer explanations for this worksheet show one way you might use the process to arrive at the right answer.

All tests will likely have questions you cannot immediately answer. On paper and pencil exams and some computer-based exams, you may skip them and return to them later. This can be a good tactic in your time management and will give you more time to use the process of elimination. The Computer Adaptive Test (CAT) used by the NREMT does not calculate a score based on the number of correct answers, but rather determines your ability level based on your answers and the difficulty of the questions. Each of your answers determines the level of difficulty of the next question; therefore, you must answer each question before moving on. For this reason you may have to make an educated guess. The ability to quickly and effectively use the process of elimination will give you the best chance for success on these questions.

Use the process of elimination to answer the following questions.

1. Ilsa is as old as Meghan will be in five years. The difference between Ed's age and Meghan's age is twice the difference between Ilsa's age and Meghan's age. Ed is 29. How old is Ilsa?
   a. 4
   b. 10
   c. 19
   d. 24

2. "All drivers of commercial vehicles must carry a valid commercial driver's license whenever operating a commercial vehicle." According to this sentence, which of the following people need NOT carry a commercial driver's license?
   a. a truck driver idling his engine while waiting to be directed to a loading dock
   b. a bus operator backing her bus out of the way of another bus in the bus lot
   c. a taxi driver driving his personal car to the grocery store
   d. a limousine driver taking the limousine to her home after dropping off her last passenger of the evening

3. Smoking tobacco has been linked to
   a. increased risk of stroke and heart attack.
   b. all forms of respiratory disease.
   c. increasing mortality rates over the past ten years.
   d. juvenile delinquency.

4. Which of the following words is spelled correctly?
   a. incorrigible
   b. outragous
   c. domestickated
   d. understandible

Answers

Here are the answers, as well as some suggestions on how you might have used the process of elimination to find them.

1. d. You should have eliminated answer **a** right off the bat. Ilsa can't be four years old if Meghan is going to be Ilsa's age in five years. The best way to eliminate other answer choices is to try plugging them into the information given in the problem. For instance, for answer **b**, if Ilsa is ten, then Meghan must be five. The difference in their ages is five. The difference between Ed's age, 29, and Meghan's age, five, is 24. Is 24 two times five? No. Then answer **b** is wrong. You could eliminate answer **c** in the same way and be left with answer **d**.

2. c. Note the word *not* in the question, and go through the answers one by one. Is the truck driver in choice **a** "operating a commercial vehicle"? Yes, idling counts as "operating," so he needs to have a commercial driver's license. Likewise, the bus operator in answer **b** is operating a commercial vehicle; the question doesn't say the operator must be on the street. The limo driver in **d** is operating a commercial vehicle, even if it doesn't have a passenger in it. However, the cabbie in answer **c** is *not* operating a commercial vehicle, but his own private car.

3. a. You could eliminate answer **b** simply because of the presence of *all*. Such absolutes hardly ever appear in correct answer choices. Choice **c** looks attractive until you think a little about what you know—aren't *fewer* people smoking these days, rather than more? So how could smoking be responsible for a higher mortality rate? (If you didn't know that *mortality rate* means the rate at which people die, you might keep this choice as a possibility, but you'd still be able to eliminate two answers and have only two to choose from.) And choice **d** is plain silly, so you could eliminate that one, too. And you're left with the correct choice, **a**.

4. a. How you used the process of elimination here depends on which words you recognized as being spelled incorrectly. If you knew that the correct spellings were *outrageous*, *domesticated*, and *understandable*, then you were home free. Surely you knew that at least one of those words was wrong!

Step 6: Know When to Guess

Time to complete: 20 minutes
Activity: Complete worksheet on Your Guessing Ability

Armed with the process of elimination, you're ready to take control of one of the big questions in test taking: Should I guess? The first and main answer is "Yes." Some exams have what's called a "guessing penalty," in which a fraction of your wrong answers is subtracted from your right answers—but EMT exams don't often work that way. If you are taking a paper and pencil exam, the number of questions you answer correctly yields your raw score, so you have nothing to lose and everything to gain by guessing.

The more complicated answer to the question "Should I guess?" depends on you—your personality and your "guessing intuition." There are two things you need to know about yourself before you go into the exam:

- Are you a risk taker?
- Are you a good guesser?

You'll have to decide about your risk-taking quotient on your own. To find out if you're a good guesser, complete the worksheet Your Guessing Ability that begins on page 17. Frankly, even if you're a play-it-safe person with lousy intuition, you're probably still safe guessing every time. The best thing would be if you could overcome your anxieties and go ahead and mark an answer. But you may want to have a sense of how good your intuition is before you go into the exam.

On the CAT NREMT exam you are not given a raw score based on the number of correct responses. The CAT exam, as stated previously, evaluates your ability level based on the answers you provide and the level of difficulty of the question. Since your answer (correct or incorrect) to the previous question determines the difficulty of the next question and continually assesses your ability, the "nothing to lose and everything to gain" philosophy is not accurate in this setting. Although you must answer each question before moving on, wildly guessing increases your chances for an incorrect answer—a determination of a lower ability by the CAT. In CAT situations, the use of the process of elimination is always preferred—even if you only eliminate one answer—over just taking a random guess.

The following are ten really hard questions. You're not supposed to know the answers. Rather, this is an assessment of your ability to guess when you don't have a clue. Read each question carefully, just as if you did expect to answer it. If you have any knowledge at all of the subject of the question, use that knowledge to help you eliminate wrong answer choices. Use this answer grid to fill in your answers to the questions.

ANSWER GRID

1. ⓐ ⓑ ⓒ ⓓ
2. ⓐ ⓑ ⓒ ⓓ
3. ⓐ ⓑ ⓒ ⓓ
4. ⓐ ⓑ ⓒ ⓓ

5. ⓐ ⓑ ⓒ ⓓ
6. ⓐ ⓑ ⓒ ⓓ
7. ⓐ ⓑ ⓒ ⓓ
8. ⓐ ⓑ ⓒ ⓓ

9. ⓐ ⓑ ⓒ ⓓ
10. ⓐ ⓑ ⓒ ⓓ

1. September 7 is Independence Day in
 a. India.
 b. Costa Rica.
 c. Brazil.
 d. Australia.

2. Which of the following is the formula for determining the momentum of an object?
 a. $p = mv$
 b. $F = ma$
 c. $P = IV$
 d. $E = mc^2$

3. Because of the expansion of the universe, the stars and other celestial bodies are all moving away from each other. This phenomenon is known as
 a. Newton's first law.
 b. the big bang.
 c. gravitational collapse.
 d. Hubble flow.

4. American author Gertrude Stein was born in
 a. 1713.
 b. 1830.
 c. 1874.
 d. 1901.

5. Which of the following is NOT one of the Five Classics attributed to Confucius?
 a. the *I Ching*
 b. the *Book of Holiness*
 c. the *Spring and Autumn Annals*
 d. the *Book of History*

6. The religious and philosophical doctrine that holds that the universe is constantly in a struggle between good and evil is known as
 a. Pelagianism.
 b. Manichaeanism.
 c. neo-Hegelianism.
 d. Epicureanism.

7. The third chief justice of the U.S. Supreme Court was
 a. John Blair.
 b. William Cushing.
 c. James Wilson.
 d. John Jay.

8. Which of the following is the poisonous portion of a daffodil?
 a. the bulb
 b. the leaves
 c. the stem
 d. the flowers

9. The winner of the Masters golf tournament in 1953 was
  a. Sam Snead.
  b. Cary Middlecoff.
  c. Arnold Palmer.
  d. Ben Hogan.

10. The state with the highest per capita personal income in 1980 was
  a. Alaska.
  b. Connecticut.
  c. New York.
  d. Texas.

Answers

Check your answers against the correct answers below.

1. c
2. a
3. d
4. c
5. b
6. b
7. b
8. a
9. d
10. a

How Did You Do?

You may have simply gotten lucky and actually known the answer to one or two questions. In addition, your guessing was more successful if you were able to use the process of elimination on any of the questions. Maybe you didn't know who the third chief justice was (question 7), but you knew that John Jay was the first. In that case, you would have eliminated answer **d** and therefore improved your odds of guessing right from one in four to one in three.

According to probability, you should get 2.5 answers correct, so getting either two or three right would be average. If you got four or more right, you may be a really terrific guesser. If you got one or none right, you may be a really bad guesser.

Keep in mind, though, that this is only a small sample. You should continue to keep track of your guessing ability as you work through the sample questions in this book. Circle the numbers of questions you guess on as you make your guess; or, if you don't have time while you take the practice tests, go back afterward and try to remember on which questions you guessed. Remember, on a test with four answer choices, your chances of getting a correct answer are one in four. So keep a separate "guessing" score for each exam. How many questions did you guess on? How many did you get right? If the number you got right is at least one-fourth the number of questions you guessed on, you are at least an average guesser, maybe better—and you should always go ahead and guess on the real exam. If the number you got right is significantly lower than one-fourth of the number you guessed on, you would, frankly, be safe in guessing anyway, but maybe you'd feel more comfortable if you guessed only selectively, when you can eliminate a wrong answer or at least have a good feeling about one of the answer choices.

Step 7: Reach Your Peak Performance Zone

Time to complete: 10 minutes to read; weeks to complete!
Activity: Complete the Physical Preparation Checklist

To get ready for a challenge like a big exam, you have to take control of your physical as well as your mental state. Exercise, proper diet, and rest will ensure that your body works with your mind, rather than against it, on test day, as well as during your preparation.

Exercise

If you don't already have a regular exercise program going, the time during which you're preparing for an exam is actually an excellent time to start one. And if you're already keeping fit—or trying to get that way—don't let the pressure of preparing for an exam fool you into quitting now. Exercise helps reduce stress by pumping wonderful good-feeling hormones called endorphins into your system. It also increases the oxygen supply throughout your body, including your brain, so you'll be at peak performance on test day.

A half hour of vigorous activity—enough to raise a sweat—every day should be your aim. If you're really pressed for time, every other day is okay. Choose an activity you like and get out there and do it. Jogging with a friend or exercising to music always makes the time go faster.

But don't overdo it. You don't want to exhaust yourself. Moderation is the key.

Diet

First of all, cut out the junk. Go easy on caffeine and nicotine, and eliminate alcohol and any other drugs from your system at least two weeks before the exam. Promise yourself a celebration/party the night after the exam, if need be.

What your body needs for peak performance is simply a balanced diet. Eat plenty of fruits and vegetables, along with protein and carbohydrates. Foods high in lecithin (an amino acid), such as fish and beans, are especially good brain foods.

The night before the exam, you might carbo-load the way athletes do before a contest. Eat a big plate of spaghetti, rice and beans, or your favorite carbohydrate.

Rest

You probably know how much sleep you need every night to be at your best, even if you don't always get it. Make sure you do get that much sleep, though, for at least a week before the exam. Moderation is important here, too. Extra sleep will just make you groggy.

If you're not a morning person and your exam will be given in the morning, you should reset your internal clock so that your body doesn't think you're taking an exam at 3 A.M. You have to start this process well before the exam. The way it works is to get up half an hour earlier each morning, and then go to bed half an hour earlier that night. Don't try it the other way around; you'll just toss and turn if you go to bed early without having gotten up early. The next morning, get up another half an hour earlier, and so on. How long you will have to do this depends on how late you're used to getting up. Use the Physical Preparation Checklist on page 20 to make sure you're in tip-top form.

For the week before the test, write down 1) what physical exercise you engaged in and for how long and 2) what you ate for each meal. Remember, you're trying for at least half an hour of exercise every other day (preferably every day) and a balanced diet that's light on junk food.

Exam minus 7 days

Exercise: _____ for _____ minutes

Breakfast: _____

Lunch: _____

Dinner: _____

Snacks: _____

Exam minus 6 days

Exercise: _____ for _____ minutes

Breakfast: _____

Lunch: _____

Dinner: _____

Snacks: _____

Exam minus 5 days

Exercise: _____ for _____ minutes

Breakfast: _____

Lunch: _____

Dinner: _____

Snacks: _____

Exam minus 4 days

Exercise: _____ for _____ minutes

Breakfast: _____

Lunch: _____

Dinner: _____

Snacks: _____

Exam minus 3 days

Exercise: _____ for _____ minutes

Breakfast: _____

Lunch: _____

Dinner: _____

Snacks: _____

Exam minus 2 days

Exercise: _____ for _____ minutes

Breakfast: _____

Lunch: _____

Dinner: _____

Snacks: _____

Exam minus 1 day

Exercise: _____ for _____ minutes

Breakfast: _____

Lunch: _____

Dinner: _____

Snacks: _____

Step 8: Get Your Act Together

Time to complete: 10 minutes to read; time to complete will vary
Activity: Complete Final Preparations worksheet

You're in control of your mind and body; you're in charge of test anxiety, your preparation, and your test-taking strategies. Now it's time to take charge of external factors, such as the testing site and the materials you need to take the exam.

Find Out Where the Test Center Is and Make a Trial Run

The testing agency or your EMS instructor will notify you when and where your exam is being held. Do you know how to get to the testing site? Do you know how long it will take to get there? If not, make a trial run, preferably on the same day of the week at the same time of day. On the Final Preparations worksheet on page 22, note the amount of time it will take you to get to the exam site. Plan on arriving 10 to 15 minutes early so you can get the lay of the land, use the bathroom, and calm down. Then figure out how early you will have to get up that morning, and make sure you get up that early every day for a week before the exam.

Gather Your Materials

The night before the exam, lay out the clothes you will wear and the materials you have to bring with you to the exam. Plan on dressing in layers; you won't have any control over the temperature of the examination room. Have a sweater or jacket you can take off if it's warm. Use the checklist on the Final Preparations worksheet on page 22 to help you pull together what you'll need.

Don't Skip Breakfast

Even if you don't usually eat breakfast, do so on exam morning. A cup of coffee doesn't count. Don't eat doughnuts or other sweet foods either. A sugar high will leave you with a sugar low in the middle of the exam. A mix of protein and carbohydrates is best: Cereal with milk, or eggs with toast, will do your body a world of good.

Getting to the Exam Site

Location of exam site: _____

Date: _____

Departure time: _____

Do I know how to get to the exam site?   Yes ___   No ___

If no, make a trial run.

Time it will take to get to the exam site: _____

Things to Lay Out the Night Before

Clothes I will wear   ____

Sweater/jacket   ____

Watch   ____

Photo ID   ____

Four #2 pencils   ____

Other   ____

Step 9: Do It!

Time to complete: 10 minutes, plus test-taking time
Activity: Ace the EMT exam!

Fast-forward to exam day. You're ready. You made a study plan and followed through. You practiced your test-taking strategies while working through this book. You're in control of your physical, mental, and emotional state. You know when and where to show up and what to bring with you. In other words, you're better prepared than most other people taking the EMT exam with you. You're psyched.

Just one more thing. When you're done with the exam, you will have earned a reward. Plan a celebration. Call up your friends and plan a party, have a nice dinner for two, or go see a good movie—whatever your heart desires. Give yourself something to look forward to.

And then do it. Go into the exam, full of confidence, armed with test-taking strategies you've practiced until they became second nature. You're in control of yourself, your environment, and your performance on the exam. You're ready to succeed. So do it. Go in there and ace the exam. And look forward to your career as an EMT!

EMT PRACTICE EXAM 1

CHAPTER SUMMARY
This is the first of ten practice exams in this book based on the National Registry's EMT cognitive exam.

Like the other tests in this book, this test is based on the National Registry's cognitive exam for EMTs. See Chapter 1 for a complete description of this exam.

Take this first exam in as relaxed a manner as you can, and don't worry about timing. You can time yourself on the other nine exams. You should, however, allow sufficient time to take the entire exam at one sitting, at least two hours. Find a quiet place where you can work without being interrupted.

The answer sheet you should use is on page 25, followed by the exam itself. The correct answers, each fully explained, come after the exam. Once you have read and understood the answer explanations, turn to Chapter 1 for an explanation of how to assess your score.

1.	ⓐ	ⓑ	ⓒ	ⓓ		41.	ⓐ	ⓑ	ⓒ	ⓓ		81.	ⓐ	ⓑ	ⓒ	ⓓ
2.	ⓐ	ⓑ	ⓒ	ⓓ		42.	ⓐ	ⓑ	ⓒ	ⓓ		82.	ⓐ	ⓑ	ⓒ	ⓓ
3.	ⓐ	ⓑ	ⓒ	ⓓ		43.	ⓐ	ⓑ	ⓒ	ⓓ		83.	ⓐ	ⓑ	ⓒ	ⓓ
4.	ⓐ	ⓑ	ⓒ	ⓓ		44.	ⓐ	ⓑ	ⓒ	ⓓ		84.	ⓐ	ⓑ	ⓒ	ⓓ
5.	ⓐ	ⓑ	ⓒ	ⓓ		45.	ⓐ	ⓑ	ⓒ	ⓓ		85.	ⓐ	ⓑ	ⓒ	ⓓ
6.	ⓐ	ⓑ	ⓒ	ⓓ		46.	ⓐ	ⓑ	ⓒ	ⓓ		86.	ⓐ	ⓑ	ⓒ	ⓓ
7.	ⓐ	ⓑ	ⓒ	ⓓ		47.	ⓐ	ⓑ	ⓒ	ⓓ		87.	ⓐ	ⓑ	ⓒ	ⓓ
8.	ⓐ	ⓑ	ⓒ	ⓓ		48.	ⓐ	ⓑ	ⓒ	ⓓ		88.	ⓐ	ⓑ	ⓒ	ⓓ
9.	ⓐ	ⓑ	ⓒ	ⓓ		49.	ⓐ	ⓑ	ⓒ	ⓓ		89.	ⓐ	ⓑ	ⓒ	ⓓ
10.	ⓐ	ⓑ	ⓒ	ⓓ		50.	ⓐ	ⓑ	ⓒ	ⓓ		90.	ⓐ	ⓑ	ⓒ	ⓓ
11.	ⓐ	ⓑ	ⓒ	ⓓ		51.	ⓐ	ⓑ	ⓒ	ⓓ		91.	ⓐ	ⓑ	ⓒ	ⓓ
12.	ⓐ	ⓑ	ⓒ	ⓓ		52.	ⓐ	ⓑ	ⓒ	ⓓ		92.	ⓐ	ⓑ	ⓒ	ⓓ
13.	ⓐ	ⓑ	ⓒ	ⓓ		53.	ⓐ	ⓑ	ⓒ	ⓓ		93.	ⓐ	ⓑ	ⓒ	ⓓ
14.	ⓐ	ⓑ	ⓒ	ⓓ		54.	ⓐ	ⓑ	ⓒ	ⓓ		94.	ⓐ	ⓑ	ⓒ	ⓓ
15.	ⓐ	ⓑ	ⓒ	ⓓ		55.	ⓐ	ⓑ	ⓒ	ⓓ		95.	ⓐ	ⓑ	ⓒ	ⓓ
16.	ⓐ	ⓑ	ⓒ	ⓓ		56.	ⓐ	ⓑ	ⓒ	ⓓ		96.	ⓐ	ⓑ	ⓒ	ⓓ
17.	ⓐ	ⓑ	ⓒ	ⓓ		57.	ⓐ	ⓑ	ⓒ	ⓓ		97.	ⓐ	ⓑ	ⓒ	ⓓ
18.	ⓐ	ⓑ	ⓒ	ⓓ		58.	ⓐ	ⓑ	ⓒ	ⓓ		98.	ⓐ	ⓑ	ⓒ	ⓓ
19.	ⓐ	ⓑ	ⓒ	ⓓ		59.	ⓐ	ⓑ	ⓒ	ⓓ		99.	ⓐ	ⓑ	ⓒ	ⓓ
20.	ⓐ	ⓑ	ⓒ	ⓓ		60.	ⓐ	ⓑ	ⓒ	ⓓ		100.	ⓐ	ⓑ	ⓒ	ⓓ
21.	ⓐ	ⓑ	ⓒ	ⓓ		61.	ⓐ	ⓑ	ⓒ	ⓓ		101.	ⓐ	ⓑ	ⓒ	ⓓ
22.	ⓐ	ⓑ	ⓒ	ⓓ		62.	ⓐ	ⓑ	ⓒ	ⓓ		102.	ⓐ	ⓑ	ⓒ	ⓓ
23.	ⓐ	ⓑ	ⓒ	ⓓ		63.	ⓐ	ⓑ	ⓒ	ⓓ		103.	ⓐ	ⓑ	ⓒ	ⓓ
24.	ⓐ	ⓑ	ⓒ	ⓓ		64.	ⓐ	ⓑ	ⓒ	ⓓ		104.	ⓐ	ⓑ	ⓒ	ⓓ
25.	ⓐ	ⓑ	ⓒ	ⓓ		65.	ⓐ	ⓑ	ⓒ	ⓓ		105.	ⓐ	ⓑ	ⓒ	ⓓ
26.	ⓐ	ⓑ	ⓒ	ⓓ		66.	ⓐ	ⓑ	ⓒ	ⓓ		106.	ⓐ	ⓑ	ⓒ	ⓓ
27.	ⓐ	ⓑ	ⓒ	ⓓ		67.	ⓐ	ⓑ	ⓒ	ⓓ		107.	ⓐ	ⓑ	ⓒ	ⓓ
28.	ⓐ	ⓑ	ⓒ	ⓓ		68.	ⓐ	ⓑ	ⓒ	ⓓ		108.	ⓐ	ⓑ	ⓒ	ⓓ
29.	ⓐ	ⓑ	ⓒ	ⓓ		69.	ⓐ	ⓑ	ⓒ	ⓓ		109.	ⓐ	ⓑ	ⓒ	ⓓ
30.	ⓐ	ⓑ	ⓒ	ⓓ		70.	ⓐ	ⓑ	ⓒ	ⓓ		110.	ⓐ	ⓑ	ⓒ	ⓓ
31.	ⓐ	ⓑ	ⓒ	ⓓ		71.	ⓐ	ⓑ	ⓒ	ⓓ		111.	ⓐ	ⓑ	ⓒ	ⓓ
32.	ⓐ	ⓑ	ⓒ	ⓓ		72.	ⓐ	ⓑ	ⓒ	ⓓ		112.	ⓐ	ⓑ	ⓒ	ⓓ
33.	ⓐ	ⓑ	ⓒ	ⓓ		73.	ⓐ	ⓑ	ⓒ	ⓓ		113.	ⓐ	ⓑ	ⓒ	ⓓ
34.	ⓐ	ⓑ	ⓒ	ⓓ		74.	ⓐ	ⓑ	ⓒ	ⓓ		114.	ⓐ	ⓑ	ⓒ	ⓓ
35.	ⓐ	ⓑ	ⓒ	ⓓ		75.	ⓐ	ⓑ	ⓒ	ⓓ		115.	ⓐ	ⓑ	ⓒ	ⓓ
36.	ⓐ	ⓑ	ⓒ	ⓓ		76.	ⓐ	ⓑ	ⓒ	ⓓ		116.	ⓐ	ⓑ	ⓒ	ⓓ
37.	ⓐ	ⓑ	ⓒ	ⓓ		77.	ⓐ	ⓑ	ⓒ	ⓓ		117.	ⓐ	ⓑ	ⓒ	ⓓ
38.	ⓐ	ⓑ	ⓒ	ⓓ		78.	ⓐ	ⓑ	ⓒ	ⓓ		118.	ⓐ	ⓑ	ⓒ	ⓓ
39.	ⓐ	ⓑ	ⓒ	ⓓ		79.	ⓐ	ⓑ	ⓒ	ⓓ		119.	ⓐ	ⓑ	ⓒ	ⓓ
40.	ⓐ	ⓑ	ⓒ	ⓓ		80.	ⓐ	ⓑ	ⓒ	ⓓ		120.	ⓐ	ⓑ	ⓒ	ⓓ

EMT Practice Exam 1

1. EMTs should wear high-efficiency particulate air (HEPA) respirators when they are in contact with patients who have which of the following?
   a. HIV (human immunodeficiency virus) or AIDS (acquired immune deficiency syndrome)
   b. tuberculosis (TB)
   c. open wounds
   d. hepatitis B

2. You are called to assist a 60-year-old female who complains of a severe headache. Upon entering the home, you smell a strong odor of natural gas. What is your first action?
   a. Check the patient's airway, breathing, and circulation.
   b. Insert a nasopharyngeal airway and assess vital signs.
   c. Remove the patient from the house to your ambulance.
   d. Open all windows and determine the source of the gas leak.

3. The most common electrical rhythm disturbance that results in sudden cardiac arrest is called
   a. pulseless electrical activity.
   b. ventricular fibrillation.
   c. ventricular tachycardia.
   d. asystole.

4. Which of the following is the highest priority patient?
   a. 57-year-old male with chest pain and systolic blood pressure of 80
   b. 40-year-old female with moderate pain from a leg injury
   c. 75-year-old male who appears confused but responds to commands
   d. 25-year-old female in labor with contractions six minutes apart

5. Of the following, which body fluid has the most potential to transmit blood-borne diseases?
   a. nasal discharge
   b. vomitus
   c. amniotic fluid
   d. feces

6. Your patient is an 11-month-old female. How can you determine if she has a decreased mental status and is responsive to verbal stimuli?
   a. She will be upset when you take her from her mother's arms.
   b. She will be unable to tell you how old she is if you ask her.
   c. She will attempt to locate her parents' voices when they speak.
   d. She will try to pull away from a painful stimulus on her toe.

7. What is the best method to assess circulation in an infant?
   a. Palpate the carotid pulse.
   b. Palpate the brachial pulse.
   c. Palpate the radial pulse.
   d. Observe capillary refill time.

8. A 45-year-old male is experiencing chest discomfort. After placing him in his position of comfort, your next action should be to
   a. ventilate the patient with a nonrebreather mask at 15 L/min.
   b. ventilate the patient with the bag-valve mask at 15 L/min.
   c. administer oxygen by nonrebreather mask at 15 L/min.
   d. administer oxygen by the nasal cannula at 6 L/min.

9. Which patient should receive a rapid trauma survey to determine hidden injuries?
   a. alert 2-year-old child in a car seat who was in a medium-speed crash
   b. alert 20-year-old male who fell ten feet and is complaining of leg pain
   c. alert 65-year-old female who fell in the bathtub and is complaining of wrist pain
   d. alert 11-year-old female who tripped while roller-skating and fell down three steps

10. Which of the following is a sign of increased pressure in the circulatory system?
   a. flat neck veins
   b. palpable carotid pulse
   c. distended jugular veins
   d. decreased radial pulse

11. An automated external defibrillator (AED) will shock which of the following rhythms?
   a. sinus rhythm
   b. asystole
   c. ventricular fibrillation
   d. pulseless electrical activity

12. To assess the motor function in the lower extremities of a responsive patient, you would
   a. ask the patient to bend his knees.
   b. ask the patient to wiggle his toes.
   c. carefully move the patient's leg.
   d. touch the skin of the patient's foot.

13. Which patient can safely receive only a focused physical examination rather than a rapid trauma assessment?
   a. 10-year-old male with a deformed right lower leg who is responsive after falling off his bicycle
   b. 20-year-old female who complains of severe pain in her ankle after stepping off a curb
   c. 70-year-old male who complains of neck pain after a medium-speed car collision
   d. 30-year-old male who is unresponsive but has only minor cuts on the extremities

14. You are using the OPQRST acronym to assess a responsive medical patient. What question would you ask to assess the P component?
   a. What were you doing when the pain started?
   b. Can you describe the character of the pain for me?
   c. What makes the pain feel worse or better?
   d. On a scale of 1 to 10, how would you rank the pain?

15. What is the first step in the physical assessment of an unresponsive medical patient?
   a. Perform the initial assessment.
   b. Assess a complete set of vital signs.
   c. Position the patient to protect the airway.
   d. Obtain SAMPLE history from a family member.

16. Which patient needs a detailed physical examination?
   a. 48-year-old male with a history of heart disease who is complaining of chest pain
   b. 35-year-old female who has been in a single-car collision and who briefly lost consciousness
   c. 28-year-old full-term pregnant female whose water has broken and who is having contractions every two minutes
   d. 53-year-old female with a history of smoking who is distressed and short of breath

17. The purpose of the ongoing assessment is to re-evaluate the patient's condition and to
   a. find any injuries missed during the initial assessment.
   b. reassure the patient that you are still caring for him or her.
   c. check the adequacy of each intervention performed.
   d. protect the EMT against liability from malpractice.

18. Immediately after delivering a shock with an AED to a patient in cardiac arrest, you should
   a. check for a pulse.
   b. check breathing and provide rescue breaths as necessary.
   c. analyze with the AED and shock again if indicated.
   d. do CPR.

19. You should apply an AED to
   a. adult patients experiencing chest discomfort.
   b. adult patients with significant traumatic injuries.
   c. adult patients without respirations or a pulse.
   d. adult patients with low blood pressure.

20. Which of the following is a contraindication for the administration of patient-assisted nitroglycerin?
   a. The patient has epistaxis.
   b. The medication is prescribed for the patient.
   c. The patient's blood pressure is greater than 100 mmHg.
   d. The patient has taken Viagra or other erectile dysfunction medication within the past 24 hours.

21. In which of the following situations should you call for immediate assistance?
   a. You must care for two critical patients with gunshot wounds.
   b. Your patient is a 26-year-old female in active labor.
   c. Your patient is a child with fever who has had a brief seizure.
   d. Your partner is needed to stabilize the cervical spine.

22. What is the structure that prevents food and liquid from entering the trachea during swallowing?
   a. larynx
   b. cricoid cartilage
   c. epiglottis
   d. diaphragm

23. The air sacs in the lungs where oxygen–carbon dioxide exchange occurs are the
   a. bronchioles.
   b. bronchi.
   c. epiglottis.
   d. alveoli.

24. Pink or bloody sputum is often seen in patients with
  a. pulmonary edema.
  b. anaphylaxis.
  c. allergic reaction.
  d. flu.

25. Which occurs during capillary–cellular exchange?
  a. Oxygen enters the capillaries as carbon dioxide enters the alveoli.
  b. Oxygen-poor blood from the capillaries passes into the alveoli.
  c. Body cells give up carbon dioxide and capillaries give up oxygen.
  d. Body cells give up carbon monoxide and capillaries give up oxygen.

26. Which of the following is a sign of inadequate breathing?
  a. warm, dry skin
  b. no audible sounds
  c. equal chest expansion
  d. accessory muscle use

27. A patient complaining of facial paralysis on one side of his face with tearing, localized pain, and sensitivity may be suffering from the most common form of facial paralysis called
  a. dystonia.
  b. muscular dystrophy.
  c. amyotrophic lateral sclerosis (ALS).
  d. Bell's palsy.

28. A gurgling sound heard with artificial ventilation is a sign that
  a. the patient must be suctioned immediately.
  b. supplemental oxygen should be added to the bag-valve mask.
  c. the airway is most likely open, patent, and clear.
  d. the patient is trying to communicate with you.

29. You are assisting a patient's ventilations with an Automatic Transport Ventilator (ATV). What indicates that you have set the ventilator on the right tidal volume?
  a. The alarm stops sounding
  b. Capnography reading < 20 mmHg
  c. Visible chest rise
  d. Proper wave form on the screen

30. You take a report from a first responder who describes a patient as *postictal*; based on this report, you would expect to find the patient
  a. alert and oriented.
  b. confused.
  c. unresponsive.
  d. hallucinating.

31. When suctioning a patient, how far should you insert a soft suction catheter?
  a. as far as you can see
  b. as far as the base of the tongue
  c. until resistance is encountered
  d. past the vocal cords

32. What is the correct procedure for a patient who has secretions or emesis that suctioning cannot easily remove?
   a. Insert an oropharyngeal or nasopharyngeal airway immediately.
   b. Suction for 15 seconds, ventilate for two minutes, and then repeat.
   c. Logroll the patient and clear the oropharynx and nasopharynx.
   d. Hyperventilate the patient with a bag-valve-mask unit.

33. What is the purpose of the head-tilt/chin-lift technique?
   a. to position the patient for insertion of an airway adjunct
   b. to remove foreign bodies from the upper airway
   c. to help the rescuer better visualize the larynx and vocal cords
   d. to lift the tongue and epiglottis out of their obstructing position

34. After opening the airway, the next step in patient management is to
   a. insert an endotracheal tube.
   b. assess adequacy of respirations.
   c. begin mouth-to-mouth ventilation.
   d. apply bag-valve-mask ventilation.

35. A patient should receive high-flow oxygen if he or she exhibits
   a. fever.
   b. anxiety.
   c. dehydration.
   d. cyanosis.

36. When providing mouth-to-mask ventilation with supplementary oxygen, what is the first step after sealing the mask to the patient's face?
   a. Follow body substance precautions before touching the patient.
   b. Connect the one-way valve and filter (if available) to the mask.
   c. Exhale slowly over the ventilation port for one and a half to two seconds.
   d. Attach oxygen tubing to the mask and set the flow rate at 15–30 L/min.

37. The correct rate of artificial ventilations for an adult patient is
   a. three ventilations per minute.
   b. five ventilations per minute.
   c. ten ventilations per minute.
   d. twelve ventilations per minute.

38. When using the two-person bag-valve-mask procedure, one EMT ventilates the patient while the other
   a. suctions the patient and administers CPR.
   b. administers mouth-to-mask ventilation.
   c. inserts the oral or nasopharyngeal airway.
   d. maintains the mask seal and monitors chest rise.

39. Where is the cricoid cartilage located?
   a. inferior to the larynx
   b. superior to the epiglottis
   c. at the carina
   d. in the oropharynx

40. Your patient is awake, confused, and disoriented. How would you grade her using the AVPU scale?
   a. A
   b. V
   c. P
   d. U

41. A bulb syringe is used to suction infants up to the age of
   a. one month.
   b. three to four months.
   c. six to eight months.
   d. one year.

42. You are on the scene of a 6-year-old patient in cardiac arrest. CPR is being performed by EMRs and you are preparing the AED. The pads should be placed
   a. to the right of the sternum and below the right clavicle and on the left lower ribs in the anterior axillary line.
   b. on the lower left anterior chest and on the upper left posterior thorax.
   c. nowhere, as children under eight do not defibrillate.
   d. on the lower right anterior chest and on the lower left posterior thorax.

43. The right ventricle pumps blood into the
   a. body via the aorta.
   b. lungs via the pulmonary vein.
   c. lungs via the pulmonary artery.
   d. left atrium.

44. A 56-year-old female patient complains of mild chest discomfort. You should
   a. decide what type of heart problem it might be.
   b. decide whether the patient has a heart problem.
   c. maintain a high index of suspicion for cardiac compromise.
   d. apply the AED.

45. Your patient is a 62-year-old male with a history of heart disease. He is experiencing chest pain. Your first action should be to
   a. place the pads for the AED on his chest.
   b. begin CPR while preparing the AED.
   c. ask him if he has taken his nitroglycerin, and if not, offer to assist him.
   d. place him in a comfortable position and administer high-flow oxygen.

46. The EMT-Basic should request prehospital ACLS for the care of the cardiac arrest patient because
   a. ACLS intervention provides higher survival rates.
   b. EMT-Basics must have prehospital ACLS present to perform defibrillation.
   c. only paramedics can transport cardiac arrest patients.
   d. the EMT-Basic is not adequately trained to manage cardiac arrest.

47. Your patient is a 29-year-old male who has fallen off a ladder. He is bleeding profusely from a wound on his right forearm and has an obvious deformity of his left thigh. Which of the following is an appropriate initial treatment for this patient?
   a. Perform a quick initial assessment to assess his ABCs.
   b. Stop the bleeding by applying pressure on the brachial artery.
   c. Maintain an open airway and ventilate the patient with a bag-valve mask.
   d. Elevate the patient's legs 20–30 cm to treat him for shock.

48. Touching the patient when the semiautomatic external defibrillator (SAED) is analyzing the rhythm
   a. is acceptable with today's modern defibrillators.
   b. is indicated to maintain cardiac compressions.
   c. is indicated to maintain artificial ventilation.
   d. can cause the SAED to misinterpret a rhythm.

49. What should you do for the cardiac arrest patient found in the rain?
   a. Perform one rapid defibrillation, then move the patient inside.
   b. Defibrillate three times, then move the patient inside.
   c. Move the patient inside, away from the rain.
   d. Perform one rapid defibrillation, then start CPR if pulseless.

50. Your patient is bleeding profusely from a wound on her right forearm. You have applied direct pressure, which has failed to stop the bleeding. What is your next step?
   a. Apply pressure to the brachial pressure point.
   b. Apply a tourniquet proximal to the wound.
   c. Add a bulky sterile dressing and apply a tourniquet over it.
   d. Apply a tourniquet distal to the wound.

51. Kinetic energy is described as the
   a. energy an object has while in motion.
   b. measure of matter.
   c. capacity to do work.
   d. tendency for an object to stay in motion.

52. A bystander is performing CPR when you arrive. You evaluate the scene, practice body substance isolation, and begin your initial assessment by having the bystander
   a. verify pulselessness.
   b. continue CPR.
   c. stop CPR.
   d. provide a history of cardiac arrest.

53. Your patient is bleeding from a wound to the forearm. The blood flows in a steady, dark-red stream. What type of bleeding should you suspect?
   a. venous
   b. arterial
   c. capillary
   d. internal

54. Your patient is restless, anxious, and complaining of thirst. She exhibits increased heart rate and pale, clammy skin. You should do all the following EXCEPT
   a. maintain an open airway and provide oxygen.
   b. elevate her legs if not contraindicated.
   c. cover the patient with a blanket to keep her warm.
   d. give the patient small amounts of liquid to drink.

55. If a person was hit by an object described in the following, which would have the potential to cause the most damage?
   a. one-pound object traveling at 10 mph
   b. two-pound object traveling at 20 mph
   c. one-pound object traveling at 30 mph
   d. one-pound object traveling at 20 mph

56. You have responded to a call for a 63-year-old female complaining of chest pain and shortness of breath. You arrive to find her sitting up. Your patient exam reveals clear and equal breath sounds, jugular vein distention, and bilateral pedal edema. The patient states she takes Lasix. What is the most likely cause of these symptoms?
  a. Left-sided heart failure
  b. Secondary drowning
  c. Right-sided heart failure
  d. Atherosclerosis

57. Which heart rhythm often converts to ventricular fibrillation?
  a. asystole
  b. ventricular tachycardia
  c. atrial fibrillation
  d. atrial tachycardia

58. What is the reason for stopping CPR while the AED is analyzing?
  a. To give the patient a chance to breathe on his or her own
  b. To allow the ACLS system to take over patient care
  c. To minimize interference and allow the AED to analyze the cardiac rhythm
  d. To allow other rescuers to get out of the way

59. You have analyzed the cardiac rhythm with an AED and it is indicating "no shock advised." What should your next action be?
  a. Contact medical control for direction
  b. Check the AED battery/power supply
  c. Resume CPR
  d. Discontinue CPR as the patient has a pulse

60. You are transporting a patient who has been resuscitated but is still unresponsive. You should check the patient's pulse every
  a. thirty seconds.
  b. minute.
  c. five minutes.
  d. ten minutes.

61. The medical direction physician orders you to deliver additional shocks to a patient in cardiac arrest while en route to the hospital. What is the correct procedure to follow?
  a. Wait for the arrival of the ACLS team.
  b. Deliver the shocks without stopping CPR.
  c. Stop the vehicle before reanalyzing the rhythm.
  d. Refuse to defibrillate the patient while en route.

62. What is the primary action of nitroglycerin?
  a. lower the blood pressure
  b. contract the heart muscles
  c. slow the heart rate down
  d. dilate the coronary vessels

63. Patients commonly describe heart attack pain as which of the following characteristics?
  a. like pins and needles
  b. crushing or squeezing
  c. intermittent (comes and goes)
  d. less severe than indigestion

64. In pedestrian versus automobile impacts, which of the following statements is true?
  a. Children often turn toward the impact and are often thrown down and under the vehicle.
  b. Adults tend to turn toward the vehicle before impact.
  c. Children often turn toward the impact and are often scooped and thrown over the vehicle.
  d. There tends to be no difference in the way adults and children respond in these situations.

65. Your patient has profuse bleeding from a wound on her lower leg but no signs of skeletal injury. The steps you should take to stop the bleeding, in the correct order, are which of the following?
  a. Direct pressure, elevation, pressure dressing, and tourniquett
  b. Pressure point, tourniquet, and concentrated or diffuse direct pressure
  c. Pneumatic anti-shock garments (PASG), lower extremity elevation, and diffuse direct pressure
  d. Direct pressure, elevation, pressure point, tourniquet, and pressure dressing

66. Where should you place your hands when using the head-tilt/chin-lift maneuver to open an unconscious patient's airway?
  a. on the nose, with the fingertips pinching it closed, and under the neck
  b. on the nose, with the fingertips pinching it closed, and on the forehead
  c. on the forehead, with the other hand under the neck
  d. on the forehead, with the fingertips of the other hand under the lower jaw

67. Your patient is found lying on the ground after falling off a roof. He is unconscious and apneic. Which method should you use to open the patient's airway?
  a. head-tilt/chin-lift
  b. modified jaw thrust
  c. head-tilt only
  d. head-tilt/neck-lift

68. Following an explosion, a patient is trapped in a collapsed structure and suffers crush injuries to both lower extremities. How would the injuries be classified based on the blast-injury phase?
  a. primary blast injury
  b. secondary blast injury
  c. tertiary blast injury
  d. none of the above

69. When splinting an injured limb, you should assess pulse, motor function, and sensation distal to the injury
  a. after applying the splint.
  b. before applying the splint.
  c. while applying the splint.
  d. before and after applying the splint.

70. When performing the modified jaw-thrust maneuver to open your patient's airway, which of the following steps is NOT correct?
  a. Stabilize the patient's cervical spine with your forearms.
  b. Rest your elbows on the same surface as the patient.
  c. Tilt the head by applying gentle pressure to the forehead.
  d. Use your index fingers to push the angles of the lower jaw forward.

71. The *golden period* in emergency medicine refers to the first 60 minutes after the
   a. arrival of EMS.
   b. occurrence of multisystem trauma.
   c. arrival at the emergency room.
   d. start of surgery.

72. Your unconscious patient has blood in his airway. You should
   a. use a suction unit to immediately clear the airway.
   b. apply oxygen using a nonrebreather mask at 15 L/min.
   c. use a bag-valve mask to clear the airway.
   d. perform a finger sweep to remove the blockage.

73. What are the three factors the EMT should consider when evaluating the MOI of a patient who has fallen?
   a. Height of the fall, surface the patient landed on, and body part making first contact
   b. Height of the fall, surface the patient landed on, and body part making first contact
   c. Weight of the patient, surface the patient landed on, and loss of consciousness
   d. Height of the fall, body part making first contact, and papillary response

74. You should not suction a patient's airway for more than 15 seconds because
   a. the patient's tongue may be injured.
   b. the suction unit's battery may drain too quickly.
   c. the patient will become hypoxic during this time.
   d. you may cause the patient to vomit.

75. Which of the following is true regarding using a pocket mask to ventilate a nonbreathing patient?
   a. There is direct contact between the rescuer and the patient's mouth.
   b. Oxygen cannot be connected to the mask.
   c. A one-way valve prevents exhaled air from contacting the rescuer.
   d. Oxygen levels of 100% may be achieved.

76. To which patient should you administer oral glucose?
   a. 60-year-old female behaving as if she is intoxicated, and whose daughter informs you that she takes insulin by injection
   b. 45-year-old male with a history of diabetes behaving erratically after falling and hitting his head in the bathtub
   c. 70-year-old male with a long history of diabetes who is unconscious and cannot swallow
   d. 52-year-old female who tells you that she is feeling dizzy and has low blood sugar

77. The focused history for patients with altered mental status should include questions about a history of trauma, diabetes, seizures, and which of the following?
   a. heart disease
   b. pregnancy
   c. fever
   d. stress

78. All of the following may be signs of allergic reaction EXCEPT
   a. headache and dizziness.
   b. rapid, labored breathing.
   c. decreased blood pressure.
   d. decreased heart rate.

79. Under medical direction, the EMT may administer epinephrine to a patient with respiratory distress or hypoperfusion resulting from an allergic reaction if the
    a. patient has no history of heart disease.
    b. patient is tachypneic with clear breath sounds.
    c. medication has been prescribed for this patient.
    d. medication has been stored in the refrigerator.

80. What is the pediatric dosage of epinephrine for anaphylaxis?
    a. 0.1 mg per kg
    b. 0.15 mg
    c. 1 ml per kg
    d. 0.5 mg

81. Your patient is a 25-year-old female who is severely hypothermic after having plunged into an icy river. Although she was rescued after only a few minutes in the water, she is showing a diminished level of responsiveness. Your care should include
    a. encouraging the patient to walk in order to improve her circulation.
    b. covering the patient in blankets and turning up the heat in the ambulance.
    c. giving her hot coffee or tea to drink and massaging her extremities.
    d. beginning active rewarming measures under direct medical direction.

82. A sign of generalized cold emergency, or hypothermia, is cool skin on the
    a. feet or hands.
    b. ears.
    c. face.
    d. abdomen.

83. Two important principles in the emergency treatment of local cold injuries are to remove the patient from the cold environment and to
    a. rewarm the cold extremity quickly.
    b. warm the whole body as soon as possible.
    c. prevent further tissue damage.
    d. prevent or treat pain.

84. Which of the following indicates that a patient with hyperthermia is in serious danger?
    a. hot skin
    b. moist skin
    c. muscle cramps
    d. dizziness

85. Your patient has been stung by a bee, and the stinger is present in the wound. You should attempt to remove it by
    a. grabbing it with sterile tweezers.
    b. cutting around it with a knife.
    c. scraping it away with a rigid object.
    d. grabbing it with your fingers.

86. Patients exposed to a nerve agent or organophosphate poisoning may show signs and syptoms that are described by the mnemonic SLUDGE. What does this mnemonic stand for?.
    a. Swelling, Lacrimation, Urination, Decerebrate posturing, Gastric distress, Emesis
    b. Salivation, Laceration, Urticaria, Defecation, Gastric distress, Elevated temperature
    c. Salivation, Lacrimation, Urticaria, Dyspnea, Gastric distress, Emesis
    d. Salivation, Lacrimation, Urination, Defecation, Gastric distress, Emesis

87. Which of the following are the signs of early respiratory distress in children and infants?
 a. breathing rate of less than ten per minute, limp muscle tone, slow or absent heart rate, weak or absent distal pulses
 b. increased rate of breathing, nasal flaring, intercostal or supraclavicular retractions, mottled skin color, abdominal muscle use
 c. altered mental status, respiratory rate of over 60 or under 20 breaths per minute, severe retractions, severe use of accessory muscles
 d. inability to cough, crying with tears but no sounds, cyanosis, abdominal or chest-wall movements with absent breath sounds

88. Your patient is an 8-year-old female who had a single, brief seizure at school. Her mother arrives at the same time you do and reports that her daughter has seizures often and is under medical treatment. What should you do?
 a. Request advanced life support (ALS) and law enforcement backup so you can transport the child.
 b. Administer a dose of the child's prescribed seizure-control medication.
 c. Maintain ABCs, monitor vital signs, and transport the patient immediately.
 d. Ensure a patent airway and request medical direction regarding transport.

89. All of the following are signs of possible child abuse EXCEPT
 a. the presence of multiple bruises in various stages of healing.
 b. a single, severe traumatic event that occurred for no reason.
 c. injuries inconsistent with the mechanism described.
 d. conflicting histories of the injury from the guardians/parents.

90. The head of a newborn infant has just delivered. You should
 a. suction the baby's mouth and nostrils with a bulb syringe.
 b. push down on the baby's upper shoulder to facilitate the rest of the delivery.
 c. push up on the baby's lower shoulder to facilitate the rest of the delivery.
 d. ventilate the baby with a pediatric bag-valve mask and high-flow oxygen.

91. Emergency care for a responsive 7-year-old child with a foreign-body airway obstruction includes
 a. holding the child on your knee and performing back blows.
 b. standing behind the child and performing sub-diaphragmatic thrusts.
 c. placing the child supine on the floor and attempting to see the obstruction.
 d. placing the child supine on the floor and performing abdominal thrusts.

92. A 2-year-old male is in respiratory failure when he has
 a. altered mental status and breathing rate of 68 per minute.
 b. limp muscle tone and weak or absent distal pulses.
 c. nasal flaring and mottled skin color.
 d. breathing rate of 6 per minute and heart rate of 50 per minute.

93. A sign or symptom of a predelivery emergency is
 a. the mother's skin is dry.
 b. profuse vaginal bleeding.
 c. the presence of a bloody show.
 d. a contraction every 20 minutes.

94. Select the correct-size oral airway for a small child by measuring from the corner of the patient's mouth to what structure?
   a. central incisor
   b. angle of the jaw
   c. tip of the nose
   d. pinnea of the ear

95. Vitreous humor is found
   a. behind the lens of the eye.
   b. in the bone marrow of the upper arm.
   c. in front of the lens of the eye.
   d. in the joint lubrication of the upper arm.

96. You are assisting with childbirth in the field. As the infant's head is delivered, you discover that the umbilical cord is wrapped tightly around the neck. You should immediately
   a. place the mother on her side and transport rapidly.
   b. deliver the infant with the cord wrapped around its neck.
   c. clamp the cord in two places and cut it between clamps.
   d. suction the infant's mouth and nose to clear secretions.

97. You have just assisted in delivering an infant with a pink body, a pulse rate of 106 per minute, and good muscle tone. The infant is crying lustily. How should you care for this newborn?
   a. Wrap the newborn in clean towels and give her to the mother to hold during transport.
   b. Provide positive pressure ventilations at the rate of 60 per minute with a bag-valve mask.
   c. Monitor the infant for one minute and reassess vital signs to see if the heart rate increases.
   d. Administer free-flow oxygen by holding an oxygen mask or tubing over the newborn's face.

98. The presence of a bloody show during the first stage of labor is a sign that
   a. the delivery of the infant is imminent.
   b. the newborn is in danger of respiratory distress.
   c. labor is progressing normally.
   d. the second stage of labor has begun.

99. Your patient has experienced a spontaneous abortion or miscarriage. You should
   a. remove any tissues from the vagina.
   b. discard any expelled tissues.
   c. place a sanitary napkin in the vagina.
   d. treat the patient for shock.

100. What is the first treatment when a mother bleeds excessively from her vagina after delivery?
   a. Massage her abdomen gently.
   b. Administer oxygen.
   c. Transport her immediately.
   d. Treat her for shock.

101. Emergency care for an infant when meconium is present in the amniotic fluid includes
   a. stimulating the infant to cough to expel the meconium.
   b. performing bag-valve-mask ventilation to improve lung compliance.
   c. performing back blows and chest thrusts to remove the meconium.
   d. suctioning and notifying the hospital that meconium was present.

102. In addition to caring for injuries, emergency care for a rape victim should focus on which of the following?
   a. performing a pelvic or rectal exam on the patient
   b. collecting evidence of the rape and bagging it in plastic
   c. allowing the patient to shower and change clothes
   d. preserving evidence in a paper bag and reassuring the victim

103. The reason to position a pregnant woman on her left side is to
   a. reduce the pressure of the fetus on maternal circulation.
   b. make labor proceed more slowly by slowing down contractions.
   c. help turn a breech fetus in the birth canal to the vertex position.
   d. ensure that there is sufficient blood flow to the placenta.

104. The patient is a 29-year-old female pregnant with her second child. She is 39-weeks pregnant and saw a bloody show approximately four hours ago. Her contractions are two minutes apart and lasting 60 seconds. Transport time is approximately 45 minutes. You should
   a. protect the airway and monitor vital signs while transporting.
   b. prepare for an imminent on-scene delivery.
   c. position the mother on her left side and begin transport.
   d. notify dispatch of the need for ALS assistance.

105. When arriving at the scene of a possible hazardous materials incident, you would identify hazards by
   a. thoroughly investigating the scene yourself.
   b. interviewing victims and bystanders.
   c. scanning with binoculars from a safe distance.
   d. assisting law enforcement officers in the search.

106. Which of the following situations represents your abandonment of a patient?
   a. You begin assessing a patient, but turn responsibility for that patient over to a first responder.
   b. You begin CPR on a cardiac arrest patient, but stop when the ALS team takes over care.
   c. With the approval of medical direction, you do not transport a patient who feels fine after having a seizure.
   d. You refuse to help a patient administer nitroglycerin that has been prescribed for someone else.

107. You are called to a store where a holdup has been committed. Police are already on the scene searching for the gunman. Through the store window, you see the store manager, who has been shot. You should
   a. enter the store immediately to care for the manager.
   b. leave immediately and seek cover a distance away.
   c. wait until the police tell you it is safe to enter the scene.
   d. request medical direction to determine if you can enter.

108. What is the first thing you should do after receiving orders from the medical direction physician?
 a. Carry out the orders immediately.
 b. Repeat the orders exactly as you heard them.
 c. Question anything you did not understand.
 d. Document the orders in your report.

109. Your pregnant patient is experiencing contractions. She feels like she needs to move her bowels. This may indicate that
 a. birth is still some time away.
 b. birth is imminent.
 c. she is going into shock.
 d. the baby is still very high in the birth canal.

110. Which statement about a patient's right to refuse care is correct?
 a. A child who is old enough to understand danger is old enough to refuse care and transport.
 b. An adult patient who is of sound mind and understands the consequences can refuse treatment.
 c. No one can authorize treatment or transport for any other individual, regardless of his or her age.
 d. EMTs should leave immediately whenever a patient says that he or she will refuse care.

111. Which situation requires that an emergency patient be moved?
 a. Your patient has undergone cardiac arrest while seated in a chair.
 b. Your patient is found on the ground, unresponsive, and alone.
 c. Your patient is found in his bed, displaying early symptoms of shock.
 d. Your patient is showing signs of inadequate breathing and shock.

112. Bacterial meningitis has an incubation period of
 a. weeks to months, depending on the type.
 b. 11–21 days.
 c. 2–10 days.
 d. 2–6 weeks.

113. You can assess a pregnant woman's uterine contractions by placing your gloved hand on
 a. her abdomen, below the naval.
 b. her abdomen, above the naval.
 c. the right side of her abdomen.
 d. the left side of her abdomen.

114. You are assessing a 24-year-old male patient who is unresponsive with the following vital signs: Pulse – 60; BP – 118/76; R – 8 and shallow; Skin is warm and dry; Pupils are pinpoint and nonreactive. There are needles near the patient and what appear to be fresh punctures in the patient's arm. What is your primary focus for this patient?
 a. Administer 2 mg Narcan IV
 b. Maintain a patent airway and assist ventilations with a bag-valve mask.
 c. Place the patient on oxygen at 4 lpm via nasal cannula
 d. Remove the patient immediately to fresh air

115. A 23-year-old pregnant female is bleeding profusely from her vagina. All of the following actions are appropriate EXCEPT
 a. providing high-concentration oxygen.
 b. placing a sanitary napkin in the vagina.
 c. replacing pads as they become soaked.
 d. rapid transport to the hospital.

116. In a multiple-casualty situation, which patient should be assigned the highest priority?
   a. adequate breathing, responsive, venous bleeding
   b. adequate breathing, responsive, suspected spine injury
   c. inadequate breathing, responsive, suspected broken tibia
   d. inadequate breathing, unresponsive, suspected internal bleeding

117. Your patient is an 84-year-old female having difficulty breathing. Her daughter, age 45, is with her. When communicating with this patient, you should assume that she is
   a. incompetent; speak directly with the daughter.
   b. hard of hearing; speak extremely slowly and loudly.
   c. competent and able to understand; speak respectfully.
   d. confused; explain your treatment clearly to the daughter.

118. Which statement about patient confidentiality is correct?
   a. Patients who are cared for in a public place lose their right to confidentiality.
   b. The right to confidentiality does not apply to minors or to wards of the state.
   c. The patient who signs a statement releasing confidential information relinquishes all rights to privacy.
   d. A patient must sign a written release before any confidential information can be disclosed.

119. Your patient, a 69-year-old male, is in cardiac arrest. His wife informs you that their physician has written a do not resuscitate order for the patient, but she does not have the written order. You should
   a. provide all necessary care to save the patient's life.
   b. obey the do not resuscitate order and leave immediately.
   c. leave right after documenting the wife's statement.
   d. call the patient's doctor and try to confirm the order.

120. Your patient is a 6-year-old female who fell off her bicycle. She has a suspected broken ankle, no respiratory compromise, and no suspected internal injuries. After providing necessary care at the scene, you are transporting the child and her father to the hospital. The father loudly insists that you use your siren and lights en route. You should
   a. request medical direction in dealing with the father.
   b. request permission from dispatch to use lights and siren.
   c. refuse, because it may cause an unnecessary hazard.
   d. comply, it will relax the father and comfort the patient.

Answers

1. b. HEPA respirators are worn when in contact with patients who have airborne infections such as TB. HIV/AIDS and hepatitis B are both blood-borne pathogens. Contaminants from open wounds would also be blood borne.

2. c. Your first action should be to remove your crew and the patient from the possible noxious gas and to notify the gas company of the leak. You may also be required to alert the hazardous-materials response team. You should not attempt to locate the gas leak yourself. Treatment for the patient will begin with an ABC assessment and management of any problems you might encounter.

3. b. Because ventricular fibrillation is the most common cause of sudden cardiac arrest, it is critical to apply an AED on an unconscious apneic and pulseless patient as quickly as possible. The other rhythms can also cause a patient to be in cardiac arrest, but they do not occur as frequently as "V-fib."

4. a. The patient with chest pain and systolic blood pressure less than 100 is the highest priority patient of the four. A leg injury may be life threatening if the femoral artery is injured, but most often, a single extremity injury is not a threat to life. The elderly gentleman may be exhibiting his normal mental status, or he may be having problems due to an ongoing health problem. You need more information before you can make that determination, but he is not in any imminent danger right now. Labor with contractions six minutes apart is not considered imminent delivery. If you have any questions, however, you should continue assessing this patient as well by asking pertinent questions and checking for crowning.

5. c. Fluids containing blood have the highest potential for disease transmission.

6. c. An infant who is alert to verbal stimuli will still try to locate the parents' voices; choice **a** describes an alert infant; choice **d** describes an infant who is responsive to painful stimuli; choice **b** is incorrect because infants of this age are not developed enough to tell you their age regardless of their mental status.

7. b. Assess circulation in an infant by palpating the brachial pulse in the upper arm. The carotid and radial pulses are difficult to locate in infants. Capillary refill time shows that the patient has impaired circulation, but it is not the first tool to use in assessing circulation because it is affected by external factors (like the environment) as well as internal factors like poor perfusion.

8. c. There is no information to indicate that the patient requires ventilatory support. Any patient experiencing chest discomfort should receive the highest possible concentration of oxygen.

9. a. The rapid trauma survey is used when you are unsure of the presence of hidden injuries or if the mechanism of injury (MOI) is unclear or severe enough to suggest the need for a rapid assessment. A 2-year-old child could be severely injured by a medium-speed collision, even if he or she appears alert and was properly restrained. The other choices do not represent MOIs considered to be high risk for hidden injury.

10. c. A supine patient may or may not have jugular veins that are prominent enough to palpate. However, even if the neck veins are normally present when an individual is supine, they will not be engorged in blood and overly firm to the touch. This is what is meant by the phrase *distended neck veins*. Distended neck veins (in any position) are a sign of increased circulatory pressure. The carotid pulse should always be palpable. A decreased radial pulse may indicate hypovolemic shock or an injured extremity.

11. c. The other rhythms do not benefit from an electrical shock. The purpose of early defibrillation is to stop a highly chaotic, disorganized electrical rhythm such as ventricular fibrillation, with the hope that an organized rhythm will begin and generate a pulse.

12. b. Assess motor function by asking the patient to wiggle his toes; moving the leg or having the patient bend the knee can compromise spinal stability; option **d** describes assessment of sensation, not motor function.

13. b. Patient **b** is the only one both responsive and who has no significant mechanism of injury.

14. c. The P component of the OPQRST acronym refers to provocation or palliation, or what makes the pain feel worse or better.

15. a. You should perform the initial assessment first, because the unresponsive patient cannot direct you to the specific complaint. Vital signs are completed during your second phase of patient assessment after you determine treatment priority and have a baseline ABC assessment. You cannot determine the appropriate course of treatment of any airway problem (including the need for positioning— choice **c**) until you have first assessed the airway. The SAMPLE history is important information to gather, but it should never come before any treatment that may be needed to correct an ABC abnormality.

16. b. Trauma and medical patients who are unresponsive, and all patients who have altered mental status, should receive a detailed physical assessment. It is easy to overlook something when the patient is not conscious enough to tell you what hurts or if the MOI and nature of illness (NOI) are unclear.

17. c. The purpose of ongoing assessment is to check the adequacy of your initial interventions. The detailed examination is designed to find missed injuries.

18. d. Do CPR. American Heart Association guidelines advise that even if there is an organized rhythm, a pulse will not be palpable immediately after a shock. CPR is crucial to maintain blood flow and ventilation during this time.

19. c. Only those patients who are unresponsive, pulseless, and apneic should have the AED applied.

20. d. A patient who has taken an erectile dysfunction drug within the past 24 hours is at increased risk of a rapid decrease in blood pressure and is therefore a contraindication for the administration of nitroglycerin. The other choices are either indications or are unrelated to the administration of nitroglycerin.

21. a. You could make the argument that you need additional help in the management of each of these situations; however, the one with the most critical need is when you must care for more than one critical patient. Both patients with gunshot wounds need immediate attention, so you should call for backup. In the other three situations, you should not require assistance unless some complicating factor presents itself. Patient **b** may or may not require ALS assistance, but most (over 80%) deliveries are simple and uncomplicated and can be easily managed by basic life support (BLS) providers. Patient **c** is having a febrile seizure, which is managed by stabilizing the ABCs and transporting. In patient **d**, even if your partner is required to stabilize the cervical spine, you should be able to manage the patient for the time being until other assistance arrives to assist with packaging and moving the patient.

22. c. The epiglottis is the leaf-shaped structure that closes off the trachea during swallowing. The larynx is the voice box, the structure that produces speech vibrations; the cricoid cartilage forms the lower portion of the larynx; the diaphragm is a large muscle that contracts to initiate inhalation.

23. d. The alveoli are the numerous minute air sacs that make up the lungs; bronchioles are small branches of the bronchi, which are the two main tubes branching from the trachea; the epiglottis is the structure that closes off the trachea during swallowing.

24. a. Other symptoms of pulmonary edema may include difficulty breathing, excessive sweating, anxiety, and pale skin.

25. c. During capillary–cellular exchange, oxygen enters the body cells and carbon dioxide enters the capillaries; choices **a** and **b** describe alveolar-capillary exchange; choice **d** has carbon monoxide, not carbon dioxide.

26. d. Accessory muscles may be seen in use in the neck and as retractions above the clavicles and/or between the ribs. These muscles are used when greater than normal inspiratory and/or expiratory pressures are needed to

move air. Normal breathing does not produce any audible sounds, but it will produce auscultatory sounds (heard with a stethoscope). Warm, dry skin and equal chest expansion are both signs of adequate breathing.

27. d. Bell's palsy is the most common form of facial paralysis. Muscular dystrophy is a degenerative disease characterized by the weakening of skeletal muscle fibers. ALS, also known as Lou Gehrig's disease, affects the nerve cells that control voluntary movement. Dystonia describes repetitive motions or abnormal posturing.

28. a. A gurgling sound means that the patient needs to be suctioned immediately; ventilation cannot be adequate when the airway is blocked from mucous, blood, or other secretions.

29. c. The best indication of the proper tidal volume with any assisted ventilations is visible rise and fall of the chest. The alarm on an ATV indicates increased airway pressures and has nothing to do with the tidal volume setting. Capnography is a good indicator of ET tube placement and respiration, but does not truly indicate an adequate tidal volume.

30. b. The seizure event is referred to as *ictal,* hence *postictal* refers to the period after the seizure wherein a patent is often confused for a period of time.

31. b. Choice **b** is the correct procedure. Choice **a** is correct for a rigid catheter, choice **c** is the correct method for inserting an oropharyngeal airway, and choice **d** is applicable only to endotracheal intubation.

32. c. Choice **c** is the correct procedure for clearing the airway when simple suctioning is not working. Choice **b** is appropriate for a patient with copious frothy secretions like the kind produced with pulmonary edema. Choices **a** and **d** are inappropriate without first clearing the airway.

33. d. The purpose of the head-tilt/chin-lift is to move the tongue and epiglottis out of the way of the airway; it is not useful for intubation (use the sniffing position), to remove foreign bodies, or to visualize the larynx.

34. b. After opening the airway, the EMT should assess the rate and depth of ventilations; choices **a**, **c**, and/or **d** would occur only after respiratory adequacy has been assessed and they are appropriate to use.

35. d. Cyanosis, or a bluish coloration of the mucus membranes and skin, is caused by inadequate oxygen supply to the body tissues; the other choices are unrelated to oxygen supply.

36. c. After sealing the mask to the patient's face, you should begin mouth-to-mask ventilation with a long, slow breath; steps **a**, **b**, and **d** should be done before applying the mask.

37. d. The correct rate is 12 ventilations per minute for an adult (one breath every five seconds), and the correct rate for a child is 20 ventilations per minute.

38. d. During a two-person bag-valve-mask procedure, one EMT ventilates the patient while the other maintains the airway and monitors the patient's chest rise.

39. a. The cricoid cartilage forms a ring of firm cartilage and is located inferior to (below) the larynx.

40. a. A means alert. The other letters in the acronym stand for verbal, pain, and unresponsive.

41. b. A bulb syringe is used to suction an infant's nasal passage or mouth and is generally used with infants up to age three to four months.

If you are using mechanical or hand-powered suction equipment in infants of this age, be very careful to use the lowest possible pressures needed to accomplish the job.

42. b. The standard pad placement for a child between the ages of one and eight or weighing less than 55 lbs is to place one on the lower left anterior chest (apex of the heart) and one on the upper right or left posterior thorax. Placement of both pads on the anterior thorax is used on adults; children's chests are generally too small to accommodate both pads on the front.

43. c. The right ventricle receives oxygen-poor blood from the right atrium. It then pumps the blood to the lungs via the pulmonary artery, where it receives oxygen and releases carbon dioxide.

44. c. The role of the EMT is not to diagnose the exact cause of the patient's chief complaint. Maintaining a high suspicion for a cardiac emergency will guide your next step in managing this patient appropriately.

45. d. Your first action would be to administer oxygen and place the patient in a comfortable position; next, if not contraindicated, you would request permission to administer nitroglycerin. You should first obtain a set of vital signs to ensure he is not in cardiogenic shock. Never put defibrillator pads onto a conscious patient with a pulse; this procedure is contraindicated. AED pads are not serving the same function as the electrodes used by ALS providers to monitor the heart rhythm.

46. a. Prehospital ACLS provides additional medications and other therapies that may help either terminate the cardiac arrest state or help prevent the patient who has regained a pulse from going back into cardiac arrest.

47. a. Although you note several injuries, you still need to perform a rapid initial assessment to determine if there are any problems with the ABCs that may be more life threatening than what you can obviously see. Controlling the bleeding is a high priority, but the use of pressure points is no longer a recommended procedure. You should treat the patient for shock, but the deformity to his leg contraindicates elevating his legs. Once on a backboard the patient could be placed in the Trendelenburg position. There is no indication that this patient needs ventilation assistance.

48. d. When the SAED is attempting to analyze the patient's electrical rhythm, any movement of the patient or the unit could cause the machine to misinterpret the signal.

49. c. Safety is critical when performing defibrillation. Any defibrillation attempt in the rain may possibly harm anyone near the patient during the discharge of the unit.

50. c. Tourniquet application has replaced pressure points as the next step in the control of profuse bleeding. A tourniquet should be placed proximal to the wound and in accordance with your local protocol.

51. a. Kinetic energy is the energy an object has while in motion. Choice **b** describes mass, choice **c** describes energy, and choice **d** describes inertia.

52. c. Having the bystander stop CPR will allow you to reassess the patient's ventilatory and circulatory status. This will tell you whether you need to continue CPR or whether the patient has regained a pulse or is breathing.

53. a. Venous bleeding flows in a steady, dark-red stream. Arterial bleeding is bright red and spurts from the wound, while capillary bleeding oozes. Internal bleeding may or may not present externally recognizable signs or symptoms.

54. d. This patient has the classic signs and symptoms of shock. Do not offer anything to eat or drink to a patient you suspect of being in shock, since surgery may be necessary later.

55. c. Speed is squared in the calculation of kinetic energy. A one-pound object traveling at 30 mph is nine times more injurious than a one-pound object traveling at 10 mph.

56. c. The patient is most likely suffering from right-sided heart failure. Her signs and symptoms indicated blood is backing up in the peripheral circulation due to the weakened right ventricle. Left-sided failure would present with wet lung sounds as the blood backed up into the pulmonary system.

57. b. Ventricular tachycardia often converts to ventricular fibrillation, a life-threatening heart rhythm that the AED is designed to correct.

58. c. Apply the AED in a manner that does not interrupt cardiac compressions. Once the AED is applied and ready to analyze the cardiac rhythm, stop CPR and allow the AED to analyze the rhythm. Stopping CPR allows the AED to evaluate the cardiac rhythm and minimizes interference from muscle movement.

59. c. When an AED either indicates "no shock advised" or has delivered a shock to a patient the EMT's next action should be to continue CPR. Research has shown that even if a patient has regained a pulse the next round of cardiac compressions is not harmful and may be beneficial. When the AED indicates "no shock advised" it has detected a non-shockable rhythm, but the AED has no way of assessing a patient's pulse.

60. a. If the patient has been resuscitated but is still unresponsive, check the pulse every 30 seconds during transport and keep the AED leads attached to the patient.

61. c. If it becomes necessary to deliver shocks while en route with the patient, the proper procedure is to stop the vehicle before reanalyzing the rhythm because the AED has a motion detector sensor in place that will not allow the unit to operate in the presence of motion.

62. d. The primary action of nitroglycerin is to dilate the myocardial (coronary) arteries, therefore easing the heart's workload by increasing the blood flow. Lowering of blood pressure is a secondary effect seen with vessel dilation. Reflex tachycardia, not bradycardia, may occur as a result of nitroglycerine administration. It does not have any direct effects on the muscles of the heart.

63. b. Myocardial pain is often difficult to determine because it can take on many different characters; however, patients most commonly (more than 40% of the time) describe the pain of a myocardial infarction as a crushing, squeezing pressure that radiates outward to the arms and upper back.

64. a. Children often turn toward the impact and are often thrown down and under the vehicle.

65. a. The combination of direct pressure, elevation, and pressure dressings is almost always successful in controlling hemorrhage in an extremity. In the event these three methods do not work a tourniquet is your next choice. Pressure points are no longer recommended and PASG is never the first method for controlling hemorrhage.

66. d. Lifting the jaw is necessary to dislodge the tongue from the back of the throat and provide a patent airway.

67. b. The head-tilt/chin-lift may jeopardize the patient's cervical spine. The other two procedures will not adequately open the airway.

68. c. Tertiary blast injury includes those injuries resulting from structural collapse.

69. d. Assess pulse, motor function, and sensation distal to a splint both before and after applying the splint to ensure that the splint is not adversely affecting circulation to the limb.

70. c. Tilting the head may compromise the stabilization of the cervical spine when using the modified jaw thrust.

71. b. The first 60 minutes after the occurrence of multisystem trauma is the *golden period*.

72. a. Blood is too fluid to be cleared adequately by a finger sweep. The other answers are not appropriate unless the airway was cleared first by suction.

73. a. The factors the EMT should consider when evaluating the MOI of a fall are the height of the fall, surface landed on, and body part making first contact. In adults, a fall of > 15' or 3 times their height is significant, whereas a child falling > 10' or falling < 10' with loss of consciousness is significant. The surface landed on will dictate how much energy the surface can absorb and the first body part making contact will help you determine the path of the energy and which systems are damaged.

74. c. While the other answers may be true, they may occur regardless of the time interval.

75. c. The one-way valve minimizes potential cross-exposure of the patient's secretions and exhaled breath to the rescuer.

76. a. Administer oral glucose on medical direction (through protocol or standing order) only to patients with altered mental status and history of diabetes. Patient **b** should be first treated as a trauma patient, and because research shows poor outcomes following brain injuries and glucose administration, it is best to withhold its use until blood sugar can be checked (which is an ALS-provider skill in many areas). Patient **c** is not appropriate because of an inability to swallow properly; ALS should be called to provide IV dextrose to this patient. Glucose should be withheld until you can better determine if patient **d** is actually diabetic or not. (A blood glucose reading would be helpful with this patient as well.)

77. c. Common causes of altered mental status include trauma, diabetes, seizures, and infectious disease. Asking about fever helps determine if there is a history of recent infection.

78. d. Signs of allergic reactions include increased heart rate, as the heart attempts to compensate for hypoperfusion. The two primary life-threatening events that occur during an allergic reaction are profound vasoconstriction (resulting in shock) and compromised airway due to swelling, constriction, or mucous production.

79. c. EMTs can administer epinephrine for anaphylactic reactions under medical direction. In many areas the medication must be prescribed for the patient; in some states epinephrine is carried by the EMT and can be administered according to local protocol. Always adhere to your local protocols when providing medications to a patient.

80. b. The pediatric dose of epinephrine for anaphylaxis is 0.15 mg and is administered with a pediatric autoinjection device (EpiPen Jr or Twinject). The other dosages are all too high.

81. b. Care for a hypothermic patient with a diminished level of responsiveness should include passive rewarming (blankets and heated room) only; active rewarming should take place only in the hospital environment, and hypothermic patients should not be allowed to exercise or to take stimulants, such as coffee or tea. However, your protocols may allow you to give warmed liquids that are not alcoholic or caffeinated to slightly hypothermic patients with a normal mental status.

82. d. Cool skin on the abdomen is a reliable sign of hypothermia in a patient because the abdomen is in the central core of the body and is generally covered under layers of clothing.

83. c. The goal of care in cases of localized cold damage is to prevent further damage by removing the patient from the cold environment and protecting the damaged tissues from further injury. Rewarming is best accomplished in the hospital setting, where pain medication can be administered and the danger of reinjury due to recooling is diminished.

84. a. A hyperthermic patient with hot skin must be treated aggressively before permanent organ damage sets in. When the skin is hot and dry, the normal sweating mechanisms have stopped functioning and the patient is in danger of brain damage due to excessive high body temperature.

85. c. Grabbing a stinger with tweezers or your fingers can squeeze more venom into the wound (also, there is personal risk of accidental exposure to the venom if you use your hands). Instead, scrape the stinger out of the skin with a piece of cardboard or rigid plastic (a credit card is ideal). Cutting around the stinger causes more tissue damage.

86. **d.** SLUDGE stands for salivation, lacrimation (tearing), urination, defecation, gastric distress, and emesis resulting from the inhibition of acetylcholinesterase, which allows the neurotransmitter acetylcholine to accumulate. Atropine, an anticholinergic, is the antidote for these symptoms. SLUDGE can also be seen in patients exposed to organophosphate poisonings.

87. **b.** Choice **b** describes early respiratory distress. Choice **a** describes the signs of impending respiratory arrest from insufficiency, choice **c** describes respiratory failure, and choice **d** describes airway obstruction.

88. **d.** For patients who have routine seizures and whose condition returns to normal quickly after a seizure, you should request medical direction about whether to transport.

89. **b.** Multiple injuries, conflicting stories of the cause, and repeated calls to the same address are characteristic of child abuse.

90. **a.** Suctioning the baby's mouth and nose will help to open the airway while the baby has not yet begun breathing. You should not force any part of the delivery process.

91. **b.** Care for a responsive child consists of standing behind the child and attempting to relieve the obstruction with a series of subdiaphragmatic thrusts.

92. **a.** Signs of respiratory failure include altered mental status and a slow or fast breathing rate with fatigue. There is not enough information to determine if patients **b** and **c** are in respiratory insufficiency, respiratory failure, or impending respiratory arrest. Patient **d** is in impending respiratory arrest.

93. **b.** Profuse vaginal bleeding may indicate a true obstetrical emergency such as uterine rupture or torn placenta.

94. **b.** Select the correct-size oral airway for an infant or child by measuring from the corner of the patient's mouth to the angle of the jaw.

95. **a.** Vitreous humor is found behind the lens of the eye. It is the clear gel that fills the space between the lens and the retina. Aqueous humor is a thick, watery substance that fills the space between the lens and the cornea.

96. **c.** If the cord is wrapped around the infant's neck and you cannot easily loosen and remove it, you should clamp it in two places and cut the cord.

97. **a.** This newborn has a high Apgar score; there is no need for respiratory support unless the condition changes. You should always follow the steps in the inverted pyramid for neonatal resuscitation by drying and warming, positioning the head down for drainage, suctioning the airway and nose as needed, and providing tactile stimulation to stimulate breathing.

98. **c.** The presence of a bloody show (which is the expulsion of the mucous plug from the mouth of the cervix) occurs during the first stage of labor. It is normal and indicates that the cervix is beginning to open or dilate and may occur several hours prior to delivery. The second stage of labor continues until the baby is born.

99. **d.** There can be large blood loss suffered by the mother during a miscarriage. The EMT should treat the patient for possible shock as well as provide emotional care.

100. **a.** More than 500 mL of blood loss after delivery is excessive; massage the mother's abdomen by rubbing firmly in one direction from

the symphasis pubis bone toward the umbilicus. This will help the uterus contract and stop the bleeding. Oxygen administration, shock treatment, and rapid transport will follow uterine massage.

101. d. If meconium is present in the amniotic fluid, suction the infant before stimulating it to cry, then notify the hospital of the presence of meconium. An ALS crew may be able to perform tracheal suctioning and intubate the infant. If the lungs are stiff and noncompliant, it may indicate that aspiration of the meconium has occurred. Aspiration pneumonia due to meconium is often fatal.

102. d. In addition to providing routine emergency care, care for a rape victim should focus on preserving evidence and providing comfort and reassurance. Although you want to provide comfort to the patient, you should not allow him or her to shower or change clothes, as this will destroy evidence. Any clothing or personal effects that are removed from the patient should be placed in paper bags to prevent the growth of bacteria that might occur if stored in plastic bags. You should not need to examine the genital or rectal area unless you note significant bleeding.

103. a. This condition, called supine hypotension syndrome, is the result of compression that the enlarged uterus causes on the vena cava of the maternal circulatory system. This corrective position, called the left lateral recumbent position, is accomplished by placing the mother on her left side with her legs bent slightly or kept straight. Maternal positional changes have no effect on the speed of labor or the position of the infant in the birth canal. By assisting in venous blood return in

the mother, you will get the secondary effect of increasing blood flow to the uterus, but this is a secondary effect seen in correcting supine hypotension syndrome.

104. b. The patient is likely to deliver imminently, so prepare for a normal delivery.

105. c. Never enter a scene where hazardous materials are present until you have verified that the scene is safe. Use binoculars to survey the scene from a distance in order to identify hazardous materials placards. Consider victims and bystanders contaminated and take appropriate precautions.

106. a. Abandonment occurs when you relinquish care without a patient's consent or without insuring that care is continued by someone of the same or higher level, such as a paramedic, ALS unit, or physician.

107. c. EMTs should not enter a crime scene until it has been secured by police. As you travel to the scene, you should determine where it is most appropriate to park your vehicle. Generally, you want cover (protection from attack) and concealment (out of direct visual range) in your staging area.

108. b. To avoid misunderstanding, always repeat medical orders exactly as you heard them. Once you have done that, you can question any order you do not understand or about which you are unclear. When you complete your written patient-care report, you should include the order in your report.

109. b. The sensation of needing to move one's bowels during labor is the result of the head pressing down on the anal sphincter as the baby passes through the birth canal. The head is very close to the opening of the birth canal, and delivery is imminent.

110. b. An adult of sound mind can refuse treatment, but the EMT should first make an effort to clearly explain the consequences; refusal of treatment should be documented in writing.

111. a. An emergency move is required in a situation where a patient is in immediate life-threatening danger. Emergency moves require only cervical spine stabilization (if it is a trauma situation) and should be performed quickly. Once the patient is in a safer location, you should begin with your initial assessment as you do in all patient situations.

112. c. Bacterial meningitis has an incubation period of 2–10 days. Bacterial infections of the meninges are extremely serious illnesses, and may result in death or brain damage even if treated.

113. b. The uterus is most easily felt just above the navel.

114. b. This patient is most likely suffering from an opioid overdose and subsequent CNS depression. He is in immediate need of a patent airway and assisted ventilations at 10–12 breaths per minute. Some states are allowing EMTs to administer Narcan, but not by IV. Always refer to your local protocol.

115. b. Placing napkins in the birth canal will not stop the source of bleeding. Placing bulky dressings or sanitary napkins at the vaginal opening will help prevent the blood from spreading.

116. d. Patients with breathing difficulties and serious bleeding receive the highest priority in a multiple-casualty situation.

117. c. Do not assume that an elderly patient is incompetent, deaf, or confused. Address all patients respectfully.

118. d. Patient information can be released only if the patient has signed a specific consent form.

119. a. If you are informed of a do not resuscitate order but do not actually see it, you must still provide all necessary care.

120. c. You are responsible for helping make your patient feel at ease, but you are also responsible for operating your ambulance in the safest possible way.

4 ▶ EMT PRACTICE EXAM 2

CHAPTER SUMMARY
This is the second of ten practice exams in this book based on the National Registry's EMT cognitive exam. Having taken one test before, you should feel more confident of your ability to pick the correct answers. Use this test to continue your study and practice. Notice how knowing what to expect makes you feel better prepared!

Like the first exam in this book, this test is based on the National Registry exam. It should not, however, look exactly like the first test you took, because you know more now about how the test is put together. You have seen how different types of questions are presented and are perhaps beginning to notice patterns in the order of questions. You see that questions on each area are grouped together. This pattern will help you develop your own test-taking strategy.

If you're following the advice of this book, you've done some studying between this exam and the first. This second exam will give you a chance to see how much you've improved.

The answer sheet, the test, and the answer key appear next (in that order). Read the answer explanations carefully, especially the explanations for the questions you missed.

1.	ⓐ	ⓑ	ⓒ	ⓓ
2.	ⓐ	ⓑ	ⓒ	ⓓ
3.	ⓐ	ⓑ	ⓒ	ⓓ
4.	ⓐ	ⓑ	ⓒ	ⓓ
5.	ⓐ	ⓑ	ⓒ	ⓓ
6.	ⓐ	ⓑ	ⓒ	ⓓ
7.	ⓐ	ⓑ	ⓒ	ⓓ
8.	ⓐ	ⓑ	ⓒ	ⓓ
9.	ⓐ	ⓑ	ⓒ	ⓓ
10.	ⓐ	ⓑ	ⓒ	ⓓ
11.	ⓐ	ⓑ	ⓒ	ⓓ
12.	ⓐ	ⓑ	ⓒ	ⓓ
13.	ⓐ	ⓑ	ⓒ	ⓓ
14.	ⓐ	ⓑ	ⓒ	ⓓ
15.	ⓐ	ⓑ	ⓒ	ⓓ
16.	ⓐ	ⓑ	ⓒ	ⓓ
17.	ⓐ	ⓑ	ⓒ	ⓓ
18.	ⓐ	ⓑ	ⓒ	ⓓ
19.	ⓐ	ⓑ	ⓒ	ⓓ
20.	ⓐ	ⓑ	ⓒ	ⓓ
21.	ⓐ	ⓑ	ⓒ	ⓓ
22.	ⓐ	ⓑ	ⓒ	ⓓ
23.	ⓐ	ⓑ	ⓒ	ⓓ
24.	ⓐ	ⓑ	ⓒ	ⓓ
25.	ⓐ	ⓑ	ⓒ	ⓓ
26.	ⓐ	ⓑ	ⓒ	ⓓ
27.	ⓐ	ⓑ	ⓒ	ⓓ
28.	ⓐ	ⓑ	ⓒ	ⓓ
29.	ⓐ	ⓑ	ⓒ	ⓓ
30.	ⓐ	ⓑ	ⓒ	ⓓ
31.	ⓐ	ⓑ	ⓒ	ⓓ
32.	ⓐ	ⓑ	ⓒ	ⓓ
33.	ⓐ	ⓑ	ⓒ	ⓓ
34.	ⓐ	ⓑ	ⓒ	ⓓ
35.	ⓐ	ⓑ	ⓒ	ⓓ
36.	ⓐ	ⓑ	ⓒ	ⓓ
37.	ⓐ	ⓑ	ⓒ	ⓓ
38.	ⓐ	ⓑ	ⓒ	ⓓ
39.	ⓐ	ⓑ	ⓒ	ⓓ
40.	ⓐ	ⓑ	ⓒ	ⓓ

41.	ⓐ	ⓑ	ⓒ	ⓓ
42.	ⓐ	ⓑ	ⓒ	ⓓ
43.	ⓐ	ⓑ	ⓒ	ⓓ
44.	ⓐ	ⓑ	ⓒ	ⓓ
45.	ⓐ	ⓑ	ⓒ	ⓓ
46.	ⓐ	ⓑ	ⓒ	ⓓ
47.	ⓐ	ⓑ	ⓒ	ⓓ
48.	ⓐ	ⓑ	ⓒ	ⓓ
49.	ⓐ	ⓑ	ⓒ	ⓓ
50.	ⓐ	ⓑ	ⓒ	ⓓ
51.	ⓐ	ⓑ	ⓒ	ⓓ
52.	ⓐ	ⓑ	ⓒ	ⓓ
53.	ⓐ	ⓑ	ⓒ	ⓓ
54.	ⓐ	ⓑ	ⓒ	ⓓ
55.	ⓐ	ⓑ	ⓒ	ⓓ
56.	ⓐ	ⓑ	ⓒ	ⓓ
57.	ⓐ	ⓑ	ⓒ	ⓓ
58.	ⓐ	ⓑ	ⓒ	ⓓ
59.	ⓐ	ⓑ	ⓒ	ⓓ
60.	ⓐ	ⓑ	ⓒ	ⓓ
61.	ⓐ	ⓑ	ⓒ	ⓓ
62.	ⓐ	ⓑ	ⓒ	ⓓ
63.	ⓐ	ⓑ	ⓒ	ⓓ
64.	ⓐ	ⓑ	ⓒ	ⓓ
65.	ⓐ	ⓑ	ⓒ	ⓓ
66.	ⓐ	ⓑ	ⓒ	ⓓ
67.	ⓐ	ⓑ	ⓒ	ⓓ
68.	ⓐ	ⓑ	ⓒ	ⓓ
69.	ⓐ	ⓑ	ⓒ	ⓓ
70.	ⓐ	ⓑ	ⓒ	ⓓ
71.	ⓐ	ⓑ	ⓒ	ⓓ
72.	ⓐ	ⓑ	ⓒ	ⓓ
73.	ⓐ	ⓑ	ⓒ	ⓓ
74.	ⓐ	ⓑ	ⓒ	ⓓ
75.	ⓐ	ⓑ	ⓒ	ⓓ
76.	ⓐ	ⓑ	ⓒ	ⓓ
77.	ⓐ	ⓑ	ⓒ	ⓓ
78.	ⓐ	ⓑ	ⓒ	ⓓ
79.	ⓐ	ⓑ	ⓒ	ⓓ
80.	ⓐ	ⓑ	ⓒ	ⓓ

81.	ⓐ	ⓑ	ⓒ	ⓓ
82.	ⓐ	ⓑ	ⓒ	ⓓ
83.	ⓐ	ⓑ	ⓒ	ⓓ
84.	ⓐ	ⓑ	ⓒ	ⓓ
85.	ⓐ	ⓑ	ⓒ	ⓓ
86.	ⓐ	ⓑ	ⓒ	ⓓ
87.	ⓐ	ⓑ	ⓒ	ⓓ
88.	ⓐ	ⓑ	ⓒ	ⓓ
89.	ⓐ	ⓑ	ⓒ	ⓓ
90.	ⓐ	ⓑ	ⓒ	ⓓ
91.	ⓐ	ⓑ	ⓒ	ⓓ
92.	ⓐ	ⓑ	ⓒ	ⓓ
93.	ⓐ	ⓑ	ⓒ	ⓓ
94.	ⓐ	ⓑ	ⓒ	ⓓ
95.	ⓐ	ⓑ	ⓒ	ⓓ
96.	ⓐ	ⓑ	ⓒ	ⓓ
97.	ⓐ	ⓑ	ⓒ	ⓓ
98.	ⓐ	ⓑ	ⓒ	ⓓ
99.	ⓐ	ⓑ	ⓒ	ⓓ
100.	ⓐ	ⓑ	ⓒ	ⓓ
101.	ⓐ	ⓑ	ⓒ	ⓓ
102.	ⓐ	ⓑ	ⓒ	ⓓ
103.	ⓐ	ⓑ	ⓒ	ⓓ
104.	ⓐ	ⓑ	ⓒ	ⓓ
105.	ⓐ	ⓑ	ⓒ	ⓓ
106.	ⓐ	ⓑ	ⓒ	ⓓ
107.	ⓐ	ⓑ	ⓒ	ⓓ
108.	ⓐ	ⓑ	ⓒ	ⓓ
109.	ⓐ	ⓑ	ⓒ	ⓓ
110.	ⓐ	ⓑ	ⓒ	ⓓ
111.	ⓐ	ⓑ	ⓒ	ⓓ
112.	ⓐ	ⓑ	ⓒ	ⓓ
113.	ⓐ	ⓑ	ⓒ	ⓓ
114.	ⓐ	ⓑ	ⓒ	ⓓ
115.	ⓐ	ⓑ	ⓒ	ⓓ
116.	ⓐ	ⓑ	ⓒ	ⓓ
117.	ⓐ	ⓑ	ⓒ	ⓓ
118.	ⓐ	ⓑ	ⓒ	ⓓ
119.	ⓐ	ⓑ	ⓒ	ⓓ
120.	ⓐ	ⓑ	ⓒ	ⓓ

EMT Practice Exam 2

1. Which patient's vital signs are NOT within normal limits?
   a. newborn: pulse, 100; respirations, 30; BP, 70/30
   b. 3-year-old child: pulse, 90; respirations, 28; BP, 86/50
   c. 10-year-old child: pulse, 88; respirations, 18; BP, 100/60
   d. adult: pulse, 76; respirations, 17; BP, 116/86

2. A 45-year-old male is breathing at a rate of 32 times per minute with shallow respirations. He is altered, and his skin signs are cool, cyanotic, and diaphoretic. You should
   a. provide oxygen at 6 L/min using a nasal cannula.
   b. provide oxygen at 12 L/min using a nonrebreather mask.
   c. provide artificial ventilation with a bag-valve mask and high-flow oxygen.
   d. place the patient into the left lateral "recovery" position.

3. Your patient is behaving abnormally but refuses treatment after falling down a flight of stairs. Before transporting the patient without consent, you should
   a. document the presence of any injury.
   b. ask bystanders to serve as witnesses.
   c. have bystanders help talk him into care.
   d. contact medical direction for advice.

4. A 45-year-old female is breathing at a rate of 22 times per minute with adequate tidal volume. She is alert, but her skin signs are cool, pale, and diaphoretic. You should
   a. provide oxygen at 6 L/min using a nasal cannula.
   b. provide oxygen at 12 L/min using a nonrebreather mask.
   c. provide artificial ventilation with a bag-valve and high-flow oxygen.
   d. place the patient into the left lateral "recovery" position.

5. You would locate a patient's carotid pulse by first finding the Adam's apple and then
   a. pressing hard on only one side of the patient's neck.
   b. placing one hand gently on each side of the neck.
   c. pressing with your thumb on one side of the neck.
   d. sliding two fingers toward one side of the neck.

6. Your patient's pupils react unequally to light. You should suspect the presence of
   a. head injury.
   b. shock.
   c. airway obstruction.
   d. cardiac arrest.

7. A 70-year-old female is complaining of shortness of breath. She has a history of emphysema. You should
   a. withhold oxygen, since these patients do not respond to oxygen.
   b. withhold oxygen, because you could eliminate the hypoxic drive.
   c. administer oxygen, because in most cases, the hypoxic drive will not be a problem.
   d. withhold oxygen, because these patients become apneic if they receive high-flow oxygen.

8. *Ecchymosis* refers to
   a. an unreactive left pupil.
   b. bruising or discoloration.
   c. motion sickness.
   d. a bad taste in the mouth.

9. In which situation should you determine the patient's blood pressure through palpation?
   a. Your patient is under one year old.
   b. The setting is unusually quiet, such as a private home.
   c. Your patient's pulse is very weak and difficult to hear.
   d. Your patient cannot tolerate pressure to the cartoid artery.

10. The correct way to select the proper size oropharyngeal airway (OPA) is to measure the distance from the
    a. corner of the mouth to the tip of the earlobe.
    b. nose to the tip of the earlobe.
    c. corner of the mouth to the nose.
    d. nose to the tip of the chin.

11. Which patient should receive only a focused physical exam and SAMPLE history?
    a. 46-year-old male, unresponsive after falling from a 10-meter scaffold
    b. 80-year-old male, responsive to painful stimuli after being hit by a car
    c. 5-year-old female, responsive and in pain after falling from a standing position
    d. 16-year-old female, responsive to verbal stimuli after a gunshot wound

12. Ethics is best described as
    a. the principles of conduct; concerns for what is right or wrong, good or bad.
    b. a code of conduct put forward by a society or some other group such as a religion.
    c. the principle of doing good for the patient.
    d. the obligation to treat all patients fairly.

13. Continuous monitoring of a patient's mental status is best accomplished by
    a. repeatedly asking the patient's name and address.
    b. continuously monitoring the patient's vital signs.
    c. continuously interacting with the patient.
    d. repeatedly assessing the peripheral circulation.

14. You should assess the brachial pulse in patients who
    a. have a weak peripheral pulse.
    b. are younger than one year old.
    c. have a history of cardiac problems.
    d. have a pulse rate less than 60/min.

15. Which patient is showing early signs of shock (decreased tissue perfusion)?
    a. 23-year-old female: pulse, 104; respiration, 25/min; BP, 118/78; cool, clammy skin
    b. 45-year-old female: pulse, 68; respiration, 20/min; BP, 110/72; warm, moist skin
    c. 5-year-old male: pulse, 110; respiration, 22/min; BP, 88/52; cool, dry skin
    d. 60-year-old male: pulse, 76; respiration, 10/min; BP, 96/60; hot, dry skin

16. Which of the following is the most important sign of a diabetic emergency?
    a. altered mental status
    b. warm, dry skin
    c. decreased heart rate
    d. nausea and vomiting

17. Of the following diseases, which poses the most risk to EMTs?
    a. hepatitis C
    b. staphylococcal infection
    c. HIV
    d. AIDS

18. In legal terms, a *tort* is a(n)?
   a. civil wrong committed by one individual against another.
   b. criminal wrongdoing.
   c. action by an employee for a workers' compensation claim.
   d. breach of contract.

19. The zygomatic bones are found in
   a. the face.
   b. the wrist.
   c. the nasal passages.
   d. none of the above.

20. What is the most common cause of airway obstruction in an unconscious patient?
   a. vomitus
   b. mucous
   c. the tongue
   d. blood

21. All of the following are reasons that infants and children are prone to respiratory difficulties EXCEPT that they
   a. breathe faster than adults.
   b. have smaller air passages.
   c. use their diaphragm rather than their intercostal muscles.
   d. are prone to respiratory infections.

22. Your patient is a newborn. You should consider the possibility of breathing difficulty if the respiratory rate is
   a. 40/min.
   b. 50/min.
   c. 60/min.
   d. 70/min.

23. When assessing your patient's airway, you hear snoring sounds. You should suspect that
   a. there is fluid in the airway.
   b. the tongue is blocking the airway.
   c. the bronchioles are constricted.
   d. the patient is forcefully exhaling.

24. How many vertebrae are there in the human spinal column?
   a. 33
   b. 66
   c. 44
   d. 77

25. You hear gurgling in your patient's airway. You should immediately
   a. administer high-flow oxygen.
   b. open and suction the airway.
   c. insert a nasopharyngeal airway.
   d. insert an oropharyngeal airway.

26. According to the American Heart Association, at least _____ of air should be delivered to the patient when using an adult bag-valve mask.
   a. 800 mL
   b. 1,000 mL
   c. 80 L
   d. 8 L

27. The advantages of using an Automatic Transport Ventilator (ATV) include
   a. the relief valve prevents barotrauma.
   b. once tidal volume is set all oxygen goes to the lungs.
   c. it can allow the EMT to perform other tasks.
   d. oxygen powered ATVs never stop working.

28. In what position should you place a child's head for ventilation?
   a. in the neutral position
   b. slightly hyperextended
   c. slightly flexed foward
   d. in the recovery position

29. You are out walking in the park and you find a 6-year-old male unresponsive, pulseless, and apneic. Your first action is to
   a. locate the closest AED and apply it to the patient.
   b. begin CPR.
   c. find the closest phone and call for help.
   d. attempt to locate the parent(s) to obtain consent to treat.

30. After obtaining medical direction, you are helping your patient use a prescribed inhaler. You should tell the patient to
   a. take three quick, shallow breaths.
   b. inhale deeply and hold her breath.
   c. exhale as slowly as she can.
   d. lie down to prevent dizziness.

31. Your patient, a 78-year-old male, has no pulse and agonal respirations. You should
   a. begin CPR immediately.
   b. administer high-flow oxygen via bag-valve mask.
   c. transport immediately to the closest medical facility.
   d. request the patient's permission to administer nitroglycerin.

32. You have assisted a patient in administering a prescribed inhaler. After one dose of the medication, the patient's pulse rate increases, and he reports feeling nauseated. You should
   a. administer another dose of the medication.
   b. assess respiratory rate, rhythm, and quality.
   c. document and report the signs and symptoms.
   d. begin cardiopulmonary resuscitation.

33. You should remove your patient's dentures in order to provide ventilation when
   a. head trauma has occurred.
   b. it is necessary to insert an oral airway.
   c. they become dislodged.
   d. they make the patient uncomfortable.

34. During the management of a cardiac arrest, the AED gives a "no shock indicated" message. Which of the following statements will most likely prompt this condition?
   a. The patient's rhythm is asystole.
   b. The patient has a pulse.
   c. The patient is in ventricular tachycardia.
   d. The patient is in ventricular fibrillation.

35. Which patient is breathing adequately?
   a. 3-month-old male: respiratory rate, 62/min, using diaphragm and muscles in chest and neck
   b. 7-year-old female: respiratory rate, 12/min, irregular rhythm, using diaphragm primarily
   c. 18-year-old male: respiratory rate, 28/min, shallow chest motions
   d. 43-year-old female: respiratory rate, 15/min, regular chest motions

36. The signs and symptoms of myocardial infarction include
   a. crushing substernal chest pain lasting longer than 20 minutes.
   b. polydipsia.
   c. chest pressure alleviated by rest.
   d. hemiparesis.

37. You have delivered a shock with the SAED. Your cardiac arrest patient has shallow, agonal respirations with a pulse. What should you do next?
  a. Deliver second shock to assure patient does not arrest again.
  b. Provide artificial ventilation with high-concentration oxygen.
  c. Give high-concentration oxygen by nonrebreather mask.
  d. Check pulse and deliver two more shocks.

38. A danger of using a rigid suction catheter with infants and young children is that stimulating the back of the throat can
  a. cause changes in the heart rhythm.
  b. be ineffective in suctioning.
  c. lead to immediate vomiting.
  d. cause the tongue to fall into the airway.

39. You have been called to a 48-year-old female patient complaining of a severe headache and a stabbing pain in the center of her chest. The patient has a history of hypertension, her vital signs include a pulse of 100 and is strong, her blood pressure is 200/110, respirations are 20 and regular, and her skin is warm and dry. You decide to check the blood pressure in both arms and find the second blood pressure is 160/96. What life threatening condition should you suspect?
  a. Acute pulmonary edema
  b. Spontaneous pneumothorax
  c. Myocardial infarction
  d. Dissecting aortic aneurysm

40. The function of the white blood cells is to
  a. form clots.
  b. fight infection.
  c. carry oxygen.
  d. carry nutrients.

41. Angina differs from a heart attack because in an attack of angina, the
  a. patient feels severe chest pain.
  b. pain radiates outward from the heart.
  c. administration of nitroglycerin provides no relief.
  d. heart muscle is not permanently damaged.

42. The following patients all have signs and symptoms of cardiac chest pain and have their own prescriptions for nitroglycerin. Which patient should you NOT assist with taking nitroglycerin?
  a. 67-year-old male: pulse, 90; respirations, 26/min; BP, 98/72
  b. 72-year-old female: pulse, 88; respirations, 23/min; BP, 140/96
  c. 78-year-old male: pulse, 98; respirations, 26/min; BP, 160/112
  d. 51-year-old female: pulse, 72; respirations, 14/min; BP, 130/80

43. When deciding whether to assist a patient in administering nitroglycerin, you should check the medicine for the patient's name, the route of administration, the dose, and the
  a. doctor who prescribed it.
  b. quantity still available.
  c. pharmacy.
  d. expiration date.

44. Your patient, a 67-year-old male with a history of cardiac disease, is unresponsive. After checking ABCs and finding no pulse, you begin CPR. The next thing you should do is
  a. administer oxygen.
  b. call for ALS backup.
  c. attach the AED.
  d. request medical direction.

45. Your patient is showing signs and symptoms of shock and has a tender abdomen. She reports vomiting material that "looked like coffee grounds." You should suspect
   a. ruptured appendix.
   b. internal bleeding.
   c. fractured pelvis.
   d. inhaled poisoning.

46. Which patient is showing signs and symptoms of cardiac compromise?
   a. 85-year-old male: difficulty breathing, high fever, rapid pulse
   b. 72-year-old female: wheezing, labored breathing, tightness in throat
   c. 53-year-old female: dull chest pain, sudden sweating, difficulty breathing
   d. 51-year-old male: headache, dizziness, gagging, chest pain

47. Which blood vessel carries oxygen-poor blood to the heart?
   a. vena cava
   b. aorta
   c. pulmonary artery
   d. pulmonary vein

48. Central pulses may be palpated at the
   a. carotid and radial arteries.
   b. radial and brachial arteries.
   c. carotid and femoral arteries.
   d. brachial and femoral arteries.

49. The diastolic blood pressure represents the pressure in the brachial artery when the
   a. ventricles contract.
   b. ventricles are at rest.
   c. cardiac artery is stressed.
   d. aorta is distended.

50. Stridor is a sign of
   a. mucus in the lower airway.
   b. accessory muscle use.
   c. upper-airway obstruction.
   d. altered mental status.

51. Your patient is complaining of chest pain. Which question would you ask to assess the O part of the OPQRST algorithm?
   a. What were you doing when the pain started?
   b. What does the pain feel like?
   c. How long ago did the pain begin?
   d. How bad is the pain now?

52. All of the following are contraindictions for the administration of nitroglycerin EXCEPT when the patient
   a. has a systolic blood pressure of less than 100 mm Hg.
   b. has taken a previous dose of nitroglycerin two minutes ago.
   c. has a heart rate less than 60 beats per minute.
   d. is an infant or child.

53. A patient is in greater danger of severe internal bleeding from fracturing which bone?
   a. pelvis
   b. rib
   c. femur
   d. tibia

54. Why is an infant more likely to suffer an airway obstruction than an adult?
   a. An infant's ribs are less flexible than an adult's.
   b. The shape of the infant's head will cause the neck to flex when the child is supine.
   c. The adult has a relatively larger tongue compared to an infant.
   d. The adult has a relatively smaller airway compared to the infant.

55. Which patient would be most likely to have a barrel chest?

    a. 10-month-old male: premature birth and history of respiratory problems

    b. 6-year-old female: history of asthma and frequent respiratory infections

    c. 58-year-old male: history of emphysema and years of smoking

    d. 70-year-old female: recent history of pneumonia and bronchitis

56. You have completed two minutes of CPR on a 4-year-old female patient who was found unresponsive, pulseless, and apneic. The patient has a cardiac history and you are preparing the AED. As you open the AED you find there are no pediatric pads or dose-attenuating system. You should

    a. not apply the AED as it will deliver an adult energy dose.

    b. apply the AED with pads on the upper right chest and lower left and defibrillate if indicated.

    c. do twice as many compressions between defibrillations.

    d. apply the AED with the pads in an anterior posterior configuration and defibrillate if indicated.

57. The primary reason you auscultate both sides of the chest is to determine whether breath sounds are

    a. strong and regular.

    b. fast or slow.

    c. noisy or quiet.

    d. present and equal.

58. For which of these procedures should you wear gloves, a gown, a mask, and protective eyewear?

    a. Performing endotracheal intubation

    b. Performing oral/nasal suctioning

    c. Cleaning contaminated instruments

    d. Bleeding control with spurting blood

59. Your patient is a 24-year-old female with a history of asthma. She is wheezing and gasping for air and has a pulse rate of 88/min. You may assist her in using an inhaler if

    a. she has not yet taken more than three doses of medication.

    b. she has her own inhaler and you obtain medical direction.

    c. her respiratory rate is greater than 24/min.

    d. her blood pressure is greater than 100/70.

60. After assisting a patient to administer nitroglycerin, you should

    a. transport the patient immediately.

    b. place the patient in Trendelenburg position.

    c. give a second dose two minutes later.

    d. reassess vital signs and chest pain.

61. The AED detects

    a. the patient's pulse rate and rhythm.

    b. electrical activity of the heart.

    c. the contraction force of the heart.

    d. the degree of cardiac compromise.

62. Your patient, the victim of a car accident, has an obvious injury to her right leg. You should splint the injury before moving her unless

    a. transport time is less than 15 minutes.

    b. the patient is in severe pain.

    c. bones are protruding through the skin.

    d. life-threatening injuries are present.

63. Your 18-month-old patient is experiencing respiratory distress. Which of the following conditions is NOT a likely cause of the difficulty in breathing?

    a. a partial foreign-body obstruction

    b. the flu

    c. epiglottitis

    d. chronic obstruction pulmonary disease (COPD)

64. A seesaw (chest and abdomen move in opposite directions) pattern of breathing is a sign of
   a. breathing difficulty in infants.
   b. normal respirations in elderly patients.
   c. adequate artificial respiration.
   d. a disease such as COPD.

65. The best treatment for cardiac arrest in the pediatric patient is
   a. immediate defibrillation.
   b. prevention with aggressive airway and ventilator management.
   c. early access to ALS medications.
   d. quality chest compressions focused on adequate depth and recoil.

66. A sign of early respiratory distress in the pediatric patient is
   a. an increased blood pressure.
   b. an increased heart rate.
   c. flush, warm skin.
   d. a decreased breathing rate.

67. Your patient is a 33-year-old female with a suspected spinal cord injury. After you have immobilized her to a long board, she vomits. What should you do?
   a. Reassess her vital signs.
   b. Ask her what she last ate.
   c. Remove the board and suction the airway.
   d. Tilt the board to clear the airway.

68. Your patient is a 28-year-old male who appears intoxicated. Bystanders report that the man seemed fine but suddenly began "acting strange." You should first suspect
   a. alcohol abuse.
   b. poisoning.
   c. diabetic emergency.
   d. allergic reaction.

69. You are treating a 58-year-old male patient complaining of respiratory distress. The patient presents sitting up, his pulse is 112, BP is 160/100, respirations are 22 and labored, you hear crackles upon auscultating his breath sounds, and he has pedal edema bilaterally. Your treatment for this patient should include
   a. high flow oxygen via non-rebreather mask and elevate the patient's legs.
   b. Fowler's position, high-flow oxygen via non-rebreather mask, assist the patient with his meter dose inhaler.
   c. Fowler's position, high-flow oxygen via non-rebreather mask, consider contacting medical direction for CPAP.
   d. recovery position, 2–4 lpm oxygen via nasal cannula, consider assisting the patient with his nitroglycerin.

70. Your patient is a 23-year-old female who calmly tells you that her thoughts are controlling the weather. Her body language and speech are nonthreatening and gentle. You should
   a. request immediate police backup for protection.
   b. talk quietly to this patient and keep her calm.
   c. request permission to restrain the patient.
   d. take a detailed medical history.

71. A 17-year-old male patient is experiencing difficulty breathing and abdominal pain after being struck with a bat in his left lower quadrant. He is alert, cool, and diaphoretic, with a tachycardic heart rate. You should provide oxygen using a
   a. nonrebreather mask at 15 L/min.
   b. nasal cannula at 6 L/min.
   c. nasal cannula at 2 L/min.
   d. nonrebreather mask at 8 L/min.

72. The last vital sign to change in a patient going into shock is
   a. an increased pulse rate.
   b. a decreased blood pressure.
   c. an increased respiration rate.
   d. cool, clammy, pale skin.

73. The central nervous system consists of the brain and the
   a. spinal cord.
   b. spinal nerves.
   c. cranial nerves.
   d. spinal vertebrae.

74. Your male patient has climbed out of his car unassisted after a car crash, but he is now complaining of back pain. You should
   a. transport him in whatever position is the most comfortable.
   b. immobilize him to a long spine board with a standing take-down.
   c. immobilize him to a short spine board in the sitting position.
   d. immobilize him with a Kendrick Extrication Device.

75. Your patient is a 37-year-old female who has been in a minor accident. The patient is alert and oriented, and baseline vital signs are pulse, 76 and regular; respirations, 16/min and unlabored; and BP, 118/78. When you check her vital signs 15 minutes later, you find that her pulse rate is now 92 and her respirations are 24/min and shallow. You should
   a. continue to reassess her every 15 minutes.
   b. call for medical direction to treat her dyspnea.
   c. administer oxygen by nonrebreather mask.
   d. treat for shock and reassess every five minutes.

76. Which of the following signs or symptoms might you expect to see in a patient suffering from hypothermia?
   a. confused behavior
   b. excessive mucous production
   c. blood tinged sputum
   d. burning or itching in the underarms

77. With medical direction, you may administer epinephrine from a patient's own autoinjector if the patient displays signs and symptoms of respiratory distress or
   a. cardiac arrest.
   b. diabetic emergency.
   c. hypoperfusion.
   d. poisoning.

78. Which set of vital signs suggests early hypothermia?
   a. pulse, 56 and faint; respirations, 9/min, shallow; BP, 96/60; cyanotic; sluggish pupils
   b. pulse, 74; respirations, 16/min, strong; BP, 124/80; cool, dry skin; reactive pupils
   c. pulse, 92; respirations, 26/min; BP, 118/76, flushed (red) skin; reactive pupils
   d. pulse, 68; respirations, 13/min, irregular; BP, 110/70; hot, moist skin; reactive pupils

79. A 2-year-old female is in severe respiratory distress. Her skin is mottled, and she does not respond to verbal or physical stimulus. You should
   a. administer oxygen by the blow-by method.
   b. assist her ventilations with a bag-valve mask and supplemental oxygen.
   c. administer blind finger sweeps to attempt removal of an obstruction.
   d. provide oxygen by pediatric nonrebreather mask.

80. What is the goal of emergency care for a hypothermic patient with a reduced level of consciousness?
  a. to actively warm the patient
  b. to keep the patient active
  c. to provide fluids and oxygen
  d. to prevent further heat loss

81. The purpose of the National Incident Management System is to provide a(n)
  a. clear chain of command in case of legal liability.
  b. means of evaluating the EMS system's response to an event.
  c. orderly method for communications and decision making.
  d. training program for first responders.

82. What does the presence of abdominal breathing signify in infants and small children?
  a. labored breathing
  b. noisy breathing
  c. shallow breathing
  d. normal breathing

83. While providing artificial ventilation to a 14-year-old drowning patient, you feel resistance during ventilations. The possible cause of the resistance is that
  a. the trachea is too short.
  b. there is water in the stomach.
  c. the patient has chronic obstructive pulmonary disease.
  d. the epiglottis is swollen, causing an obstruction.

84. The correct rate for providing artificial ventilations to infants and children is
  a. 8 breaths per minute.
  b. 12 breaths per minute.
  c. 20 breaths per minute.
  d. 24 breaths per minute.

85. Care for an unresponsive infant with a complete airway obstruction includes
  a. giving sub-diaphragmatic thrusts and ventilation.
  b. performing back blows and ventilation attempts.
  c. performing continuous chest thrusts until clear.
  d. giving back blows, chest thrusts, and ventilation.

86. Ventricular fibrillation is defined as
  a. a rapid organized heartrate that originates in the SA node.
  b. a rapid heartrate that originates in the ventricles usually greater than 150 bpm.
  c. a slow organized heartrate that originates in the SA node.
  d. a rapid disorganized and ineffective pumping of the ventricles.

87. A common side effect of high fever in infants and small children is
  a. shock.
  b. seizures.
  c. hives.
  d. cardiac arrest.

88. Your patient is an 8-month-old infant with a recent history of vomiting and diarrhea. Which signs should alert you to the possibility of shock?
  a. dry diaper and the absence of tears while crying
  b. capillary refill time of two seconds or less
  c. strong peripheral pulses; heart rate of 100
  d. skin that is flushed and hot to the touch

89. An 11-month-old crying female has swallowed a piece of a hot dog. She is coughing, and you can hear high-pitched sounds coming from the throat. You should
   a. administer back blows and chest thrusts.
   b. perform a blind finger sweep to attempt removal of the object.
   c. provide high-concentration oxygen by blow-by mask.
   d. provide ventilations by bag-valve mask and oxygen.

90. Your patient is a 26-year-old male who has been in a motor vehicle accident. The patient's radial pulse is weak, while the carotid pulse is strong. You should
   a. treat for signs and symptoms of shock.
   b. recheck by taking the brachial pulse.
   c. wait 15 minutes, then recheck vital signs.
   d. check for low blood pressure on the other arm.

91. The *sniffing position* refers to the
   a. way children position themselves when feeling respiratory distress.
   b. recovery position used for children in respiratory distress.
   c. position used to insert the oropharyngeal or nasopharyngeal airway.
   d. placement of a child's head for the head-lift/chin-tilt maneuver.

92. Diastolic pressure is a measure of the
   a. force exerted against the walls of the blood vessels when the heart contracts.
   b. force exerted against the walls of the blood vessels when the heart relaxes.
   c. rhythm and strength of the heart's contractions during arterial circulation.
   d. time it takes the capillary beds in the extremities to refill after being blanched.

93. A 5-year-old male is experiencing severe respiratory distress. He is altered with poor skin signs. You should
   a. assist ventilations with a pediatric bag-valve mask and supplemental oxygen.
   b. perform blind finger sweeps to attempt to remove an obstruction.
   c. provide oxygen by pediatric nonrebreather mask.
   d. provide oxygen by the blow-by method.

94. Fontanels are the
   a. strong contractions that signal the end of labor.
   b. soft spots located on the infant's head.
   c. blood vessels in the umbilical cord.
   d. special forceps doctors use to assist the delivery.

95. Where does blood travel when it leaves the right ventricle of the heart?
   a. to the pulmonary veins, then to the lungs
   b. to the aorta, then out to the body
   c. to the vena cava, then to the left atrium
   d. to the pulmonary arteries, then to the lungs

96. The third stage of labor consists of the
   a. delivery of the placenta.
   b. full dilation of the cervix.
   c. birth of the baby.
   d. onset uterine contractions.

97. You have just assisted in the delivery of a newborn who has good color, a strong pulse, and is not yet breathing. You should
   a. suction the infant again.
   b. slap the baby's back vigorously.
   c. massage the baby's back gently.
   d. provide artificial ventilation.

98. Amniotic fluid with a yellow or brownish color means a high likelihood of
a. miscarriage.
b. infectious disease.
c. excessive bleeding.
d. fetal distress.

99. Your patient is a 68-year-old male who is complaining of chest pain. Your focused assessment findings include a pulse rate of 92, a BP of 140/90, and some difficulty breathing. After administering oxygen, you should focus your questioning to determine if the patient has a history of
a. asthma.
b. diabetes mellitus.
c. cardiac problems.
d. strokes.

100. Your patient is a 24-year-old female who tells you that she is three months pregnant. She is experiencing profuse vaginal bleeding and severe cramping. After administering oxygen, you should
a. be alert for signs and symptoms of shock, and transport quickly.
b. prepare for an emergency on-scene delivery of a premature infant.
c. attempt to stop the bleeding before transporting the patient.
d. place the patient on her left side and call for an ALS unit.

101. Your patient is a 28-year-old pregnant female who has just been in a minor car accident. Which set of vital signs would be normal for this patient?
a. pulse, 80; respirations, 14; BP, 108/72
b. pulse, 58; respirations, 24; BP, 118/78
c. pulse, 96; respirations, 8; BP, 124/86
d. pulse, 82; respirations, 22; BP, 140/96

102. Which of the following signs and symptoms may indicate shock in children?
a. an alert mental state
b. increased urine output
c. excessive tear production
d. cool, clammy skin

103. As an EMT, you are acting as a patient advocate when you
a. document the care you provide.
b. treat patients with dignity and respect.
c. continue your education and training.
d. consult with medical direction in the field.

104. What are the earliest signs of shock?
a. fatigue and depression
b. weak pulse and low blood pressure
c. anxiety and tachycardia
d. cyanosis and shallow respirations

105. The following are all effective techniques for stress reduction EXCEPT
a. getting more exercise.
b. seeking professional help.
c. working extra hours.
d. eating a healthy diet.

106. It is necessary to wear a mask and eye protection when
a. transporting a patient.
b. suctioning a patient.
c. splinting a closed injury.
d. administering oxygen.

107. Which statement about disposable gloves is correct?

    a. You should remove gloves by grasping the ends of the fingers and pulling them off right side out.

    b. It is not necessary to wear gloves when suctioning or ventilating a patient with a bag-valve-mask device.

    c. Gloves protect both you and the patient from the transmission of infectious diseases.

    d. One pair of gloves is sufficient for any call, no matter how many patients there are.

108. Which of the following situations illustrates implied consent?

    a. You splint the broken arm and leg of a 6-year-old female with her mother's permission.

    b. You care for a cardiac patient who asks you to help him take a dose of nitroglycerin.

    c. You arrive at the scene of a car crash, and the injured driver says, "Please help my child first."

    d. You provide life support to a man who was found unconscious by bystanders who called EMS.

109. Placing a patient in the recovery position allows

    a. the patient to breathe more deeply.

    b. secretions to drain more easily.

    c. the EMT to position the airway.

    d. the EMT to provide basic life support.

110. During the scene size-up, you should determine whether the scene is safe to enter and whether

    a. you need any additional help.

    b. the patient's ABCs are normal.

    c. you need to contact dispatch.

    d. the patient is sick or a trauma victim.

111. Which of the following is NOT part of the standard medical report you give to the receiving facility?

    a. mental status

    b. history of present illness

    c. medical diagnosis

    d. vital signs

112. You are splinting the injured leg of a 5-year-old male. What should you say?

    a. "If you don't allow me to immobilize your leg the pain will get much worse."

    b. "After I strap your leg to this board, it won't hurt so much."

    c. "Stop crying! I can't work when you're making loud noises."

    d. "Mom, if your child stops crying, I'll explain what I'm doing."

113. Why is it important to maintain body heat in a patient with shock?

    a. Shivering wastes vital oxygen and energy.

    b. Patients in shock often have fever as well.

    c. Blood congeals more easily when the body is cold.

    d. Hypothermia may increase the severity of shock.

114. Which of the following is an example of a subjective statement that could be included in a prehospital-care report?

    a. Bystander stated, "He was drunk as a skunk."

    b. Patient vomited two times during transport.

    c. Bystanders assisted EMTs in moving patient.

    d. Patient is unsure of the reason for the call.

115. Your patient has a wound on her anterior left lower leg that is spurting large amounts of blood. Direct pressure alone is ineffective. What is your next action to control the bleeding?
- **a.** Place a tourniquet proximal to the injury
- **b.** Apply indirect pressure to the left side of the groin
- **c.** Place a tourniquet distal to the injury
- **d.** Apply indirect pressure to the popliteal artery

116. Your patient is an 84-year-old female who is complaining of severe abdominal pain. The abdomen is rigid and tender. What should you suspect?
- **a.** cardiac disease
- **b.** internal bleeding
- **c.** pregnancy
- **d.** thoracic aneurysm

117. Which of the following is an example of care that would be provided by the EMT performing triage at a mass-casualty incident?
- **a.** covering the patient to prevent shock
- **b.** opening the airway
- **c.** starting CPR
- **d.** applying PASGs

118. Which of the following describes an emergency patient move?
- **a.** The patient cannot be cared for adequately in the present location.
- **b.** Because of danger, there is no time to immobilize the spine.
- **c.** The patient is being moved to a more comfortable location.
- **d.** The patient is being moved against his or her will.

119. Your patient is a 6-year-old male who is having a severe nosebleed. No trauma is suspected. How should you treat this child?
- **a.** Pinch his nostrils together and transport him sitting upright, leaning forward.
- **b.** Pack the nostrils with gauze and place the patient in the recovery position.
- **c.** Apply indirect pressure to the upper lip and have the patient lie supine.
- **d.** Apply an occlusive dressing and place the patient in the recovery position.

120. How does cardiac pain differ from respiratory pain?
- **a.** Cardiac pain increases when the patient breathes.
- **b.** Cardiac pain is localized around the heart and arms.
- **c.** Cardiac pain does not change with movement or palpation.
- **d.** Cardiac pain generally occurs on the left side of the chest.

Answers

1. **a.** Normal values for a newborn are: pulse, 120–160; respirations, 40–60; BP, 80/40.

2. **c.** Based on the information provided, the patient is breathing too quickly to provide his own adequate ventilations. This patient cannot be managed with a nonrebreather alone; artificial ventilations are needed to oxygenate the patient adequately.

3. **d.** Before transporting a patient without consent, it is always best to seek medical direction.

4. **b.** Based on the information provided, the patient is ventilating adequately but has poor skin signs, indicating inadequate perfusion. High-flow oxygen via a nonrebreather mask should ensure that the patient is fully oxygenated.

5. **d.** When assessing the carotid pulse, first locate the Adam's apple and then slide two fingers toward one side of the neck; never exert strong pressure or assess the carotid pulse on both sides of the neck at the same time.

6. **a.** Head injury, eye injury, or drug use may cause the pupils to be nonreactive or unequally reactive. Shock, airway obstruction, and cardiac arrest will cause both pupils to dilate equally.

7. **c.** While it may be true that providing high levels of oxygen over prolonged time periods may cause the hypoxic drive to fail, it is a rare occurrence in the prehospital field. With the complaint of shortness of breath, it is better to ensure that the patient is fully oxygenated rather than taking a chance that she is hypoxic. The EMT is prepared to ventilate the patient if she goes into respiratory arrest due to the high levels of oxygen.

8. **b.** Blood under the skin, appearing on the surface as a bruise, is also known as *ecchymosis*.

9. **c.** Use palpation only when it is difficult to hear the pulse, either because the setting is extremely noisy or because the patient's pulse is very weak.

10. **a.** The other methods will provide an either too large or too small measurement of an OPA.

11. **c.** You can omit the detailed physical exam if your patient shows no alterations in consciousness and if the mechanism of injury does not suggest high risk of trauma.

12. **a.** Ethics are the principles of conduct; concerns for what are right or wrong, good or bad. Choice b describes morals, choice c is a better description of bioethics, and choice d describes justice for the patient.

13. **c.** The best way to monitor the patient's mental status is to interact with the patient so that you are immediately aware of any changes.

14. **b.** Assess the brachial pulse instead of the radial or carotid in patients less than one year old.

15. **a.** Patient **a**, with elevated pulse and respiratory rate and cool, clammy skin is showing early signs of shock. Patients **b** and **c** have normal vital signs. Patient **d** has a normal pulse, low blood pressure, and slow respiratory rate but hot and dry skin, so shock is not clearly evident in this patient.

16. **a.** The most important sign of a diabetic emergency is altered mental status; patients may appear intoxicated or act anxious or combative. Patients who present an altered level of consciousness should have an evaluation for diabetic emergency.

17. **a.** While many EMS workers are understandably concerned about HIV/AIDS, it presents far less risk than hepatitis or TB because the virus does not survive well outside the human body.

18. a. A *tort* is a civil wrong committed by one individual against another. Improper or negligent patient care would be considered a tort.

19. a. The zygomatic bones are found in the face. They are also known as cheekbones.

20. c. Although all the choices can cause airway obstruction, the tongue is the most common cause, especially in unconscious patients.

21. a. Infants and children are prone to breathing difficulties because they have small air passages that are easily occluded; they also rely heavily on their diaphragms and suffer frequent respiratory infections.

22. d. The normal respiratory rate for an infant is 40–60/min.

23. b. Snoring indicates that the tongue has relaxed into the upper airway, partially obstructing it.

24. a. There are 33 vertebrae in the human spinal column.

25. b. Gurgling is a sign that fluid is present in the airway; the correct procedure is to immediately open and suction the airway. An airway adjunct may be used to assist in maintaining airway patency once it is cleared.

26. a. According to the American Heart Association, at least 800 mL of air should be delivered to the patient when using an adult bag-valve mask.

27. c. ATVs can allow EMTs to perform other tasks, but the EMT must continually monitor the patient to ensure that the rate and tidal volume are adequate to ventilate the patient, the ATV is not causing barotrauma, especially in patients with poor lung compliance, and that there is enough oxygen to keep the ATV working.

28. b. A child's head should be slightly hyperextended for ventilation in a position called the sniffing position. For infants, the correct position is the neutral position with padding placed below the shoulders and upper back. You should never flex the airway forward as this will close off the airway. The recovery position is used for spontaneously breathing patients to protect their airway.

29. b. Since most children have healthy hearts, they are most likely to suffer life-threatening respiratory emergencies prior to sudden cardiac death. It is recommended to perform two minutes of CPR to see if that will revive the patient prior to going for help or locating an AED. Since the patient is suffering a life-threatening condition, you would treat the patient under implied consent.

30. b. The patient should inhale deeply and hold her breath to absorb the medicine.

31. a. Agonal respirations are a sign that the patient is nearing death. Because he is also pulseless, begin CPR immediately.

32. c. Document all side effects of medication administration and report them to the receiving facility; besides increased pulse rate and nausea, other common side effects are tremors and nervousness.

33. c. Because dentures can make it easier to obtain a good mask seal, you should remove them only if they become dislodged.

34. a. While **b** may seem correct, an AED cannot detect a pulse. It can only detect an organized rhythm that may produce a pulse.

35. d. The normal respiratory rate for an adult is 12–20 breaths per minute, and chest-wall motion should be regular and neither shallow nor very deep. Patient **a** is breathing too quickly for a 3-month-old (it should be around 40 at this age), and the use of accessory muscles in the neck shows some level of distress is present. Patient **b** has a slower than normal rate (it should be around 20), and the irregularity and diaphragmatic nature suggest a spinal cord injury may be present. Patient **c** is breathing much too fast (rate 12–20 for adults), and the shallow chest motions suggests insufficiency or distress.

36. a. Patients experiencing a myocardial infarction, death of the myocardium, complain of crushing chest pain lasting longer than 20 minutes. This is one of the signs that help to differentiate between stable angina, chest pain lasting less than 20 minutes or relieved with rest, or an infarction. Polydipsia is increased thirst and is found predominantly in diabetic emergencies and hemiparesis is one-sided weakness predominantly found in stroke patients.

37. b. A nonrebreather mask will not be adequate to provide ventilations. Additional electrical shocks may actually send the patient back into a pulseless rhythm.

38. a. When using a rigid catheter to suction infants and small children, take care not to touch the back of the throat, since stimulation here can cause bradycardia due to stimulation of the vagus nerve. Touching the back of the throat or around the base of the tongue in any patient can trigger a gag, which could lead to vomiting, but the chance of this is not any greater in pediatric patients. The tongue cannot "fall into the airway"; however, in the absence of proper positioning, a flaccid tongue can relax into a position that could lead to obstruction of the airway.

39. d. The signs and symptoms are indicative of a dissecting aortic aneurysm, which requires immediate rapid transport to the hospital.

The others have similar signs and symptoms, but the sudden onset, hypertensive emergency, and the differing blood pressure in each arm points to the aneurysm.

40. b. The white blood cells, which make up a part of the body's immune system, fight infections.

41. d. In angina, unlike a heart attack, the reduced blood flow to the heart does not result in permanent damage.

42. a. Do not administer nitroglycerin if the patient's systolic blood pressure is below 100 mm Hg.

43. d. Before assisting a patient to administer nitroglycerin, check for the right patient, the right route of administration, the right dose, and the expiration date.

44. c. After verifying that there is no pulse and opening the airway, your first priority is to attach the AED and determine if defibrillation is required.

45. b. "Coffee-grounds" vomit is digested blood and indicates the presence of internal bleeding, as do abdominal tenderness and signs and symptoms of shock. A ruptured appendix and fractured pelvis will not cause bleeding into the gastrointestinal (GI) tract. Ingested poisoning may or may not result in GI bleeding, but inhaled poisoning will result in respiratory problems.

46. c. This woman shows classic signs of cardiac compromise: dull chest pain, sudden onset of sweating, and difficulty breathing.

47. a. The vena cava carries oxygen-poor blood from the body to the right atrium, so it can be transported to the right ventricle and from there to the lungs.

48. c. Central pulses may be palpated at the carotid artery in the neck and at the femoral artery in the groin. The brachial and radial pulses are peripheral pulses.

49. b. The diastolic blood pressure represents the pressure in the brachial artery when the ventricles are at rest (diastole).

50. c. Stridor, a harsh sound usually heard during inspiration, is a sign of upper-airway obstruction.

51. c. Assess onset by asking when the pain began and how long it took to reach its greatest severity.

52. b. A patient may take up to three doses of nitroglycerin, each dose three to five minutes apart. The blood pressure should be greater than 100, and the pulse rate should be greater than 60. Nitroglycerine use is contraindicated in children.

53. a. Pelvic fractures carry danger of severe internal bleeding.

54. b. The back of an infant's head (occiput) is relatively larger compared with an adult's. Placing the infant on his or her back, without shoulder padding, may cause the head to tilt forward excessively, closing the airway.

55. c. A barrel chest is associated with a long history of respiratory disease, such as bronchitis, emphysema, or COPD. Because the alveoli are not functioning properly, air trapping occurs in the lungs. The increased effort it takes to move air in and out of the lungs results in an overdevelopment of the chest muscles and in time, leads to the barrel-shaped appearance.

56. d. You should apply the AED as if there were pediatric pads and defibrillate when indicated. The child is too small to place both pads on the anterior chest and new biphasic AEDs read the impedance of the patient and deliver and appropriate level of energy.

57. d. You auscultate (listen with a stethoscope) through the chest wall to determine if breath sounds are present and equal on both sides of the chest. As you are listening, you may also note the relative rate and quality of breathing, but those are secondary reasons for listening to the chest wall. If you are having trouble determining the respiratory rate when you are performing vital signs, you can listen to one side of the chest wall to determine the respiratory rate.

58. d. Bleeding control with spurting blood carries maximum danger of contamination; therefore, maximum protection is required. Airway suctioning or intubation does not generally require a gown. Cleaning of contaminated instruments does not generally require eye/facial protection.

59. b. An EMT may help a patient in respiratory difficulty to administer an inhaler if the inhaler was prescribed for that patient and medical direction is obtained. In some jurisdictions, you may have standing orders to assist the patient, which means medical direction is provided ahead of time in the standing order. It is important for you to determine how many doses she has already taken (choice **a**), but you must first determine if the medication she took was prescribed to her before you can assist her further. The standard dosing regimen for an EMT assisting with a prescribed inhaler is to provide a total of two doses, one every three minutes.

60. d. After helping a patient take prescribed nitroglycerin, reassess vital signs and chest pains; a second dose may be given three to five minutes later.

61. b. The AED can detect only the electrical activity within the patient's heart. It does not assess rate, mechanical activity (pumping action), or the degree of cardiac compromise.

62. d. If life-threatening conditions are present, you should focus on those injuries or begin to package the patient for rapid transport if you cannot manage her life-threatening problems.

63. d. COPD is unlikely to occur in pediatric patients. The other three choices may cause some level of respiratory distress in the pediatric patient.

64. a. A seesaw pattern is a sign of breathing difficulty in infants.

65. b. The best treatment for cardiac arrest in the pediatric patient is to prevent it all together. This can occur through aggressive public education and prevention programs or aggressive treatment of respiratory illnesses that could deteriorate into cardiac arrest.

66. b. As the body tries to compensate for a decrease in oxygen levels in the blood stream, the heart will try to beat more quickly to circulate blood to the cells more quickly. The skin will also turn pale and cool as the body shifts blood flow back to the critical organs. The patient will also breathe more quickly to draw in more oxygen and expel more carbon dioxide.

67. d. If a patient is immobilized to a long board, you can tilt the entire board to clear the airway.

68. c. Sudden onset of altered mental status strongly suggests diabetic emergency. Alcohol intoxication will have a slower onset. Poisoning may also cause altered mental status, but you should first rule out the possi-bility of a diabetic emergency as it is a more common occurrence. An allergic reaction will not cause the sudden onset of altered mental status.

69. c. This patient is most likely suffering from congestive heart failure and his treatment should include positioning him in Fowler's position (sitting up), high-flow oxygen via NRB at 10–15 lpm, and, if allowed by medical control, the use of CPAP may prevent other more invasive airway management. Elevating the patient's legs will exacerbate his respiratory compromise. His MDI is not indicated and 2–4 lpm oxygen is too low for his condition.

70. b. Talk quietly with the patient to help her remain calm and persuade her to seek medical help. Be on guard for a violent outburst. Restraints and police backup are not necessary to manage this patient. Asking too many personal questions may agitate her.

71. a. This patient may be experiencing internal bleeding and possible signs of shock. High-flow oxygen is warranted.

72. b. In shock, the body attempts to preserve perfusion by shunting blood away from the skin, increasing heart rate and increasing respiratory rate.

73. a. The central nervous system consists of the brain and the spinal cord.

74. b. Even if the patient has extricated himself from the car, immobilize him to a long spine board if the mechanisms of injury lead you to suspect spine damage. A standing take-down will allow you to immobilize the patient from the standing position.

75. d. The patient's condition has become unstable; you should treat her for shock and reassess every five minutes. She should already be on oxygen. Alert medical control of your findings, but permission is not needed to treat this patient for shock. Because she is unstable, 15 minutes is too long a time period to go between vital signs assessments.

76. a. The other choices do not make sense as potential signs or symptoms of hypothermia. As blood flow to the brain diminishes, altered mental status may occur, causing confusion and eventually unconsciousness.

77. c. Indications for use of epinephrine are signs and symptoms of respiratory distress or hypoperfusion (shock). Glucose is indicated for diabetic patients. There are no medications (other than oxygen) indicated for use by EMTs in the treatment of cardiac arrest patients.

78. c. Patients with early hypothermia have a rapid pulse and respiratory rate and red skin; patient **a** has the signs of late hypothermia. Patient **d** has hyperthermia. Patient **b** has normal vital signs.

79. b. This patient is in late stages of respiratory distress. Simply providing oxygen without ventilation will be inadequate for this child's needs.

80. d. The most important principle of care for patients with severe hypothermia is to prevent further heat loss by removing the patient from the cold environment; active rewarming should be done in the hospital.

81. c. The National Incident Management System is a coordinated system of procedures that provides standardization and flexibility, which allows for orderly communications and decision making among varied agencies in response to a disaster.

82. d. In infants and children, who rely heavily on the diaphragm for breathing, abdominal breathing is normal in the absence of other signs of labored breathing, such as supraclavicular and intercostal retractions.

83. b. Water or air in the stomach caused by involuntary swallowing during a drowning episode may cause the stomach to expand and press against the diaphragm, making it difficult to ventilate the lungs.

84. c. The correct rate of providing artificial ventilations to infants and children is 20 breaths per minute, or one breath every three seconds.

85. d. Care for an unresponsive infant with a foreign-body airway obstruction includes a series of back blows, followed by chest thrusts, alternating with ventilation attempts.

86. d. Ventricular fibrillation (V-Fib) is a disorganized and ineffective pumping of the ventricles wherein the electrical activity originates in multiple places throughout the ventricles. Choice a is tachycardia, b is ventricular tachycardia, and c is bradycardia.

87. b. Seizures, seen as body stiffness and/or shaking, are a common side effect of high fevers in infants and small children.

88. a. A dry diaper and absence of tears when the infant cries are signs of dehydration, a cause of hypovolemic shock.

89. c. The patient is not experiencing a complete foreign-body airway obstruction, and she appears to be ventilating adequately. Therefore, oxygen provided with a blow-by mask will help ensure adequate oxygenation of the patient.

90. a. Suspect shock (decreased tissue perfusion) whenever the distal pulse is weaker than the central pulse. Low blood pressure is a late sign of shock; do not wait to treat the patient for shock until the blood pressure drops.

91. d. The *sniffing position* refers to the placement of a child's head when you perform the head-tilt/chin-lift, with the face lying parallel to the surface he or she is lying on. It improves breathing by opening the airway further than hyperextending does.

92. b. Diastolic pressure is a measure of the force exerted against the walls of the blood vessels when the heart muscle relaxes; it is thus the lower of the two numbers that make up a blood pressure reading. Choice **d** describes the capillary refill test. The force of arterial circulation is not assessed in the prehospital setting as it requires very invasive procedures.

93. a. With the patient being altered in his mental status, it appears that he is not ventilating adequately. A nonrebreather mask will not be able to ventilate the child appropriately. There is no information to indicate a foreign-body obstruction.

94. b. The fontanels are the soft spots on the baby's head where the bony parts of the skull have not yet grown together, allowing the head to contract somewhat during delivery.

95. d. Oxygen-poor blood arrives in the right atrium and is pumped out through the right ventricle via the pulmonary arteries to the lungs.

96. a. The third stage of labor consists of the delivery of the placenta after the baby is delivered.

97. c. To stimulate a healthy newborn to breathe, rub his or her back, or flick the soles of his or her feet.

98. d. Meconium, or fetal stool, appears as yellow, brown, or green material in the amniotic fluid. When present, it is associated with an increased risk of fetal distress.

99. c. For a patient such as this one who is displaying signs and symptoms of cardiac compromise, use the SAMPLE survey to focus your questioning to determine if there is any past history of cardiac disease and if the patient has a prescription for nitroglycerin.

100. a. The patient is likely to be experiencing a miscarriage; shock is possible. If she delivers, the child will be too small to survive. There is no method to stop the bleeding in the pre-hospital setting. There is no need to place her in the left lateral recumbent position.

101. a. It is normal for a pregnant woman to have a slightly increased pulse and decreased blood pressure. The respiratory rate of patient **b** is too fast. Patient **c** has a too slow respiratory rate, and patient **d** is hypertensive and has a respiratory rate that is too high.

102. d. Blood is shunted away from the skin early in children with shock, causing it to pale, become cool, and sweat.

103. b. Acting as a patient advocate means treating all patients as you would like to be treated yourself.

104. c. The earliest signs of shock are subtle changes in mental status, such as anxiety and restlessness, and tachycardia. Fatigue and depression are not common signs of shock. Cyanosis is not one of the earliest signs, and shallow respirations can occur any time during the shock process. Low blood pressure is a late sign of shock.

105. c. Effective stress-reduction techniques include balancing work and recreation, getting enough rest, eating a healthy diet, getting regular exercise, and seeking help if necessary.

106. b. Wear a mask and eye protection when there is a high probability of splattering, such as when suctioning a patient.

107. c. Because gloves protect both you and your patients, most protocols now call for EMTs to wear gloves for any patient contact. Remove gloves by pulling them off inside out, so you do not touch the soiled outer surface; change gloves for each new patient contact.

108. d. Implied consent means that, because your adult patient cannot give consent to treatment, you act without it.

109. b. The recovery position, with the patient on the left side with the left arm under the head, allows secretions to drain more easily from the airway.

110. a. During scene size-up, determine whether the scene is safe for you to enter, the number of patients, if you have the appropriate BSI equipment and precautions, and whether you will need backup from additional EMS units or other services.

111. c. The EMT's report should not include a diagnosis, but rather a complete description of the patient's condition.

112. b. Always speak directly to the patient, and explain what you are doing in words he or she can understand. If the parent is present, explain your treatment to him or her as well.

113. a. Blood carries heat, and a loss of blood will result in a drop in body temperature. Shivering, the body's response to cold, increases metabolism by wasting oxygen and energy that would be better spent in fueling hypoxic cells.

114. d. This is a subjective statement. Statement **a** is inappropriate and unnecessary. Statements **b** and **c** are objective statements.

115. a. A tourniquet is now the next step in hemorrhage control for arterial bleeding. The tourniquet should be placed proximal to the injury and in accordance with your local protocol.

116. b. Internal bleeding caused by the rupture of an abdominal artery is an occasional emergency among elderly patients; symptoms are abdominal pain, tenderness, and rigidity. This patient is too old to be pregnant. A thoracic aneurysm will not cause abdominal distension.

117. b. Only the most critical care, such as opening the airway to assess respirations, is provided during triage. Unfortunately, CPR cannot be started by the individuals performing triage.

118. b. An emergency move is one required to remove the patient from imminent danger, such as a fire, or when you must move a patient to gain access to other critically wounded patients. You should stabilize the head and neck with your hands, and if possible, apply a cervical collar before moving the patient.

119. a. For a nosebleed, when no trauma is suspected, have the patient sit up and lean forward to prevent blood from entering the airway and gently pinch the nostrils together.

120. c. Cardiac pain, unlike respiratory pain, usually is not increased by movement or palpation; it is more diffuse than respiratory pain and may be felt in the shoulder, neck, and jaw, as well as in the chest.

5 ▶ EMT PRACTICE EXAM 3

CHAPTER SUMMARY
This is the third of ten practice exams in this book based on the National Registry's EMT cognitive exam. Use this test to identify which types of questions continue to give you problems.

Y ou should now be familiar with the format of the National Registry's EMT exam. Your practice test-taking experience will help you most, however, if you have created a situation as close as possible to the real one.

For this third exam, simulate a real test. Find a quiet place where you will not be disturbed. Have two sharpened pencils and a good eraser. Complete the test in one sitting, setting a timer or a stopwatch. You should have plenty of time to answer all of the questions when you take the real exam, but be sure to practice maintaining your concentration and maintaining a steady pace.

As before, the answer sheet you should use appears next. Following the exam is an answer key, with all the answers explained. These explanations will help you see where you need to concentrate further study. When you've finished the exam and scored it, note your weaknesses so that you'll know which parts of your textbook to concentrate on before you take the remaining exams.

1.	a	b	c	d	41.	a	b	c	d	81.	a	b	c	d
2.	a	b	c	d	42.	a	b	c	d	82.	a	b	c	d
3.	a	b	c	d	43.	a	b	c	d	83.	a	b	c	d
4.	a	b	c	d	44.	a	b	c	d	84.	a	b	c	d
5.	a	b	c	d	45.	a	b	c	d	85.	a	b	c	d
6.	a	b	c	d	46.	a	b	c	d	86.	a	b	c	d
7.	a	b	c	d	47.	a	b	c	d	87.	a	b	c	d
8.	a	b	c	d	48.	a	b	c	d	88.	a	b	c	d
9.	a	b	c	d	49.	a	b	c	d	89.	a	b	c	d
10.	a	b	c	d	50.	a	b	c	d	90.	a	b	c	d
11.	a	b	c	d	51.	a	b	c	d	91.	a	b	c	d
12.	a	b	c	d	52.	a	b	c	d	92.	a	b	c	d
13.	a	b	c	d	53.	a	b	c	d	93.	a	b	c	d
14.	a	b	c	d	54.	a	b	c	d	94.	a	b	c	d
15.	a	b	c	d	55.	a	b	c	d	95.	a	b	c	d
16.	a	b	c	d	56.	a	b	c	d	96.	a	b	c	d
17.	a	b	c	d	57.	a	b	c	d	97.	a	b	c	d
18.	a	b	c	d	58.	a	b	c	d	98.	a	b	c	d
19.	a	b	c	d	59.	a	b	c	d	99.	a	b	c	d
20.	a	b	c	d	60.	a	b	c	d	100.	a	b	c	d
21.	a	b	c	d	61.	a	b	c	d	101.	a	b	c	d
22.	a	b	c	d	62.	a	b	c	d	102.	a	b	c	d
23.	a	b	c	d	63.	a	b	c	d	103.	a	b	c	d
24.	a	b	c	d	64.	a	b	c	d	104.	a	b	c	d
25.	a	b	c	d	65.	a	b	c	d	105.	a	b	c	d
26.	a	b	c	d	66.	a	b	c	d	106.	a	b	c	d
27.	a	b	c	d	67.	a	b	c	d	107.	a	b	c	d
28.	a	b	c	d	68.	a	b	c	d	108.	a	b	c	d
29.	a	b	c	d	69.	a	b	c	d	109.	a	b	c	d
30.	a	b	c	d	70.	a	b	c	d	110.	a	b	c	d
31.	a	b	c	d	71.	a	b	c	d	111.	a	b	c	d
32.	a	b	c	d	72.	a	b	c	d	112.	a	b	c	d
33.	a	b	c	d	73.	a	b	c	d	113.	a	b	c	d
34.	a	b	c	d	74.	a	b	c	d	114.	a	b	c	d
35.	a	b	c	d	75.	a	b	c	d	115.	a	b	c	d
36.	a	b	c	d	76.	a	b	c	d	116.	a	b	c	d
37.	a	b	c	d	77.	a	b	c	d	117.	a	b	c	d
38.	a	b	c	d	78.	a	b	c	d	118.	a	b	c	d
39.	a	b	c	d	79.	a	b	c	d	119.	a	b	c	d
40.	a	b	c	d	80.	a	b	c	d	120.	a	b	c	d

EMT Practice Exam 3

1. Which set of vital signs is within normal limits?
   a. newborn: pulse, 100; respirations, 36/min; BP, 60/30
   b. 3-year-old male: pulse, 98; respirations, 27/min; BP, 84/48
   c. 9-year-old female: pulse, 118; respirations, 24/min; BP, 120/80
   d. 24-year-old male: pulse, 92; respirations, 26/min; BP, 112/70

2. Use of accessory muscles, grunting, and stridor are all signs of
   a. labored respirations.
   b. noisy respirations.
   c. shallow respirations.
   d. agonal respirations.

3. You assess the color, temperature, and condition of a patient's skin to gather information about his or her
   a. capillary refill.
   b. heart rate.
   c. perfusion.
   d. respiration.

4. Which statement about assessing blood pressure is correct?
   a. If you obtain one normal reading, it is not necessary to reassess blood pressure.
   b. A single reading is not as useful as multiple readings used to look for a trend.
   c. Variations of more than 5 mm Hg from normal is considered very significant.
   d. Assess blood pressure by palpation only when the patient is in a quiet place.

5. While evaluating your 56-year-old male patient with chest discomfort, he suddenly collapses and becomes unconscious. He is apneic and pulseless. Which of the following will most likely reverse this condition?
   a. Provide high-flow oxygen with a nonrebreather mask.
   b. Begin chest compressions at a rate of 80 beats per minute.
   c. Begin the process of defibrillating the patient with an AED.
   d. Ventilate the patient with a pocket mask and supplemental oxygen.

6. Your patient is a 67-year-old female whom you found in cardiac arrest. You have resuscitated her by using an AED and are now transporting her. If she again becomes pulseless, you should
   a. request online medical direction.
   b. stop the ambulance and use the AED.
   c. begin CPR and continue en route.
   d. defibrillate quickly while en route.

7. Which trauma patient is at greatest risk for serious injury?
   a. 43-year-old male, who fell seven feet from a stepladder
   b. 24-year-old female, involved in a moderate-speed vehicle collision
   c. 17-year-old male, who fell off a bicycle onto concrete
   d. 5-year-old female, involved in a moderate-speed vehicle collision

8. A bystander is doing CPR on a patient in cardiac arrest. You size up the scene, practice body substance isolation, and begin your initial assessment by having the bystander
    a. verify pulselessness.
    b. continue CPR.
    c. stop CPR.
    d. provide a history of cardiac arrest.

9. Your patient, a trauma victim, has flat jugular veins while she is lying down. What is this a sign of?
    a. increased intracranial pressure
    b. respiratory distress
    c. spinal injury
    d. severe blood loss

10. The myocardium generates its own impulse to cause coordinated contractions so the heart can pump blood throughout the body. The normal electrical pathway is
    a. AV Node, Bundle of His, SA Node, and Purkinje Fibers.
    b. SA Node, AV Node, Bundle of His, and Purkinje Fibers.
    c. SA Node, Bundle of His, AV Node, and Purkinje Fibers.
    d. SA Node, Purkinje Fibers, Bundle of His, and AV Node.

11. The valve between the right atrium and the right ventricle is the
    a. tricuspid valve.
    b. pulmonary valve.
    c. mitral valve.
    d. aortic valve.

12. You are treating a 39-year-old female who has been in a motor vehicle accident. She has a suspected broken arm and leg, moderate bleeding from the leg wound, and signs and symptoms of early shock. Vital signs are pulse, 96 and thready; respirations, 28 and shallow; BP, 110/78. Your treatment should focus on
    a. stabilizing the patient and transporting her to the hospital.
    b. carefully splinting and bandaging all the patient's injuries.
    c. performing a detailed trauma assessment in the field.
    d. opening the airway and monitoring vital signs every 15 minutes.

13. You are en route to the receiving facility with a 71-year-old male patient with a history of heart disease. The patient's distress has been relieved with nitroglycerin, and his vital signs are stable. How often should you reassess the patient's vital signs?
    a. every five minutes or more often
    b. every 15 minutes
    c. every 30 minutes
    d. There is no need to reassess a stable patient.

14. The major purpose of the EMT's interactions with a patient during transport is to continuously evaluate the patient's
    a. mental status and airway.
    b. pulse and respirations.
    c. anxiety and restlessness.
    d. skin color and pupils.

15. Your trauma patient has an amputated foot. How should you care for an amputated foot?
   a. Wrap it in a sterile dressing, then in plastic, and keep it cool.
   b. Immerse it in a tub of ice water and transport it with the patient.
   c. Put it inside the PASG and inflate the other leg of the garment.
   d. Put the foot back on the leg and then splint it in place.

16. If a patient's respiratory rate is irregular, you should count the respirations for how long?
   a. 15 seconds and multiply by four
   b. 30 seconds and multiply by two
   c. one full minute
   d. two full minutes

17. Which patient's vital signs are abnormal?
   a. 67-year-old male: pulse, 68; respirations, 15; BP, 130/88
   b. 44-year-old female: pulse, 92; respirations, 22; BP, 120/80
   c. 14-year-old male: pulse, 88; respirations, 18; BP, 110/70
   d. 7-year-old female: pulse, 100; respirations, 23; BP, 96/50

18. Which statement about the assessment of a patient with cardiac compromise is correct?
   a. You cannot determine the degree of cardiac damage in the field.
   b. You should not ask patients about nitroglycerin or other drug use.
   c. The purpose of the focused history is to determine whether to use the AED.
   d. Patients usually describe cardiac pain as localized and moderately severe.

19. The proper hand position for providing chest compressions for a child is
   a. two hands on the sternum two fingers below the sternal notch.
   b. the heel of one hand on the sternum just above the nipple line.
   c. the heel of one hand on the middle of the sternum in between the nipples.
   d. the heel of one hand on the lower half of the sternum over the xyphoid process.

20. The main purpose of the detailed physical examination is to
   a. reveal hidden or less obvious injuries.
   b. detect changes in the patient's condition.
   c. obtain a complete medical history.
   d. check vital signs and breath sounds.

21. While performing a rapid trauma assessment of a patient who was injured in a motor vehicle accident, you note paradoxical motion. This indicates the presence of
   a. pelvic fracture.
   b. internal bleeding.
   c. chest injury.
   d. head injury.

22. The glottis is the
   a. soft tissue at the base of the tongue.
   b. nasopharynx and oropharynx.
   c. midaxillary intercostal muscles.
   d. opening between the pharynx and the trachea.

23. Your patient is a 19-year-old male who has been in a motorcycle crash. Vital signs are pulse, 92 and weak; respirations, 24 and shallow; BP 116/80. He has a suspected spinal injury, as well as a painful, deformed, swollen right foot. Blood loss is not significant. What should your treatment plan focus on?
    a. immobilizing the injured foot in position of function
    b. immobilizing the patient and transporting him rapidly
    c. opening the airway and ventilating the patient
    d. applying the PASG and inflating all compartments

24. What is the general rule for administration of high-flow oxygen in the field?
    a. Administer high-flow oxygen only under specific online medical direction.
    b. Do not administer high-flow oxygen to children, elderly, or pregnant patients.
    c. Do not administer high-flow oxygen to patients with obvious signs of shock.
    d. Administer high-flow oxygen to all patients who are in respiratory distress.

25. The use of reasonable force when dealing with a patient with a behavioral disorder refers to
    a. the force necessary to incapacitate the patient.
    b. calling in police backup in a reasonable way.
    c. using soft restraints rather than handcuffs.
    d. the force necessary to restrain the patient.

26. Rapid onset of altered mental status in a diabetic patient often results when the patient
    a. decreases their insulin dose.
    b. gets too little exercise.
    c. skips a meal.
    d. drinks alcohol.

27. While suctioning, if you cannot clear a patient's mouth in 15 seconds, you should
    a. immediately suction the airway again.
    b. suction the nose along with the mouth.
    c. suction for 15 more seconds and reassess.
    d. logroll the patient to clear the mouth.

28. A 65-year-old female is complaining of chest pressure, difficulty breathing, and is pale. She presents supine in bed. What should you do before sitting her up?
    a. Check her blood pressure to make sure it is adequate.
    b. Do nothing; sit her up right away.
    c. Help the patient administer her own nitroglycerin tablets.
    d. Check her pupils to make sure they are reactive.

29. Your patient is a 20-year-old male who has been in a motorcycle accident. Because of clues from the mechanism of injury on the scene, spinal and head injuries are suspected. After your initial assessment, how often should you reassess vital signs?
    a. after every intervention
    b. every 15 minutes
    c. continuously during transport
    d. every 30 seconds

30. A 70-year-old male is complaining of chest pain and shortness of breath. He is alert with pale, cool, sweaty skin. His pulse is 100; BP, 136/64; and respirations, 24. Upon auscultation, you can hear crackles in the lung fields. Which of the following actions would be appropriate?

  a. Have the patient lie flat because he could be in shock.

  b. Provide oxygen at 2 L/min using a nasal cannula.

  c. Administer nitroglycerin that is prescribed to the patient's wife.

  d. Have the patient sit up to assist with his breathing effort.

31. Your patient is a 23-year-old male who has suffered possible spinal trauma while playing football. He is still wearing his sports helmet as you begin your initial assessment. When should you remove his helmet?

  a. when it is time to apply a cervical collar

  b. if it prevents you from assessing the airway

  c. before you position him on the long board

  d. when you assess his level of consciousness

32. You would assess a patient's breath sounds by placing your stethoscope over the midaxillary line and the

  a. midclavicular line.

  b. sternum.

  c. cricoid notch.

  d. xiphoid process.

33. Your patient, a 45-year-old female, is still seated in her car after a crash. She does not appear to be in a life-threatening situation. What technique should you use to immobilize her spine?

  a. Logroll her directly onto the ground; then apply a long spine board.

  b. Have her get out of the car; then immobilize her while standing.

  c. Apply a cervical collar before assisting her out of the car.

  d. Apply a short spine board and then transfer her to a long spine board.

34. Your patient is a 68-year-old female with chronic respiratory disease. She is experiencing difficulty breathing in spite of home oxygen delivery. You should

  a. increase the flow rate of her oxygen supply.

  b. replace her nasal cannula with a face mask.

  c. consult medical direction for instructions.

  d. treat the patient for the signs of shock.

35. In which situation should you assist a patient with using a prescribed inhaler?

  a. 47-year-old male: history of severe asthma; respirations, 28/min; wheezing, unresponsive

  b. 6-year-old female: history of upper-respiratory infection; respiratory rate, 24/min; coughing

  c. 69-year-old male: history of emphysema; difficulty breathing; inhaler was prescribed for his son

  d. 14-year-old female: history of asthma; respirations, 24/min; alert; used the inhaler one time yesterday

36. Your patient is showing signs of possible carbon monoxide poisoning. What should be your first concern on this call?
  a. Secure the safety of yourself, other people, and the patient.
  b. Open the airway and administer supplemental oxygen.
  c. Transport the patient rapidly to the closest facility.
  d. Obtain medical direction to administer activated charcoal.

37. Which patient's respiratory rate is normal?
  a. 4-year-old male: respirations, 38/min
  b. 11-year-old female: respirations, 12/min
  c. 27-year-old male: respirations, 14/min
  d. 82-year-old female: respirations, 10/min

38. In order to control the flow rate of oxygen to the patient, you must
  a. select the right size tank.
  b. select the right size tubing.
  c. open the valve on the tank.
  d. adjust the regulator setting.

39. The airway of a child can become easily obstructed because, in comparison with an adult, a child has a
  a. shorter airway and more secretions.
  b. narrower airway and larger tongue.
  c. smaller nose and mouth.
  d. faster breathing rate.

40. The major hazard associated with using and transporting oxygen tanks is that they can
  a. fail to function properly if chilled.
  b. leak and emit poisonous fumes.
  c. explode if dropped or handled roughly.
  d. run out of battery power at any time.

41. All of the following are signs of inadequate breathing EXCEPT
  a. slow rate of breathing.
  b. cool, clammy skin.
  c. respiratory rate of 12–20.
  d. shallow breathing.

42. Which of the following lists the correct order for cardiopulmonary circulation?
  a. vena cava, left atrium, left ventricle, pulmonary veins, lungs, pulmonary arteries, right atrium, right ventricle, aorta
  b. aorta, right ventricle, right atrium, pulmonary arteries, lungs, pulmonary veins, left ventricle, left atrium, vena cava
  c. aorta, right atrium, right ventricle, pulmonary veins, lungs, pulmonary arteries, left atrium, left ventricle, vena cava
  d. vena cava, right atrium, right ventricle, pulmonary arteries, lungs, pulmonary veins, left atrium, left ventricle, aorta

43. If a clinical problem is identified in the EMS service, a plan is developed and implemented to reduce further occurrences of the same problem. This is called
  a. quality improvement.
  b. call-sheet review.
  c. ongoing system redesign.
  d. quality assurance.

44. You have been called for an infant who is choking. Upon your arrival, you notice the infant is cyanotic, unresponsive, and apneic. Where will you check for a pulse on your patient?
  a. At the carotid artery closest to you
  b. At the brachial artery
  c. At the carotid artery opposite to you
  d. At the femoral artery

45. Perfusion is defined as
  a. the amount of blood pumped through the body in one minute.
  b. the exchange of gases, nutrients, and waste between the alveoli and the capillaries.
  c. the amount of blood pumped into the system with each beat.
  d. the exchange of gases, nutrients, and waste between the cells and the capillaries.

46. You would evaluate the severity of a patient's hyperthermia by assessing the
  a. temperature of the skin.
  b. color of the skin.
  c. blood pressure and heart rate.
  d. presence of muscle cramps.

47. Your patient is a 79-year-old male who is experiencing chest pain. Which question would you ask to investigate the O part of the OPQRST acronym?
  a. Have you ever felt this kind of pain before?
  b. Where were you when the pain started?
  c. How long ago did the pain begin?
  d. What does the pain feel like?

48. Your patient is a 67-year-old female with chest pains and a history of heart disease. After helping her take a dose of prescribed nitroglycerin, you find that her blood pressure is 96/68 and she is still in severe pain. Medical direction tells you to administer a second dose of nitroglycerin and transport. You should
  a. administer the medication and document the vital signs and the order.
  b. repeat the blood pressure reading and the order to medical direction.
  c. ask to speak to a senior physician.
  d. request advanced cardiac life support (ACLS) backup immediately.

49. In the case of children, airway adjuncts are used when the
  a. child is in respiratory distress and needs supplemental oxygen.
  b. usual means of opening and maintaining the airway are ineffective.
  c. child is frightened of the oxygen mask and nasal cannula.
  d. respiratory rate is less than 20/min or greater than 60/min.

50. You should select the correct size oropharyngeal airway for a child by measuring from the
  a. angle of the jaw to the corner of the mouth.
  b. central incisor to the angle of the jaw.
  c. central incisor to the tragus of the ear.
  d. corner of the mouth to the cricoid cartilage.

51. Cool, clammy skin that is a sign of shock results from
  a. a rise in the patient's temperature.
  b. the body's attempt to increase the vascular space.
  c. decreased heart rate and blood pressure.
  d. diversion of blood flow to the vital organs.

52. Delayed capillary refill is a reliable test of peripheral circulation in
   a. elderly patients.
   b. infants and children.
   c. patients in early shock.
   d. pregnant women.

53. Your medical patient is experiencing clinical signs of shock. You should
   a. lay the patient flat on his stomach.
   b. lay the patient flat on his back.
   c. sit the patient up.
   d. lay the patient flat on his back with legs elevated.

54. You are treating a patient who is anxious, has an altered mental status, complains of shortness of breath, and is sitting up in bed. You assess vital signs and obtain a pulse of 112 and weak, blood pressure is 140/98, respirations are 28, shallow, and labored, skin is pale, cool, and clammy, and breath sounds reveal crackles in all lobes. What type of shock is this patient exhibiting?
   a. Obstructive
   b. Anaphylactic
   c. Cardiogenic
   d. Distributive

55. Bleeding caused by a wound to one large artery or vein can usually be controlled by
   a. concentrated direct pressure.
   b. diffuse direct pressure.
   c. pressure points.
   d. extremity elevations.

56. The formation of plaque, through the buildup of calcium and fatty deposits, in the arteries which may lead to the formation of thromboemboli is called which of the following?
   a. Angina
   b. Arterial dissection
   c. Aortic aneurysm
   d. Atherosclerosis

57. You are treating a patient who is conscious, alert, and oriented times four. The patient is complaining of crushing chest pain that radiates to the left jaw that has lasted more than 30 minutes and is unrelieved by rest. The patient's skin is diaphoretic. You have placed the patient on oxygen and medical control has ordered the administration of aspirin. What are the actions of aspirin in the treatment of cardiac related chest pain?
   a. Fever reduction
   b. Decreases the ability of platelets to clot
   c. Inhibits the release of thrombin and breaks up the clot
   d. Inhibits the action of fibrin and decreases the ability of clots to form

58. A 14-year-old female is unconscious after a 15-foot fall off a ladder. When evaluating her chest during a rapid trauma assessment, you should assess for
   a. paradoxical motion.
   b. jugular vein distention.
   c. softness.
   d. distention.

59. Your patient is a 62-year-old male who has survived a serious car crash. He is unconscious, cyanotic, and bleeding profusely from a thigh wound. Breathing is rapid and shallow. Other injuries are suspected. In which order should you provide care?
  a. open the airway and provide oxygen, control bleeding, immobilize, transport
  b. immobilize, control bleeding, transport, open the airway and provide oxygen
  c. open the airway and provide oxygen, immobilize, control bleeding, transport
  d. control bleeding, open the airway and provide oxygen, immobilize, transport

60. For which type of wound should you use an occlusive dressing that is taped on only three sides?
  a. an impaled object
  b. a sucking chest wound
  c. an abdominal evisceration
  d. an amputation

61. When treating a patient who has suffered an electrical burn, you should be alert for the possibility of
  a. cardiac arrest.
  b. internal bleeding.
  c. heat shock.
  d. allergic reaction.

62. The outer layer of the heart is called the
  a. parietal pleura.
  b. peritoneum.
  c. myocardium.
  d. pericardium.

63. Your patient has a painful deformity of the right lower leg. The pulse in the right posterior tibial artery is missing. Before splinting the injured leg, you should
  a. use gentle traction to attempt to align the limb.
  b. apply a tourniquet to stop internal bleeding.
  c. check the right brachial pulse as well.
  d. place the right foot in the position of function.

64. Which symptoms are signs of a partial upper-airway obstruction due to the presence of a foreign body?
  a. increased work of breathing during expiration with a wheezy cough
  b. gasping respiratory efforts, and the patient is unable to cough or speak
  c. no effort of breathing, absent chest-wall movement, unable to cough or speak
  d. stridor during inspiration, inability to speak, and dyspnea

65. A 23-year-old male has suffered a penetrating head wound that is bleeding profusely and a cervical spine injury. During your rapid trauma assessment, you should
  a. treat the head wound and continue your rapid assessment.
  b. stop your exam and provide appropriate care for both injuries.
  c. manage the cervical spine injury and continue your rapid assessment.
  d. make a mental note of both injuries and continue the assessment.

66. What should you do if you do not have the right size cervical collar to fit a patient with a suspected spinal injury?
   a. Use the next larger or smaller size collar.
   b. Use rolled towels secured with tape.
   c. Leave the neck unsecured and tape the head.
   d. Place the patient on a backboard without a collar.

67. A 12-year-old female fell while skating. She did not strike her head and is alert, complaining of pain to the left wrist. How should you assess this patient?
   a. Assess just the areas that the patient tells you are painful.
   b. Assess every body part from head to toe.
   c. Focus on just the patient's airway and cervical spine.
   d. Complete only the initial and ongoing assessment.

68. Which statement by a patient is most likely to suggest that the patient's thinking is psychotic?
   a. "I've never felt this bad before."
   b. "I know you can't help me."
   c. "Am I going to die now?"
   d. "They sent you to lock me up."

69. Your patient is agitated and confused and seems to be displaying symptoms of drug use. The best way to prevent the situation from becoming dangerous to the patient, yourself, or others is to
   a. restrain the patient as soon as possible.
   b. speak calmly and quietly to the patient.
   c. refuse to treat the patient until he calms down.
   d. inform the patient of your self-defense techniques.

70. A 20-year-old female complains of leg and hip pain after falling off a 20-foot ladder. You should conduct a
   a. focused physical exam.
   b. rapid trauma assessment.
   c. an OPQRST on the pain only.
   d. detailed physical exam.

71. Which of the following patients is showing signs and symptoms of imminent respiratory arrest?
   a. 2-year-old male: respirations, 60/min; severe retractions; cyanosis
   b. 3-year-old female: respirations, 50/min; nasal flaring; wheezing
   c. 4-year-old male; respirations, 8/min; unresponsive; limp muscle tone
   d. 3-year-old female: respirations, 10/min; cyanosis; decreased muscle tone

72. When caring for a patient whose baby is delivering in a breech presentation, you should do all of the following EXCEPT
   a. position the mother with her knees flexed, drawn up, and widely separated.
   b. administer high-flow oxygen to the mother and begin transport quickly.
   c. pull gently on the infant's trunk or legs if delivery of the head is delayed.
   d. allow the delivery to occur spontaneously until the trunk is delivered.

73. You are assessing an awake, alert patient complaining of abdominal pain. He denies any trauma. When conducting a focused history and physical exam, what should you do first?
   a. Conduct a rapid physical exam.
   b. Reassess vital signs.
   c. Gather the history of the present illness.
   d. Question the patient about past medical problems.

74. The correct way to stimulate a newborn to breathe is to
   a. rub his or her back or flick the soles of his or her feet.
   b. position him or her with the head higher than the body.
   c. suction his or her nose and then the mouth.
   d. smack him or her gently on the buttocks.

75. During your focused history and physical exam of an unresponsive patient, you should first
   a. obtain vital signs and then gather OPQRST from the patient.
   b. obtain vital signs and then gather OPQRST from the family.
   c. gather a SAMPLE history and OPQRST from the family.
   d. request ALS and begin a detailed head-to-toe exam.

76. To help determine what poison a patient has ingested, you should be alert for chemical burns around the mouth as well as
   a. burns on the hands.
   b. red-colored vomitus.
   c. moist or dry skin.
   d. unusual breath odors.

77. Baseline vital signs in the unresponsive medical patient include the patient's
   a. past medical history.
   b. signs and symptoms.
   c. blood pressure.
   d. allergies.

78. Your patient has accidentally sprayed insecticide in his eye. What should immediate first aid involve?
   a. placing an airtight dressing over the eye
   b. administering activated charcoal to the patient
   c. irrigating the eye with clean water for 20 minutes
   d. placing 10 cc of sterile saline solution in the eye

79. You just completed a rapid physical exam on an unresponsive 65-year-old female. Your next action should be to
   a. take a history of the present illness.
   b. gather a SAMPLE history.
   c. perform a focused physical exam.
   d. obtain baseline vital signs.

80. Your patient is a 14-year-old male who struck his head on a diving board. Your first reaction should be to
   a. remove the patient from the water and warm him.
   b. release gastric distention and provide artificial ventilation.
   c. administer oxygen and provide artificial ventilation.
   d. immobilize the patient while still in the water.

81. Your patient is a 2-year-old female who has injured her leg. The best way to calm her while you are examining her is to
  a. explain what you are doing in technical language.
  b. tell her that if she doesn't cooperate, she won't get better.
  c. examine her while she is sitting on her parent's lap.
  d. do any painful procedures first so she can calm down.

82. Which statement about suctioning infants and children is correct?
  a. Insert the suction catheter until it touches the back of the throat.
  b. Administer oxygen immediately before and after suctioning.
  c. Never suction for longer than 30 seconds at a time.
  d. The vacuum pump should be set no higher than 200 mm Hg.

83. You are caring for a victim of a motor vehicle accident who is approximately seven months pregnant. The mechanism of injury strongly suggests spinal trauma. How should you position the patient during transport?
  a. immobilized on a long backboard that is then tilted to the left
  b. immobilized and transported supine on a long backboard
  c. immobilized in whatever position she is most comfortable
  d. seated upright with her torso immobilized in a short spine device

84. In order to determine whether an infant is responsive to verbal stimuli, you would
  a. say the child's name.
  b. ask the child to say his or her name.
  c. make a sudden loud noise.
  d. have a parent speak to the child.

85. The correct procedure for inserting an oral airway in an infant or child is to
  a. use the tongue depressor to move the tongue forward, and insert the airway right side up.
  b. tip the head back and open the mouth wide, and then rotate the airway on insertion.
  c. lubricate the tip of the airway with sterile saline, and insert it until you feel resistance.
  d. insert the airway with the bevel toward the base of the throat, pushing gently if you feel resistance.

86. When caring for a rape victim, it is important to discourage the patient from
  a. bathing or douching.
  b. reporting the crime.
  c. talking about feelings.
  d. naming the assailant.

87. In order to care for a child who has a partial upper-airway obstruction, you should
  a. use a combination of back blows and chest thrusts.
  b. open the airway and attempt to ventilate the child.
  c. provide oxygen, position the child, and transport rapidly.
  d. use back blows and finger sweeps to remove the obstruction.

88. In which of the following circumstances should you suspect the possibility of child abuse?
  a. A parent tells you the 4-month-old infant's injuries were caused by rolling off the bed.
  b. A distraught parent promptly reports and requests treatment for a seriously injured child.
  c. A parent tells you that the child walked into a door at school, but the teacher disagrees.
  d. The child and parent both give you an identical account of how an injury occurred.

89. You should suspect the possibility of shock in a child who has a recent history of
    a. vomiting and diarrhea.
    b. cardiac arrest.
    c. epileptic seizures.
    d. upper-respiratory disease.

90. Your patient, a 27-year-old-female who is pregnant with her second child, tells you, "My water broke an hour ago." This should alert you that the patient
    a. has signs and symptoms of shock.
    b. is pregnant with twins.
    c. will have her baby fairly soon.
    d. is having a miscarriage.

91. You should place your hand on a pregnant woman's abdomen during contractions to determine the
    a. strength of the contractions.
    b. duration of the contractions.
    c. size of the fetus.
    d. fetal heart rate.

92. You are assisting with a delivery in the field. As the baby's head is born, you find that the cord is wrapped tightly around the infant's neck and cannot be dislodged. You should
    a. transport the mother immediately in the knee/chest position.
    b. clamp the cord in two places and cut it between the clamps.
    c. pull hard on the cord to force the placenta to deliver immediately.
    d. exert gentle pressure on the baby's head to slow the delivery.

93. When is it normal for the baby's head to rotate from the facedown position to the side?
    a. during crowning
    b. right before the head delivers
    c. right after the head delivers
    d. as the body delivers

94. You are assessing a newborn who has a pink body but blue extremities, a pulse rate of 98/min, no response to suctioning, moderate flexion of the extremities, and a respiratory rate of 38/min. What is the APGAR score for this infant?
    a. 2
    b. 4
    c. 6
    d. 8

95. When should you expect an infant to start to breathe spontaneously?
    a. one to five seconds after birth
    b. 10–15 seconds after birth
    c. 20–30 seconds after birth
    d. one minute after birth

96. Which of these situations is a true emergency that cannot be managed in the field?
    a. breech presentation
    b. meconium in the amniotic fluid
    c. multiple births
    d. limb presentation

97. Your patient is a 19-year-old female with severe vaginal bleeding. As part of the SAMPLE history, it is particularly important to ask the patient if she
    a. feels dizzy.
    b. has vomited.
    c. may be pregnant.
    d. has ingested poison.

98. All of the following are examples of indirect medical direction EXCEPT
  a. continuing education classes taught by physicians.
  b. contact between physicians and EMTs in the field.
  c. design of EMS systems by physicians.
  d. quality-improvement efforts by physicians.

99. You should allow family members to remain with a patient EXCEPT when
  a. the patient is in the process of dying.
  b. the patient has gruesome injuries.
  c. they want to reassure the patient.
  d. they interfere with patient care.

100. If a newborn infant's respiratory effort is inadequate, your first intervention should be to
  a. provide artificial ventilations at a rate of 60-120/min.
  b. provide positive pressure ventilations at a rate of 40-60/min.
  c. administer high-flow oxygen via the blow-by method.
  d. transport immediately to a hospital with a newborn intensive care unit.

101. In which situation would you be treating a patient under an assumption of implied consent?
  a. 4-year-old male, with broken leg, parent gives permission for treatment
  b. 19-year-old female, with seizure, who refuses treatment or transport
  c. 47-year-old male, with chest pain, requests transport to the hospital
  d. 80-year-old female, unconscious, no friends or family members present

102. A standard of care is the
  a. highest level of care an EMT can legally provide.
  b. list of skills EMTs are required to perform in your state.
  c. national description of all procedures the EMTs may perform.
  d. minimum level of care that is normally provided in your locality.

103. Which situation might constitute legal abandonment of a patient?
  a. You leave your patient because the fire in an adjacent building reaches the room you are in.
  b. You begin CPR on a patient and ask a bystander to continue while you assess another patient.
  c. Your patient states that he or she does not want treatment and signs a statement to that effect.
  d. You transport a patient to the hospital and leave him or her in the care of a nurse who signed your patient-care report.

104. When using an ATV the EMT should adjust which settings to achieve proper ventilations?
  a. Rate and oxygen percentage
  b. Peak inspiratory pressure and tidal volume
  c. Rate and ventilator effort
  d. Tidal volume and rate

105. Your patient is a 25-year-old male who has had two seizures within the last hour. He shows no signs of drug or alcohol use. He now states that he feels fine and refuses both transport and further treatment. You should
   a. carefully document every attempt you make to provide care.
   b. obtain an order for tranquilizers from the medical direction physician.
   c. call for police backup to help you restrain the patient.
   d. leave the patient immediately to avoid being sued for battery.

106. In which of the following situations might you be found to have committed assault against your patient?
   a. You leave your patient at the scene of an accident before additional help arrives.
   b. You tell the patient, "If you don't let me splint your leg, I'll have to tie you up."
   c. You tell the patient, "You're over 18 and you have the right to refuse treatment."
   d. You transfer care of your patient to a first responder who has just arrived on the scene.

107. An indication for the insertion of a nasopharyngeal airway would be
   a. a patient who will not tolerate an oropharyngeal airway.
   b. severe head injury with blood draining from the nose.
   c. a deviated septum.
   d. basilar skull fracture.

108. Whenever it is necessary to carry out an emergency move of a patient, it is important to
   a. pull the patient along the line of the body's long axis.
   b. immobilize the patient to a long spine board before the move.
   c. complete the detailed assessment before the move.
   d. have at least two EMTs lift the patient off the ground.

109. The first step in a rapid extrication of a patient from a car is to
   a. apply a cervical immobilization collar.
   b. place the end of the long backboard on the seat.
   c. rotate the patient until his or her back is in the open doorway.
   d. move all of the extremities into a neutral position.

110. Which patient should be placed in the recovery position?
   a. A pregnant woman who has been in a car crash
   b. A conscious cardiac patient complaining of shortness of breath
   c. A unresponsive patient who does not have a suspected spine injury
   d. A child in respiratory distress with a rate of 6/min

111. The increased pressure on arterial walls produced when the left ventricle contracts is the
   a. systolic pressure.
   b. arterial pressure.
   c. diastolic pressure.
   d. residual pressure.

112. The nervous system regulates the frequency and strength of contractions through several receptors located in the heart and blood vessels. When the beta 1-adrenergic receptors are stimulated the
  a. heart rate and strength of contractions decrease.
  b. heart rate increases and strength of contractions decrease.
  c. strength of contractions and heart rate increase.
  d. blood vessels constrict and heart rate decreases.

113. Which of the following is an example of an effective way to communicate with an elderly patient?
  a. "Sir, I'm going to try to make you comfortable until we get to the hospital."
  b. "You just sit down here on this nice, comfortable chair and don't worry."
  c. "I will try to talk very slowly so you can understand me."
  d. "Sir, I'll make sure I explain everything I'm doing to your son."

114. When assessing our patient you note the pulse rate is elevated and the pulse feels adequate and equal. If the heart rate is elevated and the stroke volume remains the same, then the cardiac output will
  a. remain the same.
  b. increase.
  c. decrease.
  d. None of the above

115. The myocardium is perfused by the
  a. coronary arteries.
  b. carotid arteries.
  c. aorta.
  d. vena cava.

Questions 116–120 refer to the following scenario:

You respond to a dispatch of an "unknown medical event." As you arrive on the scene, an elderly gentleman greets you at the door and motions you to step inside. You are directed to the rear of the house, where an elderly woman presents to you sitting on the bed. She appears to be in severe respiratory distress.

116. After assessing the scene for hazards, what should you do next?
  a. Establish the patient's baseline vital signs.
  b. Establish a SAMPLE history.
  c. Perform an initial assessment.
  d. Perform a focused assessment.

117. When should you place the patient on oxygen?
  a. after the focused assessment
  b. during the initial assessment
  c. after taking baseline vital signs
  d. after medical command gives you permission

118. Which of the following signs would you assess for first?
  a. lung sounds
  b. abdominal tenderness
  c. presence of pedal pulses
  d. swelling in her fingers

119. Which of the following questions would you NOT ask during your OPQRST of the present illness?
  a. When did you begin having trouble breathing?
  b. Does anything else cause you pain or discomfort?
  c. Does anything make the breathing easier or worse?
  d. Do you have any respiratory problems?

120. After a few minutes of supplemental oxygen therapy, the patient states that she feels much better. What would you do now?
  a. Discontinue the oxygen since she feels better.
  b. Perform a reassessment of her vital signs.
  c. Have her sign a refusal-of-care form.
  d. Contact her private physician.

Answers

1. b. This patient's vital signs are all within the normal range for his age.

2. a. Signs of labored respirations, or increased effort of breathing, include use of accessory muscles to breathe, grunting, and stridor. Stridor is a loud, high-pitched sound heard on respirations that usually indicates an upper-airway obstruction. Agonal respirations are gasping slow respirations that happen for some patients as they are dying.

3. c. The color, temperature, and condition of the skin allows you to form an indirect assessment of the patient's perfusion, or circulatory status.

4. b. A single blood pressure reading, unless it is extremely high or extremely low, is not in itself significant. Blood pressure readings are most useful in establishing a trend that can signal changes in the patient status. Blood pressure varies constantly during the day by 20 mm Hg or more during sleep, work, and relaxation activities. Assessment of BP by palpation is useful when the patient is in a very noisy environment, making auscultation difficult.

5. c. Chances are, this patient is experiencing sudden ventricular fibrillation that may be most likely reversed with a defibrillation attempt.

6. b. For a pulseless patient, defibrillation takes precedence over either administering oxygen or performing CPR, but always stop the ambulance before using the AED. Do not analyze a heart rhythm in a moving vehicle.

7. d. Children are likely to suffer serious injury in lower-speed collisions than adults; none of the other choices represents a serious mechanism of injury.

8. c. In order to accurately assess the patient's airway, breathing, and circulation status, all external compressions or ventilations must be stopped.

9. d. The jugular veins are normally somewhat distended while a patient is lying down; flat veins signify blood loss.

10. b. The normal electrical pathway through the heart begins at the SA Node, pauses at the AV Node to allow blood to fill the ventricles, continues through the Bundle of His, and then surrounds the ventricles through the Purkinje Fibers.

11. a. The tricuspid valve separates the right atrium from the right ventricle. The pulmonary valve is between the right ventricle and the pulmonary arteries. The mitral valve separates the left atrium from the left ventricle and the aortic valve separates the left ventricle from the aorta.

12. a. Although you should quickly splint the patient's wounds and stop major bleeding, treatment of a patient in shock should focus on rapidly transporting her to the hospital. You can continue to stabilize and treat her injuries while you are transporting her. Perform any other examinations while en route to the hospital. Monitor and assess her vital signs every five minutes.

13. b. Reassess a stable patient every 15 minutes while en route to the receiving facility.

14. a. Although interacting with the patient continuously will keep you informed about his or her level of anxiety and allow you to observe skin color and pupils, the main purpose is to assess changes in mental status and patency of airway.

15. a. Always transport an amputated part along with the patient, wrapped in sterile dressings and then in plastic. Keep the amputated part cool, but do not put the foot directly in contact with ice or ice water because the ice can cause further tissue damage, which may result in the inability to reimplant the amputated part.

16. c. If a patient's respiratory rate is irregular, count for one full minute; otherwise, count for 30 seconds and multiply by two to obtain the respiratory rate.

17. b. This patient's pulse and respiratory rate are both elevated.

18. a. It is impossible to determine the actual degree of tissue damage in the field, so the purpose of the focused assessment is to gather information for the receiving facility. You should always ask about medications; it is the M of SAMPLE. The focused history has nothing to do with AED use. Cardiac pain has all sorts of presentations, making it difficult to differentiate from other conditions.

19. c. The proper hand placement for compressing a child's chest is to place the heel of one or two hands in the middle of the sternum between the patient's nipples and avoid the xyphoid process.

20. a. The purpose of the detailed physical examination, which is performed while en route to the hospital on all trauma patients as well as unresponsive medical patients, is to reveal hidden injuries.

21. c. Paradoxical motion, the movement of one portion of the chest wall in the opposite direction from the rest of the chest during respirations, indicates serious injury to the chest wall.

22. d. The glottis is the opening between the pharynx and the trachea.

23. b. For a patient who is showing signs of shock as well as possible spinal injury, care focuses on immobilization and rapid transport, rather than on caring for isolated extremity injuries. This patient already has an open airway, and ventilation is not necessary, although oxygen should be administered by a nonrebreather mask and his respiratory status should be closely monitored as his respiratory rate is a little fast and his effort is shallow.

24. d. EMTs should administer high-flow oxygen to all patients who show signs and symptoms of respiratory distress.

25. d. *Reasonable force* refers to the amount of force necessary to prevent injury to the patient or anyone else, including the rescuers. It is sometimes necessary to use force to restrain a patient with a behavioral disorder. Reasonable force does not define the type of restraints needed.

26. c. Rapid onset of altered mental status in diabetic patients is associated with hypoglycemia, or low blood sugar. This most commonly occurs when patients take their normal dose of insulin but skip a meal. Excessive exercise can also bring on a hypoglycemic state.

27. d. If you cannot clear the patient's mouth of secretions, logroll the patient so the secretions can drain out. Never suction for longer than 15 seconds at a time, and oxygenate the patient between suction attempts.

28. a. The position of comfort for most people having trouble breathing is sitting; however, this patient may have low blood pressure, possibly due to a cardiac emergency. In this case, it would be important to ensure that her blood pressure is adequate to support a sudden change in body position.

29. a. Because patients with spinal injuries are at risk of paralysis and breathing difficulties, reassess vital signs after every intervention, such as cervical immobilization or whole-body immobilizations. Once the patient is a little more stable, you would continue to reassess vital signs every five minutes because he would still be a critical patient.

30. d. This patient's blood pressure is adequate to support a sitting patient. This patient also requires high-flow oxygen via nonrebreather as part of the treatment plan.

31. b. Leave a helmet in place if it fits well, does not interfere with assessment or administration of oxygen, and the patient is not in cardiac arrest. Leave the shoulder pads in place along with the helmet. You do not need to apply a cervical collar to this patient, but you should immobilize his body and head to a long spine board. You can assess his level of consciousness without moving the helmet.

32. a. Assess breath sounds bilaterally over the midaxillary and midclavicular lines.

33. d. Immobilize the patient to a short spine board like the Kendrick Extrication Device or other commercial device while she is still seated; then transfer her to a long spine board. If you suspected she was in shock or was unstable, you would perform a rapid extrication by applying a cervical collar and quickly removing her from the vehicle with the assistance of several rescuers while trying to maintain a neutral alignment to her spine.

34. c. Consult medical direction when you encounter a patient who is having difficulty breathing in spite of home administration of oxygen.

35. d. You can help a patient to use a prescribed inhaler if the patient has signs and symptoms of respiratory emergency, if the inhaler was prescribed for that patient, and if the patient is responsive. Be sure and determine if the patient has used the inhaler already and if it helped lessen the distress.

36. a. In cases of inhalation poisoning when the toxin may still be present, your first concern should be to ensure your own safety and that of other people in the area. Move the patient to your ambulance, then begin your assessment and treatment. Activated charcoal is administered in the case of ingested (swallowed) poisons, not inhaled poisons.

37. c. The normal breathing rate for an adult is between 12–20 breaths per minute.

38. d. You control the flow of oxygen to the patient by adjusting the regulator on the oxygen tank. The size of the tank has no bearing on the flow rate. Oxygen tubing size is standardized. The valve must be in the open position to deliver any oxygen, but it does not change the rate of flow.

39. b. In comparison with an adult, a child has a larger tongue, which can obstruct the airway, and a narrow airway, which can more easily be blocked by secretions.

40. c. Because oxygen tanks contain gas at very high pressure, they can explode if they are dropped or otherwise roughly handled.

41. c. A respiratory rate of 12–20 breaths per minute is normal; signs of inadequate breathing include cyanosis, increased or decreased breathing rate, shortness of breath, and irregular rhythm.

42. b. A pulse check in an infant is performed at the brachial artery on the medial aspect of the upper arm. The carotid artery is hard to palpate in an infant, as is the femoral artery.

43. a. Quality assurance is the process that identifies the problem and focuses on the individual to make corrections. Quality improvement focuses on the system to identify an issue or process that is prone to failure and concentrates on making system corrections to solve the problem.

44. b. A pulse check in an infant is performed at the brachial artery on the medial aspect of the upper arm. The carotid artery is hard to palpate in an infant, as is the femoral artery.

45. d. Perfusion is the transfer of oxygen and carbon dioxide, glucose and other nutrients, and waste products from the cells to the capillaries. Choice **a** is cardiac output, **b** is respiration, and **c** is stroke volume.

46. a. Patients with hyperthermia with cool skin still retain their ability to eliminate heat; their condition is therefore not as serious as that of patients with hot skin, who have lost this ability. You should also closely monitor the patient's mental status.

47. c. O stands for onset, or when the pain began.

48. b. Nitroglycerin is not administered to a patient whose systolic blood pressure is lower than 100. Repeat the blood pressure reading and the order and request that the physician confirm it.

49. b. Airway adjuncts, such as nasopharyngeal and oropharyngeal airways, are used only when the jaw thrust and head-tilt/chin-lift are ineffective in opening the airway.

50. a. Select the correct size oral airway for a child by measuring from the angle of the jaw to the corner of the mouth.

51. d. In early shock, the body diverts blood flow away from the skin and toward the body's vital organs, resulting in decreased peripheral circulation and cool, clammy skin.

52. b. Capillary refill time is used to determine peripheral perfusion in infants and children only.

53. d. If no traumatic injury mechanism is suspected, keeping the patient flat with legs elevated will promote blood circulation back to the critical organs.

54. c. This patient is suffering from congestive heart failure, which has resulted in their deterioration to cardiogenic shock. The crackles in the lungs rules out anaphylactic shock. The crackles and lack of a narrowing pulse pressure rules out obstructive shock. The cool clammy skin and lack of a fever rules out distributive shock.

55. a. Bleeding from a single site can usually be controlled by concentrated direct applied pressure to that site. Diffuse pressure is reserved for circumstances when concentrated direct pressure is unadvisable, like when controlling bleeding from an open skull fracture. Tourniquets and elevation are steps to take if direct pressure is ineffective.

56. d. This is a definition of atherosclerosis. An aneurysm is a weakening of the arterial wall and a dissection occurs when the aneurysm ruptures.

57. b. Aspirin has an antiplatelet action that decreases the ability of platelets to form clots. This will prevent existing clots from getting bigger, but will not reduce or break up existing clots.

58. a. Paradoxical motion of the chest may indicate broken ribs or flail chest. Softness and distention during assessment generally refers to the abdomen.

59. **a.** Always open the airway first, regardless of other priorities. Since the patient is bleeding profusely, the second priority is to control the bleeding from the leg wound. Since the patient is showing signs and symptoms of shock, the next priorities are to immobilize the spine and transport rapidly.

60. **b.** For a sucking chest wound, apply an occlusive dressing that is taped on only three sides. This will allow air to escape from the chest cavity.

61. **a.** Electrical burns are frequently more serious than they appear from the entrance and exit wounds; you should be alert for the possibility of cardiac arrest and be prepared to use the AED.

62. **d.** The outer layer of the heart is called the pericardium. This thin layer of tissue encases the heart and holds a small amount of lubricant, to allow the heart to contract and relax without increased friction.

63. **a.** When a pulse is missing distal to an injury, attempt to align the limb with gentle traction. Bringing the limb into alignment may relieve pressure on the blood vessels and restore circulation.

64. **d.** Partial upper-airway obstruction due to a foreign body is differentiated from complete obstruction by the patient's ability to breathe or speak. Stridor indicates upper-airway obstruction. A wheezing sound (patient **a**) indicates a lower-airway obstruction. Patients **b** and **c** have a total airway obstruction.

65. **b.** Both life-threatening injuries to the patient must be treated as quickly as possible.

66. **b.** If the mechanism of injury of the patient's signs and symptoms suggest spinal injury, you must immobilize the neck and spine.

Use rolled-up towels if you do not have a cervical collar that fits properly.

67. **a.** Without a serious mechanism of injury being reported, a focused physical assessment of the patient's injuries is appropriate.

68. **d.** This statement reflects paranoia, a psychotic state in which people imagine that other people are conspiring to harm them.

69. **b.** You can frequently prevent situations from becoming dangerous by maintaining a calm, professional manner and speaking quietly to a distraught patient.

70. **b.** The mechanism of injury suggests that you should look through the kill zone areas to make sure there are no other underlying injuries.

71. **c.** Signs of imminent respiratory arrest are a breathing rate of less than 10/min, limp muscle tone, slow or absent heart rate, and weak or absent distal pulses; the patient will also be unresponsive. These patients need artificial ventilation and chest compression. Patients **a**, **b**, and **d** are in respiratory insufficiency and the early stages of respiratory failure, which, if uncorrected, will lead to respiratory arrest.

72. **c.** Do not pull on the infant's trunk or legs to assist delivery. If the baby's head is not delivered spontaneously, place your hand inside the birth canal to hold the cord and walls of the vagina away from the baby's face, and transport immediately.

73. **c.** Conducting an OPQRST on the pain and finding out the SAMPLE history will gather a lot of information about the patient's complaint.

74. **a.** If necessary, stimulate a newborn to breathe by gently rubbing his or her back or flicking the soles of his or her feet. You should always suction the mouth first and then the nose

because infants are obligate nasal breathers, and if you suction the nose first, it may stimulate them to take a breath, inhaling any amniotic fluid remaining in the oropharynx into the lungs.

75. b. Since the patient is unresponsive, the most effective method of obtaining information about the patient's condition is by looking for clues to the MOI/NOI and speaking with family and other witnesses to the event.

76. d. Some poisons can be identified by the unusual breath odors they cause; for example, cyanide causes an odor of bitter almonds. Choice **a** is incorrect because some substances may burn mucous membranes of the mouth but may not burn the skin. Choice **b** is incorrect because, depending upon the substance ingested, vomit may or may not be discolored or bloody. Choice **c** is incorrect because the toxin may or may not cause changes in skin temperature or color; it will depend upon the action of the poison and if it causes shock.

77. c. The other three choices are part of the SAMPLE history. Vital signs include pulse, blood pressure, respirations, skin signs, and pupil reactivity to light.

78. c. When toxins come in contact with the eye, irrigate the eye with clean water for 20 minutes, preferably while en route to the hospital.

79. d. Since the patient is unresponsive, it will not be possible to elicit a medical history directly. An early set of vital signs may help determine the underlying cause of the patient's condition.

80. d. Because of the great risk of spinal injury with this type of trauma, the EMT's first action should be to immobilize the patient while still in the water; the second step is to attend to the airway.

81. c. Calm the toddler by allowing her to remain with her parent and by explaining what you are doing in simple language. Warn her if something will hurt, and if possible, perform painful procedures (sometimes blood pressure assessment is painful) at the end of your assessment. Also, keep all your equipment out of sight until you are ready to use it so she can't get all worked up about it. Kids have incredible imaginations and will invent all sorts of painful scenarios as they look at your equipment and supplies. Sometimes you can let the child briefly examine a piece of equipment before you use it or pretend to use it on the parent to help calm her down.

82. b. When suctioning infants and children, be sure not to stimulate the back of the throat, which can lead to bradycardia. Administer oxygen before and after suctioning, suction for no more than 10–15 seconds at a time, and set the vacuum pump at 80–120 mm Hg.

83. a. The patient should be immobilized on a long backboard, but the entire board should be tilted to the left side with padding to reduce the pressure of the fetus on her circulatory systems. This condition is called supine hypotension syndrome.

84. d. An infant who is responsive to voice, or to verbal stimuli, would turn in the direction of the parent's voice.

85. a. When inserting an airway in an infant or child, use a tongue depressor and avoid rotating the airway.

86. a. The rape victim should be discouraged from bathing, douching, urinating, or cleaning any wounds, since these activities may destroy evidence.

87. c. Back blows, chest thrusts, and ventilation are performed on infants with complete airway obstructions; care for a child with partial obstruction consists of placing the child in a position of comfort and transporting rapidly.

88. c. In cases of child abuse, different people frequently give different accounts of the same accident, or parents may appear unconcerned.

89. a. Shock in children is most frequently associated with fluid loss due to vomiting and diarrhea or to blood loss.

90. c. It is normal for the amniotic sac to rupture and the fluid it contains to drain out of the woman's vagina before delivery.

91. b. You place your hand on the pregnant women's abdomen to measure the duration of the contractions. To measure the length of a contraction you begin the time from the beginning of the first contraction to the beginning of the next contraction.

92. b. If the cord is wrapped around the infant's neck and it cannot be placed back over the head, the infant is in danger of suffocation. Immediately clamp the cord in two places and carefully cut between the clamps. Never pull on the umbilical cord as this can cause uterine inversion, which is a life-threatening emergency.

93. c. The baby's head is usually born facedown in the vertex position, and the head rotates just after it emerges from the birth canal.

94. b. This infant would receive one point for skin color (appearance), one point for pulse rate, zero for grimace, one point for activity, and one point for respirations.

95. c. An infant normally starts breathing independently within about 20–30 seconds after birth; if it does not, provide tactile stimulations.

96. d. A limb presentation, in which an arm or leg is the presenting part, is a true emergency situation that cannot be managed in the field. Place the mother with her pelvis elevated, exert gentle pressure on the baby's body, and transport the mother in this position. Breech, meconium, and multiple births can all be handled in the field. Call for ALS assistance for each of these emergencies and expect fetal distress in the newborn(s).

97. c. Determine if the patient may be pregnant, and if so, treat her like a pregnant woman—administer oxygen and transport her on her left side.

98. b. Indirect medical direction includes all involvement by physicians with EMS systems except direct supervision of EMTs in the field.

99. d. Always allow family members to stay with a patient except if their presence interferes with necessary care.

100. b. If, on initial assessment, the newborn's respirations are slow, shallow, or absent, you should provide positive pressure ventilations with a bag-valve mask at the rate of 40-60/min. After about 30 seconds of this intervention, you should reassess the patient to determine if you need to continue with the bag-valve-mask ventilation.

101. d. Implied consent is applicable in cases where the patient is unable to consent; you provide treatment under the assumption that any rational person would want to receive treatment under the circumstances.

102. d. A standard of care for any locality is the minimum acceptable level of care normally provided there. All care providers, including EMTs, are legally held to this standard.

103. b. Abandonment may occur if you stop caring for a patient without his or her consent, and without transferring care to personnel of the same or higher level. For patient **a**, personal safety takes priority over patient care. If a conscious capable adult patient has signed a refusal (and he or she heard about risks/benefits first), you have not committed abandonment, ruling out case **c**. To avoid abandonment when dealing with hospitals, hospital personnel must assume care of patient before you can leave, and this occurred in case **d**.

104. d. The EMT should adjust the rate of respirations and the tidal volume on the Automatic Transport Ventilator (ATV) to achieve adequate ventilations. Adequate ventilations should be evaluated by the rise and fall of the chest. Some models may allow adjustment to the peak inspiratory pressure, but that is an alarm to indicate poor compliance or increased airway pressures, not adequate ventilations.

105. a. Refusal of treatment requires that the patient be fully aware of the consequences of refusing care. Document all attempts made to change the patient's mind by you and other caregivers.

106. b. Threatening the patient may be held to constitute assault; options **a** and **d** both constitute abandonment of a patient.

107. a. One of the indications for the insertion of a nasopharyngeal airway is a patient who is unable to tolerate an oropharyngeal airway.

108. a. An emergency move is carried out when the patient is in immediate danger. Because there is no time to protect the spine before an emergency move, you should try to protect the spine by dragging the patient in a straight line, either by pulling on his or her clothing or by placing the patient on a blanket and dragging the blanket.

109. a. Before beginning the actual extrication, the first step is to check and open the airway if necessary. You need to attempt to apply a cervical collar before performing the move. If it is a true emergency (scene is very unstable and dangerous) and you cannot do this, make every effort to keep the head and neck in a neutral alignment while you move the patient. If you can slide the patient onto a longboard, it will make moving him or her easier because you can keep him or her in alignment more easily.

110. c. Use the recovery position for a patient who is breathing spontaneously but who is unresponsive or likely to vomit and aspirate material into the airway. You should not use it for a spinal injured patient until he or she is properly immobilized. Patient **a** should be placed in the left lateral recumbent position once she is immobilized. Patient **b** should be assisted into the position of comfort with the recovery position used if the mental status decreases (and he or she is still breathing adequately). Patient **d** needs bag-valve mask ventilation.

111. a. The systolic pressure is the increased pressure in the artery when the left ventricle is contracted.

112. c. When the Beta 1 receptors are stimulated the heart rate and strength of contractions increase. Alpha stimulation causes the vessels to constrict and Beta 2 receptors cause the bronchioles to dilate.

113. a. Speak to elderly patients respectfully, directly, and clearly, and do not assume that they can't understand the situation.

114. b. Cardiac output is a function of the heart rate and stroke volume. If the heart rate increases and the stroke volume remains the same, then cardiac output will increase. You noted the pulse rate was elevated and the quality of the pulse remained normal; therefore, the heart rate had increased and stroke volume remained the same. A pulse that is bounding would tend to indicate an increase in stroke volume, while a weak pulse would tend to indicate a reduced stroke volume.

115. a. The coronary arteries provide circulation and therefore perfusion to the myocardium.

116. c. An initial assessment will determine the initial, most serious life threats first.

117. b. If the patient is having respiratory distress, provide oxygen immediately after assessing her respiratory effort.

118. a. Since her chief complaint appears to be respiratory distress, listening to lung sounds early would provide some information about her respiratory system.

119. d. This is a good question to ask during the SAMPLE history taking.

120. b. An ongoing assessment is important to perform so that you can spot trends in the patient's condition.

6 ▶ EMT PRACTICE EXAM 4

CHAPTER SUMMARY
This is the fourth of ten practice exams in this book based on the National Registry's EMT cognitive exam. Using all the experience and strategies you gained from the other three so far, take this exam to see how far you have come since taking the first test.

Multiple-choice exams are efficient and have become a common method of testing. It has been argued that fill-in or free-response testing is more challenging and provides a superior evaluation of a person's knowledge. Why not take advantage of both methods? The questions in this exam represent each of the modules found in the U.S. Department of Transportation's Emergency Medical Technician National Education Standards. The results can be used to guide your study. If necessary, use the open book technique and refer to your EMT training text as you go. Take your time—there is more to this exam than simply getting the answer correct; you must also understand the concept.

EMT Practice Exam 4

1. What is the minimum training level for ambulance personnel?

_____

_____

_____

2. True or false: The safety of your patient and bystanders is your primary responsibility on an EMS scene.

_____

_____

_____

3. Leaving your patient with another qualified individual is called

_____

_____

_____

4. An EMT should speak up for a patient and make sure the patient's needs are addressed. This is called

_____

_____

_____

5. The government department responsible for creating the EMT curriculum is

_____

_____

_____

6. The process consisting of continuous self-review with the purpose of identifying aspects that require improvement is called

_____

_____

_____

7. The person who assumes ultimate responsibility for the oversight of patient care is called

_____

_____

_____

_____

8. An EMT or other person authorized by the medical director to give medications or perform emergency care is called

_____

_____

_____

9. A policy or protocol issued by a medical director that authorizes EMTs and others to perform certain skills is called

_____

_____

_____

10. Organisms that cause infection such as viruses and bacteria are called

_____

_____

_____

_____

11. The processes and procedures designed to protect you from infection are known as

_____

_____

_____

12. The equipment used to protect you from all possible routes of contamination are collectively known as

_____

_____

_____

13. A patient has a productive cough. What potentially fatal lung disease should an EMT be concerned about with respect to personal safety and that of his or her crew?

_____

_____

_____

_____

14. What does the acronym HIV stand for?

_____

_____

_____

15. The U.S. Congress act that establishes procedures by which emergency response workers may find out if they have been exposed to life-threatening infectious diseases is called

_____

_____

_____

16. EMTs and other EMS workers are routinely given a test called a PPD test. What does PPD mean, and what can the test detect?

_____

_____

_____

_____

17. What is the difference between eustress and distress?

_____

_____

_____

18. When a patient finds out he or she is dying, it is common to go through various emotional stages including denial. Name some others.

_____

_____

_____

_____

19. What are the three Rs of reacting to a dangerous situation?

_____

_____

_____

_____

20. Explain the difference between expressed consent and implied consent.

_____

_____

_____

_____

21. In order for a patient to refuse care or transport, several conditions must be fulfilled. List as many of these conditions as possible.

_____

_____

_____

_____

22. Provide an example of an advance directive.

_____

_____

_____

_____

23. Name two of the most significant causes of lawsuits against EMTs.

_____

_____

_____

_____

24. A finding of negligence against an EMT requires that a number of circumstances be proved. List these circumstances.

_____

_____

_____

_____

25. Leaving a patient after care has been initiated and before proper transfer to someone with equal or greater medical training is known as

_____

_____

_____

_____

26. The anatomical term for the front of the body is

_____

_____

_____

27. The anatomical term for the rear of the body is

_____

_____

_____

28. The anatomical term to describe a position closer to the torso is

_____

_____

_____

29. The anatomical term to describe a position farther from the torso is

_____

_____

_____

30. The anatomical term for an imaginary line drawn down the center of the body passing between the eyes and past the umbilicus is

_____

_____

_____

31. Provide the positional term for the following patients (e.g., a patient lying on his or her back is in the supine position):
- A patient lying on his or her abdomen
- A patient sitting
- A patient lying with the head slightly lower than the feet

_____

_____

_____

_____

32. What is the name of the bone of the lower jaw?

_____

_____

_____

33. What is the name of the bone found at the base of the sternum?

_____

_____

_____

34. The spinal column is made up of individual bones called vertebrae. How many vertebrae are there in the human spine?

_____

_____

_____

35. Name the five divisions of the spine and state the number of vertebrae in each division.

_____

_____

_____

36. Tarsals and metatarsals are found where?

_____

_____

_____

37. The bone that sits anterior to the knee joint is known as

_____

_____

_____

38. Describe the difference between voluntary and involuntary muscles. Give at least one example of each.

_____

_____

_____

39. A leaf-shaped structure that closes to prevent food and other objects from entering the trachea is known as

_____

_____

_____

40. Small sacs within the lungs where gas exchange takes place with the bloodstream are called

_____

_____

_____

41. The component of blood primarily instrumental in the formation of blood clots is called

_____

_____

_____

42. What is a key function of the white blood cells?

_____

_____

_____

43. What is perfusion?

_____

_____

_____

44. The division of the nervous system that controls involuntary motor function and affects such things as digestion and heart rate is the

_____

_____

_____

45. Epinephrine is sometimes called

_____

_____

_____

46. During the initial assessment, how do you determine signs of adequate breathing?

_____

_____

_____

47. Your patient presents with skin that appears blue or gray. This condition is called

_____

_____

_____

48. What is respiratory failure?

_____

_____

_____

_____

49. List as many signs of inadequate breathing as you can.

_____

_____

_____

50. What is the normal breathing rate for an adult?

_____

_____

_____

_____

51. The technique used to provide the maximum opening of a patient's airway is

_____

_____

_____

52. The technique used to open the airway of a patient with a head, neck, or spine injury is

_____

_____

_____

_____

53. What is the best method to evaluate adequate ventilation of a patient when using a bag-valve mask?

_____

_____

_____

_____

54. What percentage of oxygen will a bag-valve mask with a reservoir deliver?

_____

_____

_____

55. Based on American Heart Association guidelines, how much air should be delivered to a patient using an adult bag-valve mask?

_____

_____

_____

_____

56. What is the best method to size an oropharyngeal airway (OPA)?

_____

_____

_____

_____

57. What does the term _contraindication_ mean?

_____

_____

_____

_____

58. What is the best method to size a nasopharyngeal airway (NPA)?

_____

_____

_____

_____

59. To be effective, how much air intake (measured in mm Hg) should a suction unit be able to maintain?

_____

_____

_____

60. Never suction a patient for more than _____ seconds at a time.

61. The atmosphere contains approximately _____ % oxygen.

62. A portable oxygen cylinder, when filled, is pressurized to approximately _____ pounds per square inch (psi).

63. Oxygen should not be allowed to empty below a safe residual pressure. The safe residual pressure for a portable cylinder is

_____

_____

_____

_____

64. An oxygen cylinder should be hydrostatically tested every _____ years. Cylinders with a star after the date may be hydrostatically tested every _____ years.

65. You are the first on the scene of a motor vehicle accident (MVA). List a number of priorities to consider during your scene size-up.

_____

_____

_____

_____

66. On the scene of the same MVA, you have determined that you have one patient. As part of your initial assessment, your primary objectives will be

_____

_____

_____

_____

67. What is a frequently used mnemonic when assessing how alert a patient is?

_____

_____

_____

68. What type of injury patterns are likely in a head-on motor vehicle collision?

_____

_____

_____

69. What type of vehicle damage would be noteworthy when making a determination of the mechanism of injury?

_____

_____

_____

_____

70. Textbooks often describe three collisions in a motor vehicle crash. List them.

_____

_____

_____

_____

71. Falls from greater than _____ feet, or _____ times the height of the patient, are usually considered severe.

72. List examples of low-velocity weapons.

_____

_____

_____

_____

73. List examples of medium-velocity weapons.

_____

_____

_____

_____

74. Provide examples of a high-velocity weapon.

_____

_____

_____

_____

75. A normal adult pulse rate at rest is between
_____ and _____ beats per minute.

76. What would the pulse rate of a patient be if he
or she was described as tachycardic?

_____

_____

_____

_____

77. List possible reasons for an elevated pulse rate.

_____

_____

_____

_____

78. List possible reasons for a slow pulse rate.

_____

_____

_____

_____

79. In addition to the rate, what other assessment
should be made with respect to the pulse?

_____

_____

_____

_____

80. In patients under 1 year of age, the
_____ pulse should be assessed.

81. Why shouldn't you use your thumb when
assessing a patient's pulse?

_____

_____

_____

_____

82. Provide a possible cause and an appropriate
intervention for each of the following
respiratory sounds: snoring, wheezing,
gurgling.

_____

_____

_____

_____

83. The memory aid HEENT can be used during patient assessment. What do the letters mean?

_____

_____

_____

_____

84. What is crepitation?

_____

_____

_____

_____

85. What would be the normal pulse rate for a child between ages one and three years?

_____

_____

_____

_____

86. How should a correction be made on a patient-care report?

_____

_____

_____

_____

87. When would an NPA be contraindicated?

_____

_____

_____

_____

88. What is a medication side effect?

_____

_____

_____

_____

89. When giving a medication, we should consider the "four rights," starting with the right patient. What are the other three?

_____

_____

_____

_____

90. What medication route would you use to administer sublingual nitroglycerin tablets to your patient complaining of chest pain?

_____

_____

_____

_____

91. What do the letters *COPD* mean?

_____

_____

_____

_____

92. List some contraindications for the use of a medication inhaler.

_____

_____

_____

_____

93. What is the largest artery in the cardiovascular system?

_____

_____

_____

_____

94. After the use of the AED, your patient is awake. While on the stretcher, your patient becomes unresponsive again. An assessment reveals no breathing and no pulse. What is your next action?

_____

_____

_____

_____

95. You have delivered one shock to your patient who is in cardiac arrest. What is the next action you should take?

_____

_____

_____

_____

96. Your patient complains of shortness of breath and a feeling of heavy pressure in his chest. His respirations are 38, shallow. His pulse is 56 and irregular, and he reports a history of angina. Do you have enough information to assist the patient with his prescribed nitroglycerin?

_____

_____

_____

_____

97. What distinctive lung sounds would you expect to hear if your patient has pulmonary edema?

_____

_____

_____

_____

98. What type of medication is often taken by a patient who has a history of congestive heart failure (CHF)?

_____

_____

_____

_____

99. What types of medications are described as clot busters?

_____

_____

_____

_____

100. Which organ produces insulin?

_____

_____

_____

101. What does the term *hypoglycemia* mean?

_____

_____

_____

_____

102. Your patient's family member reports that the patient accidentally took too much insulin. Would you expect to find the blood sugar too low or too high?

_____

_____

_____

_____

103. What can cause low blood sugar in a diabetic patient?

_____

_____

_____

_____

104. What are common findings in a patient with low blood sugar?

_____

_____

_____

_____

105. What units of measure are typically used to measure blood sugar levels in the United States?

_____

_____

_____

_____

106. What is the most common cause of seizures in children?

_____

_____

_____

107. What type of information should you report on a seizure patient?

_____

_____

_____

108. What is the term to describe two or more seizures without regaining full consciousness?

_____

_____

_____

_____

109. What do the letters _CVA_ mean?

_____

_____

_____

_____

110. What are the two main causes of a stroke?

_____

_____

_____

111. What are the three items of assessment used in the Cincinnati Prehospital Stroke scale?

_____

_____

_____

_____

112. Describe how arm drift is assessed in a suspected stroke patient.

_____

_____

_____

_____

113. What is the term used to describe a severe, life-threatening allergic reaction?

_____

_____

_____

114. What signs and symptoms would you expect to find in order to distinguish between anaphylaxis and a mild allergic reaction?

_____

_____

_____

115. What is the medication used in autoinjectors to treat anaphylaxis?

_____

_____

_____

_____

116. What are the contraindications to consider before using a prescribed epinephrine autoinjector on a patient presenting signs of severe allergic reaction, including difficulty breathing?

_____

_____

_____

_____

117. What is the dose contained in an adult epinephrine autoinjector?

_____

_____

_____

118. What are the contraindications for the use of activated charcoal?

_____

_____

_____

_____

119. List the information that should be gathered for a patient suspected of poison inhalation.

_____

_____

_____

_____

120. What is the most commonly inhaled poison that is characterized by its lack of odor, color, and taste?

_____

_____

_____

_____

121. List some common signs and symptoms of carbon monoxide poisoning.

_____

_____

_____

_____

122. You are called to a patient suspected of taking an overdose of codeine. What symptoms might you expect to see in this patient?

_____

_____

_____

_____

123. What is the term for the severe reaction to alcohol withdrawal characterized by sweating, trembling, anxiety, and hallucinations?

_____

_____

_____

_____

124. List the four ways a poison can enter the body.

_____

_____

_____

_____

125. Do most poisons have an antidote?

_____

_____

_____

_____

126. Conduction is one way the body loses heat. What are the other possible methods?

_____

_____

_____

_____

127. A condition in which the body temperature drops below that required for normal bodily functions is known as

_____

_____

_____

128. What is normal body temperature?

_____

_____

_____

_____

129. What are the likely changes that may be observed in the condition of the skin of a person in the early stages of frostbite?

_____

_____

_____

_____

130. Describe heat exhaustion.

_____

_____

_____

_____

131. What causes decompression sickness?

_____

_____

_____

132. In the interest of personal safety, what rescue methods should be considered before going into the water and swimming to a patient?

_____

_____

_____

_____

133. List some medical problems that can cause a person to exhibit abnormal behavior.

_____

_____

_____

134. What does the term *afterbirth* describe?

_____

_____

_____

_____

135. What type of personal protection equipment should be part of an obstetrical kit?

_____

_____

_____

_____

136. What is meconium staining?

_____

_____

_____

_____

137. What are the signs and symptoms of preeclampsia?

_____

_____

_____

_____

138. How would you define a premature infant?

_____

_____

_____

_____

139. What happens during the third stage of labor?

_____

_____

_____

_____

140. In what position should a third-trimester pregnant patient be transported and why?

_____

_____

_____

_____

141. A patient has a deep laceration to the medial aspect of the right upper arm, which presents with profuse, spurting, and bright red bleeding. You have attempted to control the bleeding with direct pressure and elevation and the bleeding continues. List the next step to control bleeding including the technique, location, and evaluation of effectiveness.

_____

_____

_____

_____

142. Name three major types of shock.

_____

_____

_____

_____

143. What would be the typical skin condition of a patient in shock?

_____

_____

_____

_____

144. Define _compensated shock_.

_____

_____

_____

_____

145. What does the term _golden period_ refer to?

_____

_____

_____

_____

146. What type of shock would be a contraindication for the use of PASGs?

_____

_____

_____

_____

147. What is the maximum on-scene time for a call involving serious trauma?

_____

_____

_____

_____

148. A collection of blood under the skin at an injury site describes what?

_____

_____

_____

_____

149. What are the signs of a tension pneumothorax?

_____

_____

_____

_____

150. Your adult patient has moderate burns to the chest and the entire right arm. Using the rule of nine formula, what is the body surface area involved?

_____

_____

_____

_____

Answers

1. The minimum training level is EMT. The other levels include Emergency Medical Responder, Advanced EMT (AEMT), and Paramedic.
2. This is false. Your personal safety comes first. It is not possible for you to help a patient if you are injured first.
3. This describes transfer of care. You must never leave your patient until proper transfer has taken place.
4. Sticking up for a patient and making sure the patient's needs are met is called patient advocacy. Among other things, you must make sure the hospital personnel have all the information that you have learned about your patient.
5. The U.S. Department of Transportation created the EMT curriculum.
6. A quality-improvement committee is often formed to carry out consistent review of operations and personnel performance.
7. The medical director assumes responsibility for the oversight of patient care. This is a physician who also oversees training and the development of protocols.
8. A person authorized by the medical director to give medication or perform emergency care is the designate agent. The transfer of such authority is an extension of the medical director's license to practice medicine.
9. This policy or protocol is called standing orders. Additional orders can also be issued by telephone while the patient is in the care of the EMT.
10. These organisms are called pathogens. Blood-borne pathogens can be found in blood and other body fluids. Airborne pathogens are spread by tiny droplets sprayed during breathing, coughing, etc.
11. The processes and procedures designed to protect you from infection are known as body substance isolation precautions (BSI).

12. This equipment is called personal protective equipment (PPE). Such equipment would include masks, eye protection, gowns, etc.

13. The patient may have TB. EMS workers can become infected even without direct contact. It is impossible to determine why a patient has a productive cough. Assume the worst for safety reasons.

14. HIV stands for human immunodeficiency virus.

15. This act is called the *Ryan White CARE Act*. It was named in honor of Ryan White, an Indiana teenager who contracted AIDS through a tainted hemophilia treatment in 1984 and was expelled from school because of the disease.

16. PPD means purified protein derivative. The test can detect exposure to TB. There are currently no immunizations against TB.

17. *Eustress* is defined as stress that is healthy or gives one a feeling of fulfillment. This type can help people work under pressure. *Distress* can occur when a situation becomes overwhelming. Distressed EMTs will not be as effective.

18. In addition to denial, other emotions may include anger ("Why me?"), bargaining ("OK, but first let me . . ."), depression ("But I haven't had a chance to . . ."), and acceptance ("I am not afraid").

19. The three Rs are retreat, radio, and re-evaluate.

20. Expressed consent is given by adults who are of legal age and are mentally competent to make a rational decision. Implied consent assumes that a patient would give consent if he or she were conscious.

21. The patient must be legally able to consent (legal age or emancipated minor), mentally competent and oriented, and fully informed. The patient must sign a release form.

22. A common advance directive found in EMS is a do not resuscitate (DNR) order. Other advance directives can direct specific care and treatment.

23. Patient refusal of care and/or transport and ambulance collisions are the two most common reasons for legal action against EMTs.

24. The EMT had a duty to act. The EMT did not provide the standard of care. The EMT's action or inaction caused harm to the patient.

25. Leaving a patient after care has been initiated but before transfer to someone of equal or greater medical training is called abandonment.

26. The anatomical term for the front of the body is anterior.

27. The anatomical term for the rear of the body is posterior.

28. The anatomical term to describe a position closer to the torso is proximal.

29. The anatomical term to describe a position farther from the torso is distal.

30. Midline describes the imaginary line drawn down the center of the body.

31. A patient lying on his or her abdomen is prone. A patient sitting is in Fowler's position. A patient lying with the head slightly lower than the feet is in Trendelenburg position.

32. Mandible is the lower jawbone. (The fused bones of the upper jaw are called the maxillae.)

33. Xiphoid process is at the base of the sternum. Hand placement during CPR is important to avoid breaking this bone.

34. There are 33 vertebrae in the human spine.

35. The five divisions of the spine are the cervical (neck), with seven vertebrae; thoracic (thorax, ribs, upper back), with twelve; lumbar (lower back), with five; sacral (back wall of pelvis), with five; and coccyx (tailbone), with four.

36. Tarsals and metatarsals are found in the ankle and foot, respectively.

37. This bone is the patella, or kneecap.

38. Voluntary muscle, or skeletal muscle, is under conscious control of the brain. Examples would include any muscle used to do things like walk, reach, or pick something up. Involuntary muscle, or smooth muscle, responds automatically to orders from the brain; there is no conscious thought in their operation. Examples are found in the digestive and respiratory systems.

39. The epiglottis prevents food from entering the trachea.

40. Alveoli are small sacs within the lungs where gas exchange with the blood stream takes place.

41. Platelets are instrumental in the formation of blood clots.

42. White blood cells, also known as leukocytes, are involved in the destruction of germs and the production of antibodies.

43. Perfusion is the adequate supply of oxygen and nutrients to the organs and tissues of the body with the removal of waste products.

44. The autonomic nervous system controls involuntary muscle function. Other divisions include the central and peripheral nervous systems.

45. Epinephrine is also called adrenaline.

46. Look for equal chest expansion in inhalation. Listen for air exchange at the nose or mouth. Feel for air movement at the nose or mouth.

47. A patient with skin that appears to be blue or gray has cyanosis. This could be an indication of hypoxia.

48. Respiratory failure is the reduction of breathing to the point where oxygenation is not sufficient to support life.

49. Signs of inadequate breathing are uneven, minimal, or absent chest rise; breathing effort limited to abdominal motion; no air can be felt or heard; breath sound diminished or absent, and the patient makes noises such as wheezing, crowing, stridor, snoring, and gurgling; rate of breathing too rapid or too slow; breathing very shallow, deep, or labored; there is prolonged inspiration or expiration; the patient is unable to speak in full sentences, and there is nasal flaring.

50. The normal adult breathing rate is 12–20 breaths per minute.

51. The head-tilt/chin-lift maneuver provides the maximum opening of a patient's airway.

52. The jaw-thrust maneuver opens the airway of a patient with a head, neck, or spine injury.

53. Observe the patient's chest rise and fall with ventilations.

54. It should deliver nearly 100% oxygen.

55. An adult bag valve mask should deliver 800 mL of air.

56. Place the OPA to the side of the patient's face and make sure that it extends from the center of the mouth to the angle of the jaw, or from the corner of the patient's mouth to the tip of the earlobe.

57. Contraindications are specific signs, symptoms, or circumstances under which the administration of a drug would not be advisable.

58. Measure from the patient's nostril to the earlobe or angle of the jaw.

59. The unit should maintain 300 mm Hg when the suction tube is closed.

60. Never suction a patient for more than 15 seconds. If the patient requires additional suctioning, ventilate for two minutes and then suction for an additional 15 seconds. This sequence may be repeated. Consider obtaining medical direction in this situation.

61. The atmosphere contains 21% oxygen. The remainder is made up of approximately 78% nitrogen, 0.93% argon, 0.038% carbon dioxide, and trace amounts of other gases and water vapor.

62. A portable oxygen cylinder is pressurized to 2,000 to 2,200 psi when filled.

63. The cylinder should be changed before the pressure drops to 200 psi to ensure proper oxygen delivery to the patient.

64. An oxygen cylinder should be hydrostatically tested every five years. A cylinder with a star after the date should be tested every ten years. Hydrostatic testing involves checking for leaks after filling the tank with a nearly incompressible liquid, usually water.

65. Ensure safety for yourself and your crew, consider the mechanism of injury, account for all people who are potentially injured, consider additional resources (haz-mat, heavy rescue, additional ambulances, etc.), and determine best access for other responders.

66. Maintain manual spine stabilization; form a general impression of the patient; determine responsiveness; look for life-threatening conditions with emphasis on airway, breathing, and circulation; and make a transport decision.

67. Use AVPU to assess how alert a patient is. The acronym means alert, responds to verbal, responds to pain, unresponsive.

68. Two types are likely. If the patient went up and over the steering wheel, head, neck, chest, and abdomen injuries should be suspected. If the patient followed a down-and-under pathway, one may find injuries to the knees, legs, and hips.

69. Noteworthy vehicle damage would be evidence of rollover; spidered windshield; bent steering wheel; damage to dashboard, seats, or floor; damage intrusion into passenger compartment; and broken axle or other major component.

70. The three collisions in a motor vehicle crash are when the vehicle strikes an object, when the body strikes the interior of the car, and when the internal organs strike the interior surface of the body.

71. Falls from greater than 15 feet or three times the height of the patient are usually considered severe.

72. Low-velocity weapons are those propelled by hand such as knives, clubs, etc.

73. Medium-velocity weapons include handguns, some shotguns, etc.

74. A high-powered weapon such as an AK47 assault rifle or a 30/30 hunting rifle are examples of high-velocity weapons. These weapons attain muzzle velocities greater than 1,500 feet/second.

75. A normal adult pulse rate is between 60–100 beats per minute.

76. A pulse rate of a tachycardic patient would be greater than 100 beats per minute.

77. Reasons for an elevated heart rate include exertion, fright, fever, blood loss, shock, drugs, and cardiac-related conditions.

78. Reasons for a slow heart rate include head injury, drugs, some poisons, and cardiac-related conditions.

79. Rhythm and quality are other assessments that should be made in respect to the pulse. For example, in addition to the number of beats per minute, an EMT should report the regularity and the feel of the force. "The pulse is 84 regular and full."

80. The brachial pulse, which is found in the upper arm, should be assessed.

81. Your thumb has its own pulse and may cause you to measure your own pulse instead of the patient's.

82. Snoring might be caused by a blocked airway. To treat, open the airway and clear as necessary. Wheezing might be caused by medical problems such as asthma. To treat, assist with prescribed meds and administer meds as allowed by local protocols. Gurgling might be caused by fluids in the airway. To treat, suction airway, provide oxygen, and transport promptly.

83. HEENT stands for head, ears, eyes, nose, and throat.

84. Crepitation describes the sound of grating bones rubbing together, often indicating a fracture.

85. The normal pulse rate for a child between ages one and three years is 80–130 beats per minute at rest.

86. A single line may be drawn through the error, the correct information written beside it, and then initialed. The erroneous information should not be obliterated.

87. An NPA should be contraindicated anytime there is a suspicion of facial or skull fractures.

88. A side effect is the action of a drug other than the desired action.

89. The three other rights are right medication, right dose, right route.

90. Sublingual means under the tongue. In this case, you would place the tablets under the tongue and allow them to dissolve.

91. COPD stands for chronic obstructive pulmonary disease. Emphysema, chronic bronchitis, black lung, and other undetermined respiratory illnesses fall into this category.

92. The patient is not alert and not able to use the device, the inhaler is not prescribed to the patient, use has been denied by medical control, or the patient has already taken maximum prescribed dose.

93. The aorta carries blood from the left ventricle to the systemic circulation.

94. Reanalyze using the AED and shock if indicated.

95. Perform two minutes of CPR. You are unlikely to find a pulse immediately after a shock even if the shock successfully converted the rhythm. CPR is required to maintain perfusion in the meantime.

96. You need a blood pressure before you can safely administer nitroglycerin. Hypotension is a contraindication for its use.

97. Crackling or bubbling lung sounds can often be heard as air passes through the fluid that has accumulated in the lungs. These sounds are called rales.

98. Diuretics, also known as water pills, are often prescribed to these patients. A common example of this type of medication is Lasix (furosemide).

99. Thrombolytics are used to dissolve blood clots that block the coronary arteries. To be used effectively, these medications must be used early in the process.

100. The pancreas produces insulin.

101. *Hypoglycemia* means low blood sugar.

102. Too much insulin would cause more sugar to be put into the cells, leaving too little in the blood. A low blood sugar reading would be expected.

103. Low blood sugar can be caused by the patient taking too much insulin, not eating, overexercising, or vomiting a meal.

104. Altered mental status and possible unconsciousness are typical in a patient with low blood sugar.

105. Use milligrams of glucose per deciliter of blood, or mg/dL. A deciliter = 100 mL.

106. High fever is the most common cause of seizures in children. These are called febrile seizures.

107. You should note what the patient was doing before the seizure, description of the seizure activity, loss of bowel or bladder control, how long the seizure lasted, and how the patient's mental status was after the seizure.

108. Status epilepticus is the term. This is a high-priority call. Rapid, safe transport and support of airway are the priorities.

109. *CVA* means cerebral vascular accident, also called a stroke.

110. A stroke, or CVA, can be caused by a blockage of an artery that supplies blood to part of the brain. This is also known as an ischemic stroke. Another cause would be bleeding in the brain, known as hemorrhagic stroke.

111. Three items of assessment are facial droop, arm drift, and speech difficulties.

112. Ask the patient to close his or her eyes and extend his or her arms out in front for ten seconds. A normal response would be for the patient to move both arms at the same time. An abnormal response would be if the patient could not move an arm or one arm drifts down.

113. Anaphylaxis, or anaphylactic shock, describes a severe, life-threatening allergic reaction.

114. Respiratory distress and signs or symptoms of shock are indicators of a severe allergic reaction (anaphylaxis).

115. Epinephrine is the medication used in autoinjections.

116. There are very few contraindications to epinephrine in cases of life-threatening anaphylaxis. These include the patient being allergic to epinephrine, the drug being out of date and, according to local protocol, either the medication is not prescribed for the patient or medical control denies permission to administer it..

117. The dose is 0.3 mg.

118. Contraindications include altered mental status, ingestion of acids or alkalis, and the inability to swallow.

119. Find out the name of the substance involved, when the exposure occurred, how long the exposure lasted, interventions taken, and effects on the patient.

120. The most commonly inhaled poison that is characterized by its lack of color, odor, and taste is carbon monoxide.

121. Common signs and symptoms of carbon monoxide poisoning are headache, dizziness, breathing difficulty, nausea, cyanosis, altered mental status, unconsciousness, and death. Note: Despite commonly accepted ideas, cherry red skin is not a common finding.

122. Symptoms of codeine overdose include reduced pulse rate, reduced breathing rate and depth, constricted pupils, lethargy, low blood pressure, and sweating. In extreme cases, coma or respiratory or cardiac arrest can follow.

123. This describes delirium tremens (DTs).

124. The four ways poison can enter the body are ingestion, inhalation, injection, and absorption.

125. Although many people think there is an antidote for many poisons, there are, in fact, very few true antidotes.

126. Convection, radiation, evaporation, and respiration are ways the body loses heat.

127. This condition is called hypothermia. The body can be significantly affected with a drop of one or two degrees.

128. Normal body temperature in humans is 98.6° Fahrenheit (37° Celsius).

129. A person in the early stages of frostbite often presents white, waxy skin; blotchy skin; loss of skin texture; and discoloration, including grays, yellows, and blues.

130. Heat exhaustion is a form of shock. An active, healthy individual can lose as much as a liter of fluid per hour through perspiration.

131. A diver ascending quickly from a dive is the most common cause of decompression sickness. Any sudden decrease in pressure can be a cause.

132. First try to reach with your arm; then consider throwing a floating object or rope and towing the victim out. Rowing to the victim would be next. Remember: reach, throw, tow, row. Swim only if you are a good swimmer and trained to do so.

133. Some medical problems include low blood sugar, lack of oxygen, stroke, head trauma, drugs, and exposure to cold or heat.

134. The afterbirth describes the placenta, the membranes that are normally expelled after the birth of the baby.

135. Personal protection should include gloves, face mask, eye shield, and gown.

136. Meconium staining refers to the discoloration of the amniotic fluid. It is an indication of fetal distress during labor.

137. Symptoms of preeclampsia include high blood pressure, fluid retention, and headache.

138. A premature infant is generally described as weighing less than 5.5 pounds or born within 37 weeks of pregnancy.

139. The placenta is delivered during the third stage of labor.

140. The patient should be transported on the left side to avoid supine hypotensive syndrome.

141. Place a tourniquet proximal to the injury and tighten the tourniquet until the bleeding stops.

142. Three major types of shock are hypovolemic shock, cardiogenic shock, and neurogenic shock.

143. Cool, pale, and sweaty skin is a typical presentation of a patient in shock.

144. *Compensated shock* is when the body senses a decrease in perfusion and compensates by raising the heart rate and concentrating blood flow to critical organs.

145. The golden period describes the ideal maximum time from the time of injury to the time corrective surgery takes place.

146. Cardiogenic shock would be a contraindication for the use of PASGs.

147. Ten minutes is the maximum on-scene time for a call involving serious trauma. This is also referred to as the platinum ten minutes.

148. A collection of blood under the skin is called hematoma. As much as a liter of blood can be lost in a hematoma.

149. Signs of a tension pneumothorax include difficulty breathing, signs of shock, distended neck veins, tracheal deviation, and diminished breath sounds on the affected side.

150. The body surface area is 18%, per the rule of nines: chest (9%) + 1 arm (9%) = 18%.

7

► EMT PRACTICE EXAM 5

CHAPTER SUMMARY
This is the fifth of ten practice exams in this book based on the National Registry's EMT cognitive exam. See Chapter 1 for a complete description of this exam.

Use this test to continue your study and practice. Notice how knowing what to expect on the exam makes you feel better prepared!

As before, the answer sheet you should use appears next. Following the exam is an answer key, with all the answers explained. These explanations will help you see where you need to concentrate further study. When you've finished the exam and scored it, note your weaknesses so that you'll know which parts of your textbook to concentrate on before you take the next exam.

1.	ⓐ	ⓑ	ⓒ	ⓓ	41.	ⓐ	ⓑ	ⓒ	ⓓ	81.	ⓐ	ⓑ	ⓒ	ⓓ
2.	ⓐ	ⓑ	ⓒ	ⓓ	42.	ⓐ	ⓑ	ⓒ	ⓓ	82.	ⓐ	ⓑ	ⓒ	ⓓ
3.	ⓐ	ⓑ	ⓒ	ⓓ	43.	ⓐ	ⓑ	ⓒ	ⓓ	83.	ⓐ	ⓑ	ⓒ	ⓓ
4.	ⓐ	ⓑ	ⓒ	ⓓ	44.	ⓐ	ⓑ	ⓒ	ⓓ	84.	ⓐ	ⓑ	ⓒ	ⓓ
5.	ⓐ	ⓑ	ⓒ	ⓓ	45.	ⓐ	ⓑ	ⓒ	ⓓ	85.	ⓐ	ⓑ	ⓒ	ⓓ
6.	ⓐ	ⓑ	ⓒ	ⓓ	46.	ⓐ	ⓑ	ⓒ	ⓓ	86.	ⓐ	ⓑ	ⓒ	ⓓ
7.	ⓐ	ⓑ	ⓒ	ⓓ	47.	ⓐ	ⓑ	ⓒ	ⓓ	87.	ⓐ	ⓑ	ⓒ	ⓓ
8.	ⓐ	ⓑ	ⓒ	ⓓ	48.	ⓐ	ⓑ	ⓒ	ⓓ	88.	ⓐ	ⓑ	ⓒ	ⓓ
9.	ⓐ	ⓑ	ⓒ	ⓓ	49.	ⓐ	ⓑ	ⓒ	ⓓ	89.	ⓐ	ⓑ	ⓒ	ⓓ
10.	ⓐ	ⓑ	ⓒ	ⓓ	50.	ⓐ	ⓑ	ⓒ	ⓓ	90.	ⓐ	ⓑ	ⓒ	ⓓ
11.	ⓐ	ⓑ	ⓒ	ⓓ	51.	ⓐ	ⓑ	ⓒ	ⓓ	91.	ⓐ	ⓑ	ⓒ	ⓓ
12.	ⓐ	ⓑ	ⓒ	ⓓ	52.	ⓐ	ⓑ	ⓒ	ⓓ	92.	ⓐ	ⓑ	ⓒ	ⓓ
13.	ⓐ	ⓑ	ⓒ	ⓓ	53.	ⓐ	ⓑ	ⓒ	ⓓ	93.	ⓐ	ⓑ	ⓒ	ⓓ
14.	ⓐ	ⓑ	ⓒ	ⓓ	54.	ⓐ	ⓑ	ⓒ	ⓓ	94.	ⓐ	ⓑ	ⓒ	ⓓ
15.	ⓐ	ⓑ	ⓒ	ⓓ	55.	ⓐ	ⓑ	ⓒ	ⓓ	95.	ⓐ	ⓑ	ⓒ	ⓓ
16.	ⓐ	ⓑ	ⓒ	ⓓ	56.	ⓐ	ⓑ	ⓒ	ⓓ	96.	ⓐ	ⓑ	ⓒ	ⓓ
17.	ⓐ	ⓑ	ⓒ	ⓓ	57.	ⓐ	ⓑ	ⓒ	ⓓ	97.	ⓐ	ⓑ	ⓒ	ⓓ
18.	ⓐ	ⓑ	ⓒ	ⓓ	58.	ⓐ	ⓑ	ⓒ	ⓓ	98.	ⓐ	ⓑ	ⓒ	ⓓ
19.	ⓐ	ⓑ	ⓒ	ⓓ	59.	ⓐ	ⓑ	ⓒ	ⓓ	99.	ⓐ	ⓑ	ⓒ	ⓓ
20.	ⓐ	ⓑ	ⓒ	ⓓ	60.	ⓐ	ⓑ	ⓒ	ⓓ	100.	ⓐ	ⓑ	ⓒ	ⓓ
21.	ⓐ	ⓑ	ⓒ	ⓓ	61.	ⓐ	ⓑ	ⓒ	ⓓ	101.	ⓐ	ⓑ	ⓒ	ⓓ
22.	ⓐ	ⓑ	ⓒ	ⓓ	62.	ⓐ	ⓑ	ⓒ	ⓓ	102.	ⓐ	ⓑ	ⓒ	ⓓ
23.	ⓐ	ⓑ	ⓒ	ⓓ	63.	ⓐ	ⓑ	ⓒ	ⓓ	103.	ⓐ	ⓑ	ⓒ	ⓓ
24.	ⓐ	ⓑ	ⓒ	ⓓ	64.	ⓐ	ⓑ	ⓒ	ⓓ	104.	ⓐ	ⓑ	ⓒ	ⓓ
25.	ⓐ	ⓑ	ⓒ	ⓓ	65.	ⓐ	ⓑ	ⓒ	ⓓ	105.	ⓐ	ⓑ	ⓒ	ⓓ
26.	ⓐ	ⓑ	ⓒ	ⓓ	66.	ⓐ	ⓑ	ⓒ	ⓓ	106.	ⓐ	ⓑ	ⓒ	ⓓ
27.	ⓐ	ⓑ	ⓒ	ⓓ	67.	ⓐ	ⓑ	ⓒ	ⓓ	107.	ⓐ	ⓑ	ⓒ	ⓓ
28.	ⓐ	ⓑ	ⓒ	ⓓ	68.	ⓐ	ⓑ	ⓒ	ⓓ	108.	ⓐ	ⓑ	ⓒ	ⓓ
29.	ⓐ	ⓑ	ⓒ	ⓓ	69.	ⓐ	ⓑ	ⓒ	ⓓ	109.	ⓐ	ⓑ	ⓒ	ⓓ
30.	ⓐ	ⓑ	ⓒ	ⓓ	70.	ⓐ	ⓑ	ⓒ	ⓓ	110.	ⓐ	ⓑ	ⓒ	ⓓ
31.	ⓐ	ⓑ	ⓒ	ⓓ	71.	ⓐ	ⓑ	ⓒ	ⓓ	111.	ⓐ	ⓑ	ⓒ	ⓓ
32.	ⓐ	ⓑ	ⓒ	ⓓ	72.	ⓐ	ⓑ	ⓒ	ⓓ	112.	ⓐ	ⓑ	ⓒ	ⓓ
33.	ⓐ	ⓑ	ⓒ	ⓓ	73.	ⓐ	ⓑ	ⓒ	ⓓ	113.	ⓐ	ⓑ	ⓒ	ⓓ
34.	ⓐ	ⓑ	ⓒ	ⓓ	74.	ⓐ	ⓑ	ⓒ	ⓓ	114.	ⓐ	ⓑ	ⓒ	ⓓ
35.	ⓐ	ⓑ	ⓒ	ⓓ	75.	ⓐ	ⓑ	ⓒ	ⓓ	115.	ⓐ	ⓑ	ⓒ	ⓓ
36.	ⓐ	ⓑ	ⓒ	ⓓ	76.	ⓐ	ⓑ	ⓒ	ⓓ	116.	ⓐ	ⓑ	ⓒ	ⓓ
37.	ⓐ	ⓑ	ⓒ	ⓓ	77.	ⓐ	ⓑ	ⓒ	ⓓ	117.	ⓐ	ⓑ	ⓒ	ⓓ
38.	ⓐ	ⓑ	ⓒ	ⓓ	78.	ⓐ	ⓑ	ⓒ	ⓓ	118.	ⓐ	ⓑ	ⓒ	ⓓ
39.	ⓐ	ⓑ	ⓒ	ⓓ	79.	ⓐ	ⓑ	ⓒ	ⓓ	119.	ⓐ	ⓑ	ⓒ	ⓓ
40.	ⓐ	ⓑ	ⓒ	ⓓ	80.	ⓐ	ⓑ	ⓒ	ⓓ	120.	ⓐ	ⓑ	ⓒ	ⓓ

EMT Practice Exam 5

1. After the head emerges when delivering a baby, you should
   a. guide the head downward as the upper shoulder appears.
   b. suction the nostrils.
   c. suction the mouth.
   d. feel at the neck to see if the umbilical cord is wrapped around it.

2. You have delivered a neonatal patient and during your APGAR assessment you note the patient has a score of five, with cyanosis in the extremities with a weak respiratory effort, slow respirations, and a brachial pulse of 80 bpm. After additional suctioning you provide assisted ventilations with a bag-valve mask. After 30 seconds you reassess the patient and find a brachial pulse of 40 and weak. Your resuscitation efforts should now include which of the following?
   a. Continue bag-valve mask ventilations, insert a BAID, and call for ALS
   b. Continue bag-valve mask ventilations, begin chest compressions, and request ALS
   c. Continue bag-valve mask ventilations for another 30 seconds and reassess for improvement in the pulse rate, request ALS
   d. Begin chest compressions, apply the AED, and prepare to defibrillate

3. You respond to a patient who has amputated two digits. What should you do with the amputated digits?
   a. Place the digits on ice.
   b. Place the digits in a biohazard bag and keep them cool with cold packs.
   c. Place the digits in sterile saline.
   d. Place the digits in a biohazard bag and dispose of them in the proper receptacle.

4. A burn that is characterized by pain, blisters, and mottled skin is a
   a. partial thickness burn.
   b. superficial burn.
   c. full thickness burn.
   d. subcutaneous burn.

5. The upper chambers of the heart are the
   a. ventricles.
   b. myocardium.
   c. septum.
   d. atria.

6. The left side of the heart receives blood from the
   a. lungs.
   b. pulmonary veins.
   c. arteries.
   d. aorta.

7. The body's three-stage response to stress is referred to as the
   a. fight-or-flight response.
   b. general adaptation syndrome.
   c. critical incident stress management.
   d. physiological response.

8. The most effective way to control disease transmission is by using
   a. universal precautions.
   b. body substance isolation.
   c. proper hand-washing.
   d. indirect contact.

9. If you suspect that your patient has tuberculosis, you should
   a. wear a standard surgical mask when treating the patient.
   b. place a HEPA respirator on the patient.
   c. wear a HEPA respirator when treating the patient.
   d. transport the patient rapidly, with the ambulance's exhaust fan on high.

10. The exchange of oxygen and carbon dioxide (respiration) occurs between the
  a. Bronchioles and alveoli
  b. Alveoli and pulmonary capillaries
  c. Pulmonary capillaries and bronchioles
  d. Pulmonary venules and alveoli

11. What is a normal systolic blood pressure for a 2-year-old?
  a. 80–100
  b. 70–95
  c. 50–70
  d. 90–110

12. Cardiopulmonary arrest in children is most commonly caused by
  a. underlying cardiac disease.
  b. traumatic injuries.
  c. child abuse.
  d. respiratory failure.

13. The chain of survival involves which of the following links, in order?
  a. Early access, early defibrillation, early CPR, and early ALS
  b. Early access, early CPR, early ALS, early defibrillation
  c. Early access, early ALS, early CPR, early defibrillation
  d. Early access, early CPR, early defibrillation, early ALS

14. The manner in which you must act or behave is called a
  a. standard of care.
  b. duty to act.
  c. standing protocol.
  d. standard operating procedure.

15. An adult burn patient with circumferential burns to his right arm, burns to the entire anterior aspect of his right leg, and burns to his genitals will have burns to a total body surface area of
  a. 14.5%.
  b. 19%.
  c. 23.5%.
  d. 28%.

16. The sinoatrial node is located within the
  a. purkinje fibers.
  b. right atrium.
  c. left atrium.
  d. right ventricle.

17. Your patient has a pulse rate of 90, a blood pressure of 132/80, and a stroke volume of 70. What is this patient's cardiac output?
  a. 6,300
  b. 630
  c. 7,200
  d. 5,600

18. Your patient complains of headache, stiff neck, fever, and has an altered mental status. You should suspect
  a. stroke.
  b. traumatic brain injury.
  c. viral syndrome.
  d. meningitis.

19. The strength or ability of a pathogen to produce a disease is
  a. transmission.
  b. virulence.
  c. effectivity.
  d. infectivity.

20. Which of the following is a definitive sign of death?
  a. no deep tendon or corneal reflexes
  b. no systolic blood pressure
  c. dependent lividity
  d. lowered or decreased core temperature

21. If you extend your arm parallel to the ground, this movement is called
  a. pronation.
  b. adduction.
  c. abduction.
  d. flexion.

22. The lower airway begins with the
  a. trachea.
  b. bronchioles.
  c. larynx.
  d. epiglottis.

23. In an unconscious patient, the most common airway obstruction is caused by
  a. foreign objects.
  b. the patient's own tongue.
  c. dentures.
  d. oral secretions.

24. A contraindication for inserting an oropharyngeal airway is that a patient
  a. is unconscious.
  b. is being ventilated with a BVM.
  c. requires airway suctioning.
  d. has an intact gag reflex.

25. Your patient is an apneic child. How should you ventilate this patient?
  a. one breath per five to six seconds
  b. one breath per three to five seconds
  c. one breath per five to eight seconds
  d. none of the above

26. The sudden blood loss of _____ in a 1- to 8-year-old can be life threatening.
  a. 1,000 cc
  b. 200 cc
  c. 1,200 cc
  d. 500 cc

27. The head accounts for what percentage of body surface area in a pediatric patient?
  a. 9%
  b. 4.5%
  c. 14%
  d. 18%

28. Your patient is a conscious, injured male, who is in control of his own actions and refusing care. You can treat this patient legally under
  a. implied consent.
  b. verbal consent.
  c. expressed consent.
  d. no circumstances.

29. You have used an EpiPen on a patient and have NOT obtained consent prior to treatment. You could be charged with
  a. fraud.
  b. battery.
  c. forcible restraint.
  d. negligence.

30. Which of the following is considered a high priority severe burn?
  a. partial thickness burns affecting 15%–30% of total body surface area
  b. full thickness burns affecting 3% of body surface area, excluding hands, face, genitals, and upper airway
  c. circumferential burns to the arm
  d. superficial burns affecting 40% of total body surface area

31. The valve that separates the right atrium from the right ventricle is the
  a. bicuspid valve.
  b. tricuspid valve.
  c. aortic valve.
  d. pulmonic valve.

32. What are the only veins in the body that carry oxygenated blood?
   a. vena cava
   b. pulmonary veins
   c. venules
   d. peripheral veins

33. Why is early CPR included in the chain of survival for cardiac arrest?
   a. CPR provides oxygen and nutrients to the heart
   b. CPR ascertains responsiveness
   c. CPR focuses on ventilations and improves oxygenation of the lungs
   d. CPR jumpstarts the electrical system of the heart

34. Your patient has fractured her lower jawbone. This bone is known as the
   a. mandible.
   b. maxillae.
   c. occiput.
   d. zygoma.

35. A normal heart rate for an adolescent patient is
   a. 60–100.
   b. 90–150.
   c. 70–120.
   d. 80–110.

36. You are treating a 58-year-old female patient for cardiac related chest pain. The patient is conscious and alert and has the following vital signs; P – 88, R – 20, BP – 132/84, skin is warm and dry, pupils are equal and reactive, and she rates her pain an 8 out of 10. Your treatment will include which of the following?
   a. Request ALS, recovery position, oxygen, aspirin, and assisting the pt. with nitroglycerin
   b. Request ALS, position of comfort, aspirin, and contact medical control for nitroglycerin
   c. Request ALS, position of comfort, oxygen, and contact medical control for aspirin and nitroglycerin
   d. Semi-Fowler's position, oxygen, transport

37. The spleen is located
   a. in the upper right quadrant.
   b. in the upper left quadrant.
   c. retroperitoneal.
   d. in the lower left quadrant.

38. You are treating a female patient who is nine months pregnant and contractions are two minutes apart and strong. She also states that her water has broken and she has felt the baby drop. You inspect for crowning and find one leg protruding from the birth canal. How do you proceed with this birth?
   a. Prepare a sterile area and continue with the birth, being careful not to pull on the presenting part
   b. Place the patient in the Trendelenburg or knee-to-chest position, advise her not to push, and place your hand into the birth canal to relieve pressure on the limb
   c. Place the patient in the Trendelenburg or knee-to-chest position, cross her legs, advise her not to push, and transport her to the hospital
   d. Cover the limb with a sterile towel, place the patient in the Trendelenburg or knee-to-chest position, encourage the patient not to push, and transport to the hospital.

39. When suctioning a pediatric patient, you should suction
   a. until the foreign body is removed.
   b. until the return of spontaneous respirations.
   c. using only a French catheter.
   d. for only ten seconds at a time.

40. A nasal cannula will deliver approximately what amount of oxygen to a patient?
   a. 5%–30%
   b. 24%–44%
   c. 10%–15%
   d. nearly 100%

41. What stage of labor begins with full dilation of the cervix?
   a. pre-labor
   b. first stage
   c. second stage
   d. third stage

42. If a newborn isn't breathing immediately after birth or suctioning of the mouth and nose,
   a. begin chest compressions.
   b. use a neonatal BVM and administer breaths at a rate of 40–60 per minute.
   c. give tactile stimulation.
   d. invert the newborn and slap his or her buttocks.

43. Good Samaritan laws protect EMT-Bs from a lawsuit
   a. only if proper care is provided.
   b. as long as willful negligence is not proven.
   c. as long as the EMT-B does not act outside his or her scope of practice.
   d. None of the above.

44. The action of nitroglycerin in the treatment of cardiac chest pain is
   a. to dilate the coronary blood vessels.
   b. to constrict coronary blood vessels.
   c. to decrease blood pressure.
   d. to reduce pain.

45. What would be the appropriate treatment of a partial thickness burn to the back with an 18% body surface area?
   a. cover the burned area with a dry, sterile dressing

   b. cover the area with a moistened, sterile dressing
   c. apply antibiotic ointment and cover with a dry, sterile dressing
   d. use a needle to decompress the fluid-filled blisters and apply a moistened, sterile dressing

46. Where do the coronary arteries originate?
   a. Apex of the heart
   b. Aortic arch
   c. Terminus of the carotid arteries
   d. Top of the left ventricle

47. What blood vessel transports blood from the left ventricle in order to begin systemic circulation?
   a. left pulmonary artery
   b. aorta
   c. right pulmonary artery
   d. superior vena cava

48. After the contraction of the right ventricle, blood enters the
   a. aorta.
   b. left atrium.
   c. pulmonary artery.
   d. pulmonary vein.

49. A patient who is found lying facedown is in what position?
   a. Fowler's
   b. semi-Fowler's
   c. prone
   d. supine

50. The gallbladder is located in the
   a. lower right quadrant.
   b. upper right quadrant.
   c. lower left quadrant.
   d. upper left quadrant.

51. The external visible part of the ear is the
a. earlobe.
b. pinna.
c. external auditory meatus.
d. mastoid process.

52. The spinal column is divided into how many sections?
a. four
b. three
c. five
d. six

53. You are treating a patient in respiratory arrest and have applied an automatic transport ventilator (ATV). As you continue care for the patient you note that the patient is becoming more cyanotic and chest rise and fall have become inadequate. What is your next course of action?
a. Check the ATV for the proper settings
b. Check the oxygen level of the ATV
c. Begin manual bag-valve mask ventilations
d. Reassess the airway

54. Painful bleeding in late pregnancy that is caused by the placenta prematurely separating from the uterine wall is called
a. placenta previa.
b. eclampsia.
c. abruptio placenta.
d. spontaneous abortion.

55. Which of the following is an accurate indicator of oxygenation and ventilation in a pediatric patient?
a. work of breathing
b. respiratory rate
c. breath sounds
d. pulse oximeter reading

56. What is the most common cause of wheezing in pediatric patients?
a. pneumonia
b. pulmonary contusion
c. upper-airway obstruction
d. asthma

57. When you and your partner arrive to a medical call that is only five minutes from the hospital, the patient is walking toward the ambulance. What should be your first course of action?
a. initial assessment
b. focused history and physical exam
c. detailed physical exam
d. scene size-up

58. The build-up of fatty deposits, which can damage the walls of the arteries, is called?
a. Arterial aneurysm
b. Thromboembolism
c. Atherosclerosis
d. Hyperlipidemia

59. A hazardous Class 7 indicates
a. flammable materials.
b. toxic materials.
c. corrosive materials.
d. radioactive materials.

60. Full thickness burns are characterized by
a. blisters.
b. redness and pain.
c. a dry, leathery appearance.
d. mottled skin.

61. At an MCI, a pediatric patient who is breathing independently at a rate of 12 breaths per minute should be tagged with what color using the Jump-Start system?
a. green
b. yellow
c. red
d. black

62. What is the best way to immobilize a hip fracture?
a. Apply a traction splint.
b. Place the patient in a position of comfort.
c. Use a long spine board with padding placed under the knees.
d. Apply a rigid splint to the lower extremity of the side that is affected.

63. After safety, what is the first priority when rendering treatment to a burn patient?
a. maintaining a sterile field
b. stopping the burning process
c. pain management
d. transport decision

64. What is the proper order for securing a patient to a long spine board?
a. head, torso, extremities
b. head, extremities, torso
c. torso, head, extremities
d. torso, extremities, head

65. At what point should you assess circulation, sensation, and movement when using a short spine board?
a. before the device is applied
b. after the device is completely secured
c. before padding the voids
d. both **a** and **b**

66. The blood vessels that supply blood to the heart muscle are the
a. coronary arteries.
b. coronary capillaries.
c. pulmonary veins.
d. pulmonary arteries.

67. What arteries supply the head and brain with blood?
a. peripheral
b. carotid
c. coronary
d. brachial

68. What allows for the exchange of waste and nutrients at the cellular level?
a. venules
b. mitochondria
c. capillaries
d. platelets

69. What is a condition of insufficient oxygen that can cause chest pain or discomfort?
a. hypercarbia
b. hypocarbia
c. hypoxia
d. ischemia

70. Disorganized quivering of the ventricles is called
a. atrial fibrillation.
b. ventricular fibrillation.
c. asystole.
d. atrial flutter.

71. Treatment of a patient in cardiogenic shock should include
a. defibrillation.
b. cardioversion.
c. preservation of body heat.
d. compressions.

72. The collection of fluid in a body part that is closest to the ground is called
a. pulmonary edema.
b. dependent edema.
c. dependent lividity.
d. congestive edema.

73. The upper section of the sternum is called the
a. angle of Louis.
b. manubrium.
c. xiphoid process.
d. thoracic cage.

74. The depression in which the femoral head fits into is called the
   a. iliac crest.
   b. acetabulum.
   c. ischium.
   d. greater trochanter.

75. The small, lower extremity bone that lies on the lateral side of the leg is the
   a. fibula.
   b. tibia.
   c. patella.
   d. lateral malleolus.

76. The Sellick's maneuver may be helpful when performed during which of the following interventions?
   a. When the patient begins to vomit
   b. When assisting the paramedic with orotracheal intubation
   c. When assisting ventilations in a conscious patient
   d. When used in conjunction with a BVM

77. When you arrive at the residence of a patient who has a possible airway obstruction, you notice that the patient is coughing forcefully. Bystanders state that he was chewing a piece of steak, laughed, and then began coughing. Your next action should be to
   a. start performing abdominal thrusts (i.e., the Heimlich maneuver).
   b. attempt to remove the object manually.
   c. tell the patient to extend his arms over his head.
   d. monitor the patient closely and encourage him to continue coughing.

78. Which type of breathing is characterized by irregular respirations followed by a period of apnea?
   a. Kussmaul's respirations
   b. agonal respirations
   c. retractions
   d. Cheyne-Stokes respirations

79. How do you measure the nasopharyngeal airway size needed prior to placement?
   a. Measure from the tip of the nose to the angle of the jaw.
   b. Measure from the tip of the nose to the earlobe.
   c. Measure from the corner of the mouth to the angle of the jaw.
   d. Measure from the tip of the nose to the top of the ear.

80. You are assessing a patient who is complaining of respiratory distress. You note the patient is sitting upright and is using her accessory muscles to facilitate breathing. The patient is cyanotic around the lips, you note she is producing frothy sputum, and she has swelling in her ankles. You listen to breath sounds and hear wheezing in all the lower lobes and crackles in the upper lobes. This patient is exhibiting signs and symptoms related to?
   a. Congestive heart failure
   b. Asthma
   c. Emphysema
   d. Anaphylaxis

81. Expiratory grunting in a pediatric patient is indicative of which of the following?
   a. An upper-airway obstruction
   b. Inflammation of the glottis
   c. Collapsing alveoli
   d. Partially blocked small airways

82. The third stage of labor is complete when
   a. the baby is born.
   b. contractions begin.
   c. contractions cease.
   d. the placenta delivers.

83. What term is used to describe the number of viable births?
   a. gravid
   b. multigravida
   c. para
   d. premipara

84. An umbilical cord that is wrapped around an infant's neck is called a
 a. prolapsed cord.
 b. granulomar umbilicus.
 c. umbilical hernia.
 d. nuchal cord.

85. When triaging at an MCI, the maximum number of seconds that should be spent assessing each patient is
 a. 30 seconds.
 b. 15 seconds.
 c. 10 seconds.
 d. 60 seconds.

86. Cardiac chest pain is caused by decreased oxygen supply to the myocardium. As this conditions progresses, the myocardium becomes irritated and may cause electrical impulses to originate in areas of the heart remote from the SA Node. One of these rhythms that originates in the ventricles and is rapid (< 180 bpm), organized, and does not allow adequate filling of the ventricles is called
 a. sinus tachycardia.
 b. ventricular fibrillation.
 c. premature ventricular contractions.
 d. ventricular tachycardia.

87. You are dispatched to a patient with a nosebleed. Upon your arrival you find a patient complaining of a nosebleed. You begin to gather the patient's history and find the patient has no medical history and no allergies. As you collect information on his current condition the patient also states having a ringing in his ears and a headache. Vital signs include a pulse of 88 strong and bounding, blood pressure is 172/102, respirations are 20, skin is warm and dry, and the pupils are equal and reactive. Your treatment of this patient should include
 a. pinching of the nostrils at the septum and patient sitting forward.

 b. placing sterile gauze into the nostrils and patient leaning forward.
 c. sterile gauze at the nostrils, patient sitting forward, oxygen, request ALS.
 d. sterile gauze at the nostrils, Semi-Fowler's position, transport.

88. You respond to a residence and find an elderly male in cardiac arrest. His caregiver states that she remembers seeing a DNR and is going to look for it. What should you do?
 a. Wait for the caregiver to return with the proper documentation before rendering treatment.
 b. Contact the patient's physician.
 c. Begin CPR.
 d. Advise the police and have them determine the next step.

89. The bottom quadrant of the diamond-shaped NFPA symbol contains information about any
 a. health hazards.
 b. special hazards.
 c. reactivity.
 d. fire hazards.

90. You are dispatched to a call for an unconscious patient. You arrive on scene and find a 6-year-old child unresponsive with gasping respirations. You immediately check for a pulse and find a weak carotid pulse at a rate of 52. Your treatment should include which of the following?
 a. Open the airway, high-flow oxygen via NRB, request ALS
 b. Open the airway, assist ventilations with a BVM, begin chest compressions, request ALS
 c. Open the airway, low-flow oxygen via NC, and request ALS
 d. Open the airway, assist ventilations with a BVM, and request ALS

91. What is the definitive care for decompression sickness?
a. High-flow oxygen
b. Epinephrine
c. Cath lab
d. Hyperbaric chamber

92. Who should direct the movement of a patient when a spinal injury is suspected?
a. the crew leader
b. the rescuer who is positioned at the head
c. the rescuer who is positioned at the feet
d. the first rescuer on scene

93. Which of the following is a sign of a superficial local cold injury?
a. swelling
b. loss of feeling and sensation in the injury area
c. blisters
d. white, waxy skin

94. What section of the vertebral column is most susceptible to injury?
a. cervical spine
b. lumbar spine
c. thoracic spine
d. coccyx

95. A condition where severe force or weight is placed upon the thorax, forcing blood from the right atrium into the circulation of the head and neck, is
a. a hemothorax.
b. pericardial tamponade.
c. traumatic asphyxia.
d. tension pneumothorax.

96. If a cold injury appears to be deep, you should NOT
a. splint the injury.
b. cover the injury.
c. remove jewelry.
d. rewarm the injury.

97. The common dosage for the administration of acetylsalicylic acid in a cardiac emergency is
a. 81 mg PO
b. 324 mg PO
c. 81 mg IO
d. 324 g PO

98. Nitroglycerine is supplied in which of the following forms?
a. sublingual tablets
b. transdermal patches
c. sublingual spray
d. all of the above

99. The bones that make up the toes are the
a. tarsals.
b. metatarsals.
c. phalanges.
d. carpals.

100. The fibrous tissues that connect bone to bone are
a. ligaments.
b. tendons.
c. joints.
d. skeletal muscles.

101. Which part of the nervous system regulates activities in which there is voluntary control, such as talking, walking, etc.?
a. voluntary nervous system
b. somatic nervous system
c. automatic nervous system
d. central nervous system

102. Which of the following is the largest part of the brain?
a. brain stem
b. cerebellum
c. cerebrum
d. cerebrospinal fluid

103. A patient suffering from heatstroke will typically have what symptoms?
- **a.** cool, diaphoretic, pale skin
- **b.** hot, dry, flushed skin
- **c.** normal-colored, warm, diaphoretic skin
- **d.** none of the above

104. Your patient has had a previous laryngectomy, is conscious, atraumatic, and has agonal respirations. He is lying supine on the floor. How would you ventilate this patient?
- **a.** Use an adult-sized mask directly over the stoma and ventilate with a BVM, using a hand to seal the patient's nose and mouth.
- **b.** Use head-tilt/chin-lift and a BVM.
- **c.** Insert an ET tube directly into the stoma and ventilate using a BVM.
- **d.** Use an infant- or child-sized mask, make a seal over the stoma, ventilate with a BVM, and use a hand to seal the patient's nose and mouth.

105. What is the normal tidal volume of the bag of an adult BVM device?
- **a.** 800–1,200 mL
- **b.** 500–700 mL
- **c.** 500–1,200 mL
- **d.** 1,200–1,600 mL

106. What method delivers the highest tidal volume to a patient?
- **a.** BVM-to-face
- **b.** mouth-to-mask
- **c.** blow by O_2
- **d.** nebulizer

107. Which of the following is a contraindication for an oxygen-powered ventilation device?
- **a.** CHF
- **b.** respiratory arrest
- **c.** COPD
- **d.** respiratory distress

108. What is the passive part of breathing?
- **a.** respiration
- **b.** inhalation
- **c.** exhalation
- **d.** ventilation

109. A pregnant female should be transported
- **a.** supine.
- **b.** left lateral recumbent.
- **c.** in a semi-Fowler's position.
- **d.** in Trendelenburg.

110. When suctioning an infant, do NOT suction for more than
- **a.** 5 seconds.
- **b.** 10 seconds.
- **c.** 15 seconds.
- **d.** 30 seconds.

111. To suction the nose of a newborn, it is recommended to use a
- **a.** French catheter.
- **b.** bulb syringe.
- **c.** rigid tip.
- **d.** oxygen-powered device.

112. A normal respiratory rate for a newborn at rest is
- **a.** 60–80.
- **b.** 40–70.
- **c.** 30–60.
- **d.** 20–30.

113. When parking at the scene of a motor vehicle crash, an ambulance should be parked
- **a.** in front of the collision.
- **b.** 100 feet away from the collision.
- **c.** behind the collision.
- **d.** downwind.

114. You and your partner arrive on the scene and find a 44-year-old male patient who presents unresponsive, apneic, and pulseless. Your care for this patient should include
  a. two minutes of CPR, application of an AED, defibrillate if indicated, and immediately resume CPR post defibrillation.
  b. two minutes of CPR, application of the AED, defibrillate if indicated, reassess the patient, and continue CPR or post-resuscitation care.
  c. apply the AED, defibrillate if indicated, reassess the patient and begin CPR if indicated.
  d. apply the AED, defibrillate if indicated, and immediately begin CPR post defibrillation.

115. What should be applied to an evisceration?
  a. moistened, sterile dressing
  b. dry, sterile dressing
  c. pressure dressing
  d. moistened bandage

116. If a patient sustains a brain injury in the temporal region, she may develop problems with
  a. memory.
  b. vision.
  c. sensory functions.
  d. emotions.

117. Why is an occlusive dressing applied to a sucking chest wound?
  a. to control bleeding
  b. to seal the wound, preventing air from going into the chest cavity
  c. to prevent infection
  d. none of the above

118. What are the principle signs of hypovolemic shock?
  a. normal blood pressure and rapid, weak pulse
  b. low blood pressure and bounding pulse
  c. low blood pressure and normal pulse
  d. low blood pressure and rapid, weak pulse

119. Your patient is complaining of dyspnea and you notice paradoxical movement upon inspiration and expiration. What does this indicate?
  a. pneumothorax
  b. tension pneumothorax
  c. flail chest
  d. umbilical hernia

120. Which of the following is a sign that a patient is NOT getting an adequate amount of oxygen?
  a. The patient is coughing.
  b. The patient is sitting forward.
  c. The patient has an increased respiratory rate.
  d. The patient states that he feels short of breath.

Answers

1. d. When delivering an infant, feel around the baby's neck after the head emerges to determine if the cord is wrapped around it. This situation, called a nuchal cord, is extremely dangerous for the baby and can cause strangulation or brain damage. The cord must be released from around the neck immediately.

2. b. During the resuscitation of a depressed newborn efforts are focused on suctioning, drying, stimulating, warming, and providing supplemental oxygen. Few neonates will require assisted ventilations and even fewer will require chest compressions or ALS. The neonate whose pulse rate drops below 60 bpm during resuscitative efforts requires chest compressions and ALS should be requested as advanced interventions may be required.

3. b. Amputated digits should be placed in a biohazard bag and cold packs should be placed outside of the bag to keep them cold. Never submerge an amputated part or place it directly on ice, as damage to the tissue can occur.

4. a. A burn that is characterized by pain, blisters, and mottled skin is a partial thickness burn.

5. d. The upper right and left chambers of the heart are the atria.

6. a. The left side of the heart receives oxygenated blood from the lungs through the pulmonary veins.

7. b. The body's three-stage response to stress is referred to as general adaptation syndrome.

8. c. The most effective way to control disease transmission is by proper hand-washing.

9. c. If you suspect that your patient has tuberculosis, you should wear a HEPA respirator when treating the patient.

10. b. Respiration takes place between the alveoli and pulmonary capillaries. The capillaries' size only allows one red blood cell through at a time and the thinness of the walls allows the carbon dioxide to leave the red blood cell and cross into the alveoli, as oxygen diffuses across the wall from the alveoli to the capillaries and attaches to red blood cells.

11. a. The normal systolic blood pressure for a 2-year-old child ranges from 80 to 100 mm Hg.

12. d. Cardiopulmonary arrest in children is most commonly caused by respiratory failure.

13. d. The correct order for the chain of survival begins with access, then CPR, then defibrillation, and finally early ALS.

14. a. The manner in which you must act or behave is called the standard of care.

15. b. This patient has burns to 19% of his body surface area. This was calculated by adding 9% for the total right arm, 9% for the anterior aspect of his right leg, and 1% for burns to his genitals.

16. b. The sinoatrial (SA) node is located within the right atrium.

17. a. The patient's cardiac output is 6,300. The equation for calculating cardiac output is stroke volume multiplied by heart rate. The blood pressure is not necessary for this calculation.

18. d. If a patient has a headache, altered mental status, and a fever, meningitis should be suspected.

19. b. Virulence is the strength or ability of a pathogen to produce a disease.

20. c. Dependent lividity is a definitive sign of death.

21. c. Abduction is motion away from the midline.

22. c. The lower airway begins with the larynx.

23. b. The most common airway obstruction in the unconscious patient is his or her own tongue.

24. d. A patient with an intact gag reflex is a contraindication for inserting an oropharyngeal airway. If your patient does have an intact gag reflex and you choose to use an airway adjunct, insert a nasopharyngeal airway.

25. b. An apneic child should be ventilated with one breath every three to five seconds.

26. d. The sudden blood loss of 500 cc in a 1- to 8-year-old child can be life threatening.

27. d. The head accounts for 18% of body surface area in a pediatric patient.

28. d. This patient may not be treated. If an adult patient is alert, oriented, and competent, he has the right to refuse care. You must have proper documentation and inform the patient of the benefits of care and the risks of refusal.

29. b. If treatment is rendered without a patient's consent, it is considered battery on the patient.

30. c. Circumferential burns to any extremity are considered a high priority and require transport to a burn center if available.

31. b. The tricuspid valve is the valve that is between the right atrium and the right ventricle.

32. b. The only veins in the body that carry oxygenated blood are the pulmonary veins. All other veins carry deoxygenated blood back to the heart.

33. a. Although chest compressions only provide approximately one-third the circulation of a perfusing rhythm, they do improve oxygenation and increase the stores of energy in the heart, which makes the heart more apt to convert into a perfusing rhythm once defibrillation is performed.

34. a. The mandible is the lower jawbone.

35. a. A normal heart rate for an adolescent patient is 60 to 100 beats per minute.

36. c. A patient believed to be suffering from cardiac chest pain requires ALS intervention and medications allowed by medical control. Always remember basic medications and oxygen while considering ALS interventions.

37. b. The spleen is located in the upper left quadrant.

38. d. You should cover the presenting part with a sterile towel, place the patient in a position that relieves pressure on the limb, and transport to the hospital. Limb presentations cannot be delivered in the field and will most likely require a Cesarean section. Do not place your hand into the birth canal, have the patient cross her legs, or attempt to deliver the baby.

39. d. Pediatric patients should only be suctioned for ten seconds at a time. Suctioning longer than ten seconds can cause hypoxia.

40. b. A nasal cannula will deliver approximately 24% to 44% of oxygen to a patient.

41. c. The second stage of labor begins with the full dilation of the cervix.

42. c. If a newborn isn't breathing immediately after birth or suctioning to the mouth and nose, give tactile stimulation by either drying the baby, rubbing the back, or flicking the feet.

43. d. Good Samaritan laws do not protect you from being sued; they only provide an affirmative defense *if* you are sued. They will also only protect you when you exercise due care and do not deviate from the standard of care.

44. a. Nitroglycerin's action is to dilate the coronary blood vessels, to increase oxygen supply to the myocardium. A side effect is a possible decrease in blood pressure and the increase in oxygenation may relieve pain, but nitroglycerin is not a pain reliever.

45. a. Burns greater than 15% body surface area should be covered with a dry, sterile dressing to reduce the amount of body heat that is lost.

46. b. The coronary arteries begin at the aortic arch. They are the first arteries to branch off of the aorta. The heart receives its blood supply from the coronary arteries, which branch into the left and right coronary arteries.

47. b. The aorta transports blood from the left ventricle out to the systemic circulation.

48. c. After the contraction of the right ventricle, blood enters the pulmonary artery to reach the lung.

49. c. A patient who is lying facedown is in the prone position.

50. b. The gallbladder is located in the upper right quadrant.

51. b. The external, visible part of the ear is the pinna.

52. c. The spinal column is divided into five sections: cervical, thoracic, lumbar, sacral, and coccyx.

53. d. Whenever there is deterioration in a patient's respiratory status the EMT must reassess all their interventions to ensure they are still adequate. This always begins with reassessing the patency of the airway. If the airway is clear, the EMT should immediately begin bag-valve mask ventilations and then check the ATV for any malfunctions that could be remedied. One disadvantage of the ATV is that it will not function if the oxygen level in the supply cylinder gets low.

54. c. Painful bleeding late in pregnancy that is caused by the placenta prematurely separating from the uterine wall is called abruptio placenta.

55. a. The best indicator for assessing the oxygenation and ventilation in a pediatric patient is his or her work of breathing.

56. d. The most common cause for wheezing in the pediatric patient is asthma.

57. d. Regardless of the transport time, always size up a scene upon arrival to ensure your safety and the safety of other personnel.

58. c. The build-up of fatty deposits that damages the inner lining of the arteries is called atherosclerosis. This damage can lead to thromboembolism, and hyperlipidemia is a risk factor for atherosclerosis.

59. d. A hazardous Class 7 indicates the presence of radioactive materials.

60. c. Full thickness burns are characterized by a dry, leathery appearance.

61. c. A pediatric patient who is breathing independently at a rate of 12 breaths per minute should be tagged with a red triage tag, due to the decreased respiratory rate.

62. c. The best way to immobilize and splint a hip fracture is to place the patient on a long spine board and place padding under the knees.

63. b. After scene safety and BSI, it is important to stop the burning process in the burn patient.

64. d. The proper order of securing a patient to a long spine board is to secure the torso first, followed by the extremities, and finally the head.

65. d. When using a short spine board, circulation, sensation, and movement should be assessed prior to and after the application of the device.

66. a. The blood vessels that supply blood to the myocardium are the coronary arteries.

67. b. The carotid arteries supply the head and brain with blood.

68. c. Capillaries allow for the exchange of waste and nutrients at the cellular level.

69. d. Ischemia is a condition of insufficient oxygen that can cause chest pain or discomfort.

70. b. Ventricular fibrillation is disorganized quivering of the ventricles.

71. c. Preservation of body heat should be included in the treatment for cardiogenic shock.

72. b. Dependent edema is the collection of fluid in the body part that is closest to the ground.

73. b. The upper section of the sternum is called the manubrium.

74. b. The acetabulum is the depression in which the femoral head fits.

75. a. The fibula is the small, lower extremity bone that lies on the lateral side of the leg.

76. b. The use of the Sellick's maneuver (cricoid pressure) is no longer recommended during artificial ventilations. It is contraindicated when a patient is vomiting and when used the patient must be unconscious. Its current recommendations are limited to assisting paramedics with orotracheal intubation.

77. d. If the patient has a mild airway obstruction, he will be able to cough forcefully. If he is able to move air, talk, or cough, continue to allow him to cough and do not interfere with his own efforts to expel the object.

78. d. Cheyne-Stokes respirations are characterized by irregular respirations followed by a period of apnea.

79. b. To choose the appropriate sized nasopharyngeal airway for a patient, measure from the tip of the nose to the earlobe.

80. a. This patient is exhibiting classic signs of CHF. The wheezing in the lower lobes is possibly due to the extreme narrowing of the bronchiole space from excess fluid.

81. c. Expiratory grunting in a pediatric patient is an attempt to keep the alveoli open.

82. d. The third stage of delivery is complete when the placenta delivers.

83. c. *Para* is the term that is used to describe the total number of viable births that a mother has had.

84. d. An umbilical cord that is wrapped around an infant's neck is called a nuchal cord.

85. a. When triaging at an MCI, no more than 30 seconds should be spent assessing each patient.

86. d. The rhythm that originates in the ventricles, is greater than 180 bpm, and does not allow the ventricles to adequately fill with blood is ventricular tachycardia. Any sinus rhythm begins in the atria, ventricular fibrillation is unorganized, and premature ventricular contractions are extra beats usually within a sinus rhythm.

87. c. The patient presents with a nosebleed, but the additional information gathered in the history taking and physical exam reveals the patient may be having a hypertensive emergency, and therefore oxygen and ALS are indicated.

88. c. Do not delay CPR if a DNR is not readily available or if there is any question as to its existence.

89. b. The bottom quadrant of the diamond-shaped NFPA symbol contains information about any special hazards.

90. b. Children between one and eight years of age and infants require chest compressions if they are not breathing adequately and have a pulse less than 60 bpm.

91. d. A patient suffering from decompression sickness will need treatment in a hyperbaric chamber after they are stabilized.

92. b. The rescuer who is positioned at the head should direct the movement of a patient when a spinal injury is suspected.

93. b. Loss of feeling and sensation is a sign of a superficial local cold injury.

94. a. The cervical spine is the section of the vertebral column that is the most susceptible to injury.

95. c. Traumatic asphyxia is a condition where severe force or weight is placed upon the thorax, forcing blood from the right atrium into the circulation of the head and neck.

96. d. If a cold injury appears to be deep, you should not reheat the injured part.

97. b. The common dosage for the administration of acetylsalicylic acid in a cardiac emergency is 324 mg by mouth (PO).

98. d. Nitroglycerine is supplied as sublingual tablets, sublingual spray, transdermal patches, and cream or ointment.

99. c. The bones that make up the toes are phalanges.

100. a. Ligaments are the fibrous tissues that connect bone to bone.

101. b. The somatic nervous system regulates the activities in which there is voluntary control.

102. c. The cerebrum is the largest part of the brain.

103. b. A patient suffering from a heatstroke will typically have symptoms of hot, dry, flushed skin.

104. d. A patient with a stoma should be ventilated by using an infant- or child-sized mask, making a seal over the stoma, and ventilating with a BVM while maintaining a seal over the patient's mouth and nose.

105. d. The normal tidal volume of the bag of an adult BVM device is 1,200–1,600 mL.

106. b. Mouth-to-mask delivers the highest tidal volume to a patient.

107. c. COPD is a contraindication for an oxygen-powered ventilation device.

108. c. Exhalation is the passive part of breathing.

109. b. A pregnant female should be transported left lateral recumbent to keep the baby positioned away from the inferior vena cava.

110. a. When suctioning an infant, suction for no more than five seconds.

111. b. A bulb syringe should be used to suction the nose of a newborn.

112. c. A normal respiratory rate for a newborn at rest is 30 to 60.

113. b. When parking at the scene of a motor vehicle crash, the ambulance should be parked at least 100 feet away from the collision.

114. a. This is an unwitnessed arrest and therefore two minutes of CPR is indicated prior to the use of the AED. You should also immediately resume CPR post defibrillation. It is no longer recommended to assess the patient post defibrillation as the rhythm generally does not recover to an adequately perfusing rhythm immediately after defibrillation.

115. a. A moistened, sterile dressing should be applied to an evisceration.

116. a. If a patient sustains a brain injury in the temporal region, she may develop problems with memory.

117. b. An occlusive dressing is applied to a sucking chest wound to seal it, preventing air from entering the pleural cavity.

118. d. The principle signs of hypovolemic shock are a rapid, weak pulse and low blood pressure.

119. c. Paradoxical movement in the chest upon inspiration and expiration is indicative of a flail chest.

120. c. If a patient has an increased respiratory rate, it is a sign that the patient is not getting an adequate amount of oxygen.

8

▶ EMT
PRACTICE EXAM 6

CHAPTER SUMMARY
This is the sixth of ten practice exams in this book based on the National Registry's EMT cognitive exam. Use this test to continue your study and practice. Notice how knowing what to expect on the exam makes you feel better prepared!

L ike the other tests in this book, this test is based on the National Registry's cognitive exam for EMT Exams. See Chapter 1 for a complete description of the exam.

As before, the answer sheet you should use appears next. Following the exam is an answer key, with explanations that will help you see where you need to concentrate your studies. When you've finished this exam and scored it, note your weaknesses, so you'll know what parts of your textbook to concentrate on before you take the next exam.

1.	a b c d		41.	a b c d		81.	a b c d
2.	a b c d		42.	a b c d		82.	a b c d
3.	a b c d		43.	a b c d		83.	a b c d
4.	a b c d		44.	a b c d		84.	a b c d
5.	a b c d		45.	a b c d		85.	a b c d
6.	a b c d		46.	a b c d		86.	a b c d
7.	a b c d		47.	a b c d		87.	a b c d
8.	a b c d		48.	a b c d		88.	a b c d
9.	a b c d		49.	a b c d		89.	a b c d
10.	a b c d		50.	a b c d		90.	a b c d
11.	a b c d		51.	a b c d		91.	a b c d
12.	a b c d		52.	a b c d		92.	a b c d
13.	a b c d		53.	a b c d		93.	a b c d
14.	a b c d		54.	a b c d		94.	a b c d
15.	a b c d		55.	a b c d		95.	a b c d
16.	a b c d		56.	a b c d		96.	a b c d
17.	a b c d		57.	a b c d		97.	a b c d
18.	a b c d		58.	a b c d		98.	a b c d
19.	a b c d		59.	a b c d		99.	a b c d
20.	a b c d		60.	a b c d		100.	a b c d
21.	a b c d		61.	a b c d		101.	a b c d
22.	a b c d		62.	a b c d		102.	a b c d
23.	a b c d		63.	a b c d		103.	a b c d
24.	a b c d		64.	a b c d		104.	a b c d
25.	a b c d		65.	a b c d		105.	a b c d
26.	a b c d		66.	a b c d		106.	a b c d
27.	a b c d		67.	a b c d		107.	a b c d
28.	a b c d		68.	a b c d		108.	a b c d
29.	a b c d		69.	a b c d		109.	a b c d
30.	a b c d		70.	a b c d		110.	a b c d
31.	a b c d		71.	a b c d		111.	a b c d
32.	a b c d		72.	a b c d		112.	a b c d
33.	a b c d		73.	a b c d		113.	a b c d
34.	a b c d		74.	a b c d		114.	a b c d
35.	a b c d		75.	a b c d		115.	a b c d
36.	a b c d		76.	a b c d		116.	a b c d
37.	a b c d		77.	a b c d		117.	a b c d
38.	a b c d		78.	a b c d		118.	a b c d
39.	a b c d		79.	a b c d		119.	a b c d
40.	a b c d		80.	a b c d		120.	a b c d

EMT Practice Exam 6

1. What is the most common cause of seizures in the pediatric patient?
   a. fever
   b. head trauma
   c. hypoxia
   d. brain tumor

2. Which of the following is a risk factor for SIDS?
   a. mother older than 40-years-old
   b. infant who was recently diagnosed with an upper respiratory infection
   c. infant with poor hygiene
   d. mother who smoked during pregnancy

3. The logistics function of the Incident Command System includes
   a. providing resources.
   b. providing support to meet the incident needs.
   c. providing all services to support the incident.
   d. all of the above.

4. Who is the only person authorized to release information to the media after approval by the incident commander is given?
   a. liaison officer
   b. public information officer
   c. logistics officer
   d. highest-ranking officer on the scene

5. Radio communications on an MCI or multi-system response incident should use
   a. radio codes.
   b. ten codes.
   c. numerical signals.
   d. clear text.

6. A fracture in which the bone is broken into more than two fragments is a(n)
   a. comminuted fracture.
   b. greenstick fracture.
   c. pathologic fracture.
   d. epiphysical fracture.

7. Your patient is a young male who appears to have a dislocated patella. How should you splint this injury?
   a. in a position of comfort
   b. straighten the leg, then splint with a rigid splint
   c. splint in the position found
   d. none of the above

8. A traumatic injury caused by fragments will most likely occur in what blast phase?
   a. tertiary
   b. primary
   c. secondary
   d. none of the above

9. What is most important when assessing for injuries sustained from a fall?
   a. the patient's height
   b. the height of the fall
   c. the patient's weight
   d. previous injuries

10. After the administration of nitroglycerine, blood pressure should be taken within _____ minutes after each dose.
   a. 5
   b. 10
   c. 15
   d. 2

11. The upper airway includes which of the following structures?
a. Nose, nasopharynx, mouth, oropharynx, carina, and larynx
b. Mouth, oropharynx, tongue, larynx, and trachea
c. Nasopharynx, tongue, oropharynx, and bronchus
d. Nasopharynx, tongue, oropharynx, and larynx

12. Where are the central chemoreceptors involved in controlling breathing located?
a. The aortic arch
b. The cerebrum
c. The medulla oblongata
d. The cerebellum

13. You have responded to a call for a patient with respiratory distress. Your patient states a history of asthma and states her distress began during exercise. The patient states she is also feeling weak and lightheaded and her inhaler is in her purse. Your assessment reveals diffuse wheezing upon auscultation and the following vital signs: P – 112, R – 26 shallow and labored, BP – 122/84, skin is warm and dry. Per medical control you are preparing to assist the patient with her MDI. What are the contraindications to the use of the MDI?
a. The medication is prescribed to the patient.
b. The patient has a history of asthma.
c. The medication is expired.
d. Medical control has been consulted.

14. Blood occupies what percentage of the cranium?
a. 10%
b. 20%
c. 80%
d. 15%

15. A body temperature of what degree and higher is considered to be abnormal?
a. 99.9°F
b. 100.0°F
c. 100.4°F
d. 100.9°F

16. What component in the blood contains hemoglobin?
a. white blood cells
b. platelets
c. plasma
d. red blood cells

17. How much blood loss can occur with a femur fracture?
a. 500 to 1,000 cc
b. 500 to 750 cc
c. 1,000 to 2,000 cc
d. 1,000 to 3,000 cc

18. In the late stages of decompensated shock, the body will have a(n) _____ in blood pressure and the pulse will _____.
a. increase, decrease
b. decrease, decrease
c. decrease, increase
d. increase, increase

19. The type of amnesia where the patient is not able to recall events that have happened after a traumatic injury or event is
a. retrograde amnesia.
b. intermittent amnesia.
c. false amnesia.
d. anterograde amnesia.

20. Your patient is found lying unconscious on the sidewalk. No obvious trauma is noted. How should you open the patient's airway?
  a. head-tilt/chin-lift maneuver
  b. jaw-thrust maneuver
  c. using the forefinger and thumb in a crossover motion
  d. none of the above

21. The correct way to select the size of a nasopharyngeal airway is to measure
  a. from the corner of the mouth to the angle of the jaw.
  a. from the earlobe to the corner of the jaw.
  a. from the tip of the nose to the earlobe.
  a. from the chin to the Adam's apple.

22. What causes the high-pitched sound in wheezing?
  a. foreign body
  b. narrowing of the airways
  c. a fall in carbon dioxide levels
  d. mucous in the airways

23. When assessing breathing, look for
  a. Rate, length, rhythm, strength
  b. Rate, strength, effort, duration
  c. Rate, length, rhythm, depth
  d. Rate, rhythm, depth, effort

24. You respond to a child with unknown respiratory problems. You find that the child has a tracheostomy tube and is on a ventilator. The ventilator is malfunctioning. You should
  a. reset the ventilator settings.
  b. disconnect the ventilator and ventilate the child using a BVM connected to a tracheostomy tube.
  c. contact medical control.
  d. suction the airway.

25. When assessing a central pulse in a pediatric patient with a weak pulse, check the _____ pulse if the patient is older than one year.
  a. brachial
  b. carotid
  c. radial
  d. popliteal

26. To mount a car seat in an ambulance, place the car seat
  a. in the front seat of the ambulance.
  b. on the bench seat.
  c. on the stretcher.
  d. None of the above.

27. The scene size-up should include
  a. the number of injuries, if known.
  b. the surrounding buildings' addresses.
  c. the number of law enforcement on the scene.
  d. none of the above.

28. You are treating a conscious patient with a complete foreign-body airway obstruction. During your attempts to relieve the obstruction the patient becomes unconscious. You should
  a. reassess the airway and if still obstructed begin CPR.
  b. call for an ALS unit as backup.
  c. request medical direction for further instructions.
  d. reassess the airway and if still obstructed begin series of five abdominal thrusts.

29. A patient with repetitive questioning after a traffic accident most likely has a
  a. cerebral hemorrhage.
  b. skull fracture.
  c. concussion.
  d. herniation.

30. What should be the next step in your assessment if a significant mechanism of injury is found?
 a. focused trauma assessment
 b. baseline vital signs
 c. rapid trauma assessment
 d. detailed physical exam

31. In the mnemonic DCAP-BTLS, what does the letter *B* stand for?
 a. bruising
 b. burns
 c. breathing
 d. Battle's sign

32. When you find a patient facedown in water, you should position yourself
 a. beside the patient.
 b. at the head.
 c. at the feet.
 d. None of the above.

33. Low blood flow to the heart is usually caused by
 a. hypovolemia.
 b. anemia.
 c. ischemia.
 d. atherosclerosis.

34. The heart has _____ chambers.
 a. four
 b. three
 c. two
 d. five

35. Blood from the abdomen, legs, and kidneys is carried through the _____ into the right atrium.
 a. inferior vena cava
 b. aorta
 c. right coronary artery
 d. femoral artery

36. You are assessing a male patient with an altered level of consciousness. The patient is talking in confused statements and your physical exam has revealed the following vital signs and physical findings: P – 112, BP – 118/76, R – 18 regular, pupils are equal and reactive, and skin is cool and clammy. You find no signs of trauma and the patient has a medic alert bracelet indicating he is a diabetic. Bystanders state the patient was working and suddenly became disoriented. This patient is most likely suffering from
 a. hypoglycemia.
 b. hyperglycemia.
 c. head injury.
 d. cerebral vascular accident.

37. What is the artery that is located in the upper arm and is palpated in infants to determine a pulse?
 a. radial artery
 b. popliteal artery
 c. femoral artery
 d. brachial artery

38. What is the condition when a diver starts acting strangely and out of character after diving too deeply or for too long?
 a. diving response
 b. mammalian diving reflex
 c. decompression sickness
 d. nitrogen narcosis

39. *Hypothermia* is defined as a core body temperature below
 a. 92°F.
 b. 96°F.
 c. 94°F.
 d. 98°F.

40. What is the membrane that is attached to the lung surface?
 a. parietal pleura
 b. diaphragm
 c. pleural membrane
 d. visceral pleura

41. Of the following, which is characterized by rapid, deep respirations that are usually present with strokes or head injuries?
 a. Kussmaul's respirations
 b. central neurogenic hyperventilation
 c. Cheyne-Stokes respirations
 d. hypoxic respirations

42. The three signs that make up Cushing's triad are
 a. decreased blood pressure, decreased pulse, and abnormal respirations.
 b. increased blood pressure, increased pulse, and abnormal respirations.
 c. decreased blood pressure, increased pulse, and abnormal respirations.
 d. increased blood pressure, decreased pulse, and abnormal respirations.

43. The type of asphyxia that can occur when you improperly restrain a patient is
 a. traumatic asphyxia.
 b. positional asphyxia.
 c. mechanical asphyxia.
 d. perinatal asphyxia.

44. Which of the following is a strong indicator of circulatory status in a child who is less than 3-years-old?
 a. blood pressure
 b. respiratory rate
 c. pulse pressure
 d. skin

45. An infant who is between 1 month and 1 year old should have a pulse rate between
 a. 90–180.
 b. 70–120.
 c. 100–160.
 d. 120–190.

46. What is the best way to determine the proper sized equipment for a pediatric patient?
 a. Look in the protocols.
 b. Memorize appropriate sizes.
 c. Refer to a pediatric resuscitation tape measure.
 d. Look on the equipment packaging.

47. The treatment unit is responsible for
 a. the direction of incoming resources.
 b. the sorting of patients according to their seriousness and injuries.
 c. obtaining resources for the transport of patients to the appropriate facility.
 d. the establishment of a treatment area, where patients can be treated and collected.

48. How many incident command posts should be established on the scene of an incident?
 a. one for every ten units
 b. one
 c. two
 d. three

49. Signs and symptoms of abnormal breathing in a child are
 a. nasal flaring, restlessness, and retractions.
 b. restlessness, tripod position, and clear breath sounds.
 c. anxiety, warm, pink skin, and stridor.
 d. alert, cyanosis, and tachypnea.

50. The most important aspect of an MCI is
   a. the appropriate number of responding units.
   b. establishing a unified command.
   c. establishing incident command.
   d. scene safety.

51. Patients who are not breathing after repositioning their airway should be tagged
   a. black.
   b. red.
   c. yellow.
   d. green.

52. When someone fractures their tailbone, what section of the spine is involved?
   a. sacrum
   b. coccyx
   c. lumbar
   d. ischium

53. In addition to obvious injuries, what information is needed to determine injuries or suspected injuries in a trauma patient?
   a. the patient's medical history
   b. bystanders' accounts of what happened
   c. the patient's account of what happened
   d. the mechanism of injury

54. The _____ refers to the time from injury to definitive care in which the treatment of a trauma patient's injuries and shock should occur in order to maximize the chance of survival.
   a. platinum ten minutes
   b. *golden period*
   c. bronze 15 minutes
   d. rapid assessment

55. Which of the following is an atypical symptom of an acute myocardial infarction?
   a. chest pain
   b. nausea
   c. neck pain
   d. fatigue

56. You arrive on the scene to find an unconscious and unresponsive patient lying supine on the ground with his lower extremities in a puddle. Bystanders state that he was complaining of chest pain prior to falling to the ground. Before defibrillating this patient, you should
   a. establish an airway.
   b. do four cycles of CPR.
   c. remove the patient from the puddle.
   d. start compressions.

57. At a minimum, AEDs should be checked every
   a. week.
   b. day.
   c. two weeks.
   d. 30 days.

58. Which of the following is a component of the cardiovascular system?
   a. blood
   b. perineum
   c. pleura
   d. insulin

59. The structures that connect muscles to bones are
   a. ligaments.
   b. cartilage.
   c. joints.
   d. tendons.

60. An injury that is caused by stretching or tearing tendons or ligaments is a
   a. fracture.
   b. strain.
   c. sprain.
   d. pull.

61. Which of the following is a sign of a tension pneumothorax?
   a. chest pain
   b. decreased oxygen saturation
   c. tachypnea
   d. tracheal deviation

62. Your partner has just intubated the patient. You should first listen over the _____ to confirm tube placement.
   a. sternum
   b. right side of chest
   c. left side of chest
   d. stomach

63. The oropharynx is the area directly
   a. posterior to the nose.
   b. posterior to the mouth.
   c. anterior to the nose.
   d. anterior to the mouth.

64. The smallest branches of the bronchi are the
   a. alveoli.
   b. pulmonary capillaries.
   d. bronchus.
   d. bronchioles.

65. When performing chest compressions on an infant, compress the chest
   a. 1 to $1\frac{1}{2}$ inches.
   b. 1 inch.
   c. $\frac{1}{3}$ to $\frac{1}{2}$ its depth.
   d. $1\frac{1}{2}$ to 2 inches

66. Which of the following injuries should raise your index of suspicion of child abuse?
   a. Arm fracture
   b. A grid pattern burn
   c. Injuries consistent with history
   d. Increased concern of the caregiver

67. Stranger anxiety usually develops when the patient is a(n)
   a. toddler.
   b. infant.
   c. preschooler.
   d. adolescent.

68. You are called to the residence of a woman who is in labor. Examination of her genitalia shows that she has a limb presentation. You should
   a. lightly pull on the exposed limb to assist in the delivery.
   b. cover the limb with a sterile towel and transport the woman immediately.
   c. coach the woman to breathe and push.
   d. insert two fingers into the vagina to relieve pressure on the limb.

69. Your first preparation for the delivery of an infant should be
   a. contacting medical control.
   b. calming the mother.
   c. making a transport decision.
   d. BSI precautions.

70. When ventilating an unconscious patient without a spinal injury, you notice what appears to be abdominal distention. You should first
   a. Reposition the head
   b. Decrease your tidal volume given
   c. Gently press on the stomach to relieve pressure
   d. Insert an oral adjunct

71. A teratogenic substance
   a. causes mutation.
   b. causes cancer.
   c. causes damage to a developing fetus.
   d. None of the above.

72. A warm zone is the area
   a. where treatment is performed.
   b. where contamination is actually present.
   c. surrounding the contamination zone.
   d. where triage is performed.

73. Where should vehicles be parked in relation to a fuel leak or hazardous materials release?
   a. downwind
   b. at least 50 feet away
   c. upwind
   d. none of the above

74. SAMPLE history, rapid trauma assessment, and baseline vital signs are all components of the
   a. detailed physical exam.
   b. initial assessment.
   c. scene size-up.
   d. focused history and medical exam.

75. If a potentially life-threatening condition is identified during the detailed physical exam, you should
   a. contact medical control.
   b. change treatment modalities.
   c. reconsider transport decision.
   d. return to the initial assessment.

76. The left and right sides of the heart are separated by the
   a. endoplasmic reticulum.
   b. septum.
   c. ventricular wall.
   d. cellular wall.

77. In addition to the atria and ventricles, _____ also contain valves to prevent the backflow of blood.
   a. veins
   b. arteries
   c. arterioles
   d. bronchioles

78. The electrical impulse is held in the _____ for a fraction of a second to allow for the filling of the ventricles.
   a. AV node
   b. SA node
   c. Purkinje fibers
   d. bundle of His

79. Upon your arrival at a respiratory distress call you encounter a 24-year-old male patient who is tachypneic at a rate of 36 times per minute and shallow. The patient states he has just lost his job and does not know what he is going to do. The patient also complains of chest tightness, anxiety, and numbness around his mouth and hands. Your treatment for this patient should include which of the following?
   a. Calm the patient and have the patient breath into a paper bag
   b. Calm the patient, place the patient on oxygen, continue your assessment, and transport
   c. Tell the patient that he needs to calm down or he will pass out!
   d. Reassure the patient and withhold oxygen as hyperventilation is caused by excessive oxygen levels in the blood

80. A geriatric patient is considered to be a patient who is _____ years or older.
   a. 65
   b. 75
   c. 55
   d. 60

81. The leaf-shaped structure that covers and prevents food and other foreign matter from entering the trachea is the
   a. uvula.
   b. larynx.
   c. thyroid cartilage.
   d. epiglottis.

82. The knee is _____ to the hip.
   a. distal
   b. proximal
   c. posterior
   d. anterior

83. When a patient has loose dentures you should _____ before ventilating.
   a. reposition them
   b. remove them
   c. ignore them
   d. hold them in place

84. When a patient hyperventilates, they have a buildup of _____ in the blood.
   a. oxygen
   b. nitrogen
   c. carbon dioxide
   d. carbon monoxide

85. What should the oxygen flow rate be set to when using a small volume nebulizer?
   a. 4–6 LPM
   b. 6–8 LPM
   c. 10–15 LPM
   d. 2–4 LPM

86. If lung sounds are present on the right side and diminished on the left side, this means that the _____ has been intubated.
   a. left mainstem bronchus
   b. right mainstem bronchus
   c. esophagus
   d. epigastrium

87. You respond to a patient complaining of respiratory distress. Upon your arrival you are directed to a tall slender male patient who complains of sudden sharp stabbing left-sided chest pain. The patient denies any medical history or allergies. The patient states he has been sick with a non-productive cough over the past week and the pain began after coughing. You listen to breath sounds and note diminished breath sounds in the lower left lobe. You suspect this patient is suffering from?
   a. angina.
   b. spontaneous pneumothorax.
   c. tension pneumothorax.
   d. pleural effusion.

88. When a mother is in true labor,
   a. there will be a brownish-colored bloody show.
   b. pain starts and stays in the lower abdomen.
   c. contractions are intermittent.
   d. change in position does not relieve contractions.

89. When preparing for the delivery of an infant, you notice that the amniotic sac is protruding from the vagina as the head is crowning. You should
   a. puncture the amniotic sac.
   b. transport immediately.
   c. support the infant's head and encourage the mother to push.
   d. apply a moist, sterile pad to the vagina and transport.

90. In addition to the APGAR score, your documentation of the infant should include the
   a. infant's name.
   b. equipment used in the delivery.
   c. names of the personnel on the scene.
   d. time of birth.

91. To slow bleeding after childbirth,
   a. place a sanitary pad on the vagina.
   b. apply direct pressure to the vagina.
   c. pack the vagina with gauze.
   d. gently massage the mother's abdomen.

92. A woman who is experiencing her first pregnancy is called
   a. primipara.
   b. multigravid.
   c. primigravida.
   d. unopara.

93. To perform a roof flap of a vehicle with an entrapped victim using a hydraulic-powered cutter, cut through the_____ with a relief cut to the roof and fold the roof over.
   a. B and C posts
   b. A and B posts
   c. nader pin
   d. windshield

94. _____ is the oversight of all patient care aspects in EMS.
   a. Incident command
   b. The emergency medical dispatcher
   c. The standard operating procedures guide
   d. Medical direction

95. If you are the initial unit to arrive on the scene of a multicasualty incident, you should first
   a. report to the command post for assignment.
   b. establish command.
   c. begin triaging patients.
   d. start treating patients appropriately.

96. A condition in which the artery walls become hard and stiff due to calcium deposits is
   a. arteriosclerosis.
   b. hypercholesterolemia.
   c. hyperlipidemia.
   d. atherosclerosis.

97. The dilation or ballooning of a weakened area in the wall of an artery is called
   a. arteriosclerosis.
   b. thrombus.
   c. embolism.
   d. aneurysm.

98. Accumulation of fluid in the lungs is called
   a. pitting edema.
   b. dependent edema.
   c. pulmonary edema.
   d. pulmonary embolism.

99. You arrive on the scene to find a 59-year-old male patient sitting in his living room, complaining of crushing chest pain. He rates the pain 10:10, his skin is pale, and he is diaphoretic. Your next action should be to immediately
   a. administer 0.4 mg NTG SL.
   b. apply AED.
   c. obtain SAMPLE history.
   d. apply oxygen.

100. In what part of the skin are nerve endings located?
   a. epidermis
   b. dermis
   c. subcutaneous layer
   d. fascia

101. You arrive to find your patient sitting upright in a chair. This position is called
   a. Trendelenburg.
   b. semi-Fowler's.
   c. Fowler's.
   d. laterally recumbent.

102. The dorsalis pedis artery is located
   a. posterior to the knee.
   b. on the posterior surface of the medial malleolus.
   c. on the anterior surface of the foot.
   d. on the lateral aspect of the anterior wrist.

103. Which of the following most closely mimics the signs and symptoms of an acute stroke?
   a. hypotension
   b. carbon monoxide poisoning
   c. hypoxia
   d. hypoglycemia

104. Your patient is an elderly female who is found lying supine in bed. She is cool to the touch with a decreased body temperature. She suffered heat loss due to
   a. evaporation.
   b. conduction.
   c. convection.
   d. radiation.

105. Pupils that are constricted are
   a. normal sized.
   b. unequal.
   c. larger than normal.
   d. smaller than normal.

106. What component of blood is responsible for transporting oxygen and carbon dioxide to and from the tissues of the body?
   a. red blood cells
   b. plasma
   c. white blood cells
   d. platelets

107. You have assisted your patient in taking his nitroglycerine. His next set of vital signs indicates that he is now hypotensive, and he is still complaining of chest pain. Your next action should be to
   a. administer a second dose of nitroglycerine.
   b. lay the patient flat.
   c. apply an AED.
   d. contact medical control for orders.

108. The first stage of labor begins with the
   a. presentation of the head.
   b. rupture of the amniotic sac.
   c. onset of contractions.
   d. full dilation of the cervix.

109. When performing CPR on an infant, deliver_____ ventilations and _____ compressions per minute.
   a. 20, 100
   b. 36, 100
   c. 60, 100
   d. 60, 120

110. What condition should be suspected in all patients with vaginal bleeding?
   a. assault
   b. pregnancy
   c. trauma
   d. shock

111. You arrive on the scene of an initial call of chest pain. You find the patient unconscious, unresponsive, pulseless, and apneic. Your first action should be to
   a. perform abdominal thrusts.
   b. apply the AED.
   c. begin chest compressions.
   d. apply oxygen.

112. Angina is often triggered by
   a. decreased oxygen demand.
   b. damage to the cardiac muscle.
   c. exertion.
   d. complete blockage of a blood vessel.

113. When using an AED after the shock is administered or when no shock is indicated, CPR should be performed for
   a. one minute.
   b. two minutes.
   c. three minutes.
   d. None of the above.

114. Your patient opens her eyes to the sound of your voice, withdraws from pain, and is confused. Her GCS is
   a. 12.
   b. 11.
   c. 13.
   d. 9.

115. Which of the following is NOT part of the assessment when using the Cincinnati Prehospital Stroke Scale?
   a. ability to swallow
   b. facial droop
   c. arm drift
   d. abnormal speech

116. When a patient is in anaphylaxis, the exaggerated immune response causes blood vessels to _____ and the airway passages to _____.
   a. constrict, dilate
   b. dilate, dilate
   c. constrict, constrict
   d. dilate, constrict

117. What is the dose for activated charcoal for adults and children?
   a. 12.5 mg activated charcoal/kg of body weight
   b. 12.5 g activated charcoal
   c. 1 g activated charcoal/kg of body weight
   d. 1 mg activated charcoal/kg body weight

118. According to the Centers for Disease Control and Prevention, which of the following is the third leading cause of death in the 15- to 24-year-old age group?
   a. suicide
   b. motor vehicle crashes
   c. head injuries
   d. respiratory disorders

119. What is a false belief in which a patient believes he or she is being harmed, followed, or persecuted?
   a. schizophrenia
   b. psychosis
   c. anxiety
   d. paranoia

120. After receiving a medication order by medical control, you should
   a. reassess vital signs.
   b. check the expiration date of the medication.
   c. administer the medication.
   d. verify the proper medication form and dose.

Answers

1. a. The most common cause for seizures in a pediatric patient is fever.

2. d. A mother who smokes during pregnancy is a risk factor for Sudden Infant Death Syndrome.

3. d. In the Incident Command System, logistics provides resources and support to meet the incident needs. It also provides all services to support the incident.

4. b. When the incident commander approves, the only person authorized to release information to the media is the public information officer.

5. d. Clear text should always be used on an MCI or when there are multiple organizations responding to an incident.

6. a. A fracture in which the bone is broken into more than two fragments is a comminuted fracture.

7. c. A dislocated patella should be splinted in the position that it is found.

8. c. A traumatic injury caused by fragments will most likely occur in the secondary blast phase.

9. **b.** The height of the fall is the most important of these answer choices when you are assessing injuries from a fall.

10. **a.** The blood pressure should be taken five minutes after the administration of nitroglycerine.

11. **d.** The upper airway includes the nose, nasopharynx, mouth, tongue, oropharynx, and the larynx. The larynx is the dividing line between the upper and lower airways.

12. **c.** The central chemoreceptors, which measure and react to the pH of the cerebral spinal fluid to control breathing, are located in the medulla oblongata.

13. **c.** Expired medications are contraindications to administering the medications. All the other choices are indications to administer the medications.

14. **a.** Blood supply occupies ten percent of the cranium.

15. **c.** A body temperature of 100.4°F or higher is considered to be abnormal.

16. **d.** Red blood cells contain hemoglobin.

17. **c.** 1,000 cc to 2,000 cc of blood loss can occur with a femur fracture.

18. **b.** In the late stages of decompensated shock, the body will have a decrease in blood pressure and the pulse will decrease.

19. **d.** A patient who is unable to recall events that happened after an incident or injury likely has anterograde amnesia.

20. **b.** The jaw-thrust maneuver should be used to open an airway if it is unknown if the patient has sustained an injury.

21. **c.** The nasopharyngeal airway is measured from the tip of the patient's nose to the earlobe.

22. **b.** Narrowing of the airways causes the high-pitched sound of wheezing.

23. **d.** To assess for normal breathing the EMT needs to look at the rate, rhythm, depth, and effort of breathing. The EMT should also assess breath sounds to complete the breathing assessment.

24. **b.** If a ventilator malfunctions, disconnect the ventilator and ventilate the patient using a BVM. In this case, the patient has a tracheostomy, so the mask portion should be removed from the BVM and the tracheostomy tube should connect directly to the BVM. Ventilate at the proper rate for the patient's age.

25. **b.** When there is a weak pulse found in a pediatric patient, the carotid pulse should be checked for circulation if the patient is one year old or older.

26. **c.** When a car seat is used, mount it to the stretcher, in order to have access to the patient.

27. **a.** When performing a scene size-up, include the number of injuries if they are known.

28. **a.** Once a patient becomes unresponsive the EMT should reassess the airway and if the obstruction persists, then CPR should be started. Abdominal thrusts and blind finger sweeps are no longer recommended.

29. **c.** A patient with repetitive questioning after a traffic accident most likely has a concussion.

30. **c.** If a significant mechanism of injury is found, a rapid trauma assessment should be performed.

31. **b.** In the mnemonic DCAP-BTLS, the *B* stands for burns.

32. **a.** When you find a patient lying facedown in water, position yourself beside him or her.

33. **d.** Decreased blood flow to the heart is typically caused by atherosclerosis.

34. **a.** The heart has four chambers. There are two atria and two ventricles.

35. **a.** Blood from the abdomen, legs, and kidneys is carried through the inferior vena cava into the right atrium.

36. a. This patient is exhibiting the signs and symptoms of hypoglycemia. The rapid onset rules out hyperglycemia. The lack of trauma rules out a head injury as do the equal pupils. A CVA is possible, but the cool clammy skin points to hypoglycemia.

37. d. To determine the presence of a pulse in an infant, palpate the brachial artery, which is located in the upper arm.

38. d. Nitrogen narcosis is a condition that occurs in divers when they have been diving too deeply or for too long. This condition is characterized by strange behavior that is out of character for the diver.

39. a. *Hypothermia* is defined as a core body temperature that is below 92°F.

40. d. The membrane that is attached to the surface of the lung is the visceral pleura.

41. b. Central neurogenic hyperventilation is characterized by rapid, deep respirations and is usually present with strokes or head injuries.

42. d. The three signs that make up Cushing's triad are increased blood pressure, decreased pulse, and abnormal respirations.

43. b. The type of asphyxia that can occur when you improperly restrain a patient is positional asphyxia.

44. d. In a child, the skin is a better indicator of circulatory status than blood pressure, pulse pressure, and respiratory rate.

45. c. The normal range for an infant's pulse rate is 100–160.

46. c. The best way to determine the proper sized equipment for a pediatric patient is to use pediatric resuscitation tape.

47. d. The treatment unit is responsible for the establishment of a treatment area, where patients can be treated and collected.

48. b. Only one command post should be established on the scene of an incident.

49. a. These are all signs of inadequate breathing in the pediatric patient. Clear breath sounds, warm, pink skin, and alert mental status are all signs of adequate breathing.

50. d. The most important aspect of any scene is scene safety.

51. a. Patients who are not breathing after repositioning their airway should be tagged black.

52. b. When a patient fractures his or her tailbone, the section of the spine that is involved is the coccyx.

53. d. The mechanism of injury is needed in order to determine or suspect injuries in the trauma patient.

54. b. The *golden period* refers to the time from injury to definitive care in which the treatment of injuries and shock should occur. This maximizes the chance of survival in the trauma patient.

55. d. An atypical symptom that can be present in an acute myocardial infarction is fatigue.

56. c. To prevent arcing, injury, or death, patients must be removed from standing water prior to defibrillating.

57. d. At a minimum, AEDs should be checked every 30 days.

58. a. Blood is a component of the cardiovascular system.

59. d. Tendons connect muscles to bones.

60. c. A sprain is an injury that is caused by the stretching or tearing of tendons or ligaments.

61. d. All the other answers may be signs of a pneumothorax, but they are also signs of a simple pneumothorax as well as other respiratory illnesses and injuries. Although a late and rare sign, you will only see tracheal deviation in the tension pneumothorax.

62. d. To decrease the chance of delay in ventilation or causing distention of the stomach, listen over the stomach initially, after a patient is intubated.

63. b. The oropharynx is the area that is directly posterior to the mouth.

64. d. Bronchioles are the smallest branches of the bronchi.

65. c. When performing chest compressions on an infant, compress the chest $\frac{1}{3}$ to $\frac{1}{2}$ its depth.

66. b. A grid pattern burn should raise the index of suspicion of child abuse.

67. a. Stranger anxiety usually develops in the toddler years.

68. b. A limb presentation during delivery is a severe emergency. Do not attempt to pull or push on the limb. Cover the limb with a sterile towel and transport immediately.

69. d. Your first preparation for the delivery of an infant should be BSI (body substance isolation) precautions.

70. a. If the abdomen becomes distended while ventilating an unconscious and unresponsive patient, reposition the airway and then be sure to allow for exhalation during ventilation.

71. c. A teratogenic substance causes damage to a developing fetus.

72. c. The area surrounding the contamination zone is the warm zone.

73. c. Vehicles should be parked upwind from a fuel leak or hazardous materials release.

74. d. The SAMPLE history, rapid trauma assessment, and baseline vital signs are all components of the focused history and medical exam.

75. d. If a potentially life-threatening condition is identified during the detailed physical exam, you should return to the initial assessment (ABCs).

76. b. The left and right sides of the heart are separated by the septum.

77. a. In addition to the atria and ventricles, veins also contain valves to prevent the backflow of blood.

78. a. The electrical impulse is held in the atrio-ventricular node for a fraction of a second to allow for the filling of the ventricles.

79. b. Although hyperventilation syndrome is manifested by anxiety attacks and is not a life threatening condition, there are numerous serious medical conditions—pulmonary embolism, AMI, and hyperglycemia—which can exhibit hyperventilation as a sign of illness.

80. a. A geriatric patient is considered to be a patient who is 65-years-old or older.

81. d. The epiglottis is the leaf-shaped structure that covers and prevents food and other foreign matter from entering the trachea.

82. a. The knee is distal to the hip.

83. b. When a patient has loose dentures you should remove them prior to ventilating the patient.

84. c. When a patient hyperventilates, they have a buildup of carbon dioxide in the blood.

85. b. The oxygen flow rate should be set on 6 LPM to 8 LPM when a small volume nebulizer is attached.

86. b. If lung sounds are present on the right side and diminished on the left, this means that the right mainstem bronchus has been intubated.

87. b. This patient's physical characteristics and presentation are highly indicative of a spontaneous pneumothorax. A tension pneumothorax is a possible complication of a spontaneous pneumothorax, but the signs and symptoms are not indicative it has progressed that far. Angina would present with chest discomfort and would not involve diminished breath sounds. A pleural effusion would present with sharp pain, but breath sounds would be clear and equal.

88. d. When a mother is in true labor, a change in her position will not relieve the contractions.

89. a. If the amniotic sac is protruding from the vagina when the infant's head crowns, puncture the sac, aiming away from the infant's face.

90. d. In addition to the APGAR score, the time of birth should be documented.

91. d. To slow the mother's bleeding after childbirth, gently massage her abdomen.

92. c. *Primigravida* is the term that is used when a woman is experiencing her first pregnancy.

93. b. To perform a roof flap of a vehicle with an entrapped victim using a hydraulic-powered cutter, cut through the A and B posts with a relief cut to the roof. Then, fold the roof over.

94. d. Medical direction is the oversight of all patient care aspects in EMS.

95. b. As the initial arriving unit on the scene of an incident, it is your responsibility to establish command.

96. a. Arteriosclerosis is a condition in which the artery walls become hard and stiff due to calcium deposits.

97. d. The dilation or ballooning of a weakened area in the artery wall is called an aneurysm.

98. c. Pulmonary edema is the accumulation of fluid in the lungs.

99. d. Oxygen should be applied to a patient who is complaining of chest pain.

100. b. Nerve endings are located in the dermis.

101. c. The Fowler's position is a position in which the patient is sitting upright.

102. c. The dorsalis pedis artery is located on the anterior surface of the foot.

103. d. The signs of hypoglycemia closely mimic those of a CVA.

104. d. A patient who is lying in bed and is sheltered by her home most likely loses body heat due to radiation.

105. d. Pupils that are constricted are smaller than normal.

106. a. Red blood cells are responsible for transporting oxygen and carbon dioxide to and from the tissues of the body.

107. b. When a patient suddenly becomes hypotensive, lay him flat.

108. c. The first stage of labor begins with the onset of contractions.

109. a. When performing CPR on an infant, deliver 20 ventilations and at least 100 compressions per minute.

110. d. Shock should be suspected in all patients with vaginal bleeding.

111. c. In an unwitnessed arrest, chest compressions should be performed for two minutes before applying the AED.

112. c. Angina is often triggered by exertion.

113. b. When using an AED after the shock is administered or when no shock is indicated, CPR should be performed for two minutes.

114. b. The Glasgow Coma Scale (GCS) of this patient is 11.

115. a. The ability to swallow is not part of the assessment in the Cincinnati Prehospital Stroke Scale.

116. d. When a patient is in anaphylaxis, the exaggerated immune response causes blood vessels to dilate and the airway passages to constrict.

117. c. The dose for activated charcoal in adults and children is 1 g activated charcoal/kg of body weight.

118. a. According to the Centers for Disease Control and Prevention, suicide is the third leading cause of death in the 15- to 24-year-old age group.

119. d. Paranoia is a false belief in which the patient believes he or she is being harmed, followed, or persecuted.

120. d. After receiving a medication order by medical control, verify the proper medication and dose.

9

▶ EMT
PRACTICE EXAM 7

CHAPTER SUMMARY

This is the seventh of ten practice exams in this book based on the National Registry's EMT cognitive exam. Use this test to continue your study and practice.

Like the previous practice exams, this test is based on the National Registry's cognitive exam for EMT Exams. Chapter 1 provides a complete description of this exam.

As before, the answer sheet you should use appears next. Following the exam is an answer key, with explanations that will help you see where you need to concentrate your studies. When you've finished this exam and scored it, note your weaknesses. This will show you what parts of your textbook to review before you take the next practice exam.

1.	(a)	(b)	(c)	(d)
2.	(a)	(b)	(c)	(d)
3.	(a)	(b)	(c)	(d)
4.	(a)	(b)	(c)	(d)
5.	(a)	(b)	(c)	(d)
6.	(a)	(b)	(c)	(d)
7.	(a)	(b)	(c)	(d)
8.	(a)	(b)	(c)	(d)
9.	(a)	(b)	(c)	(d)
10.	(a)	(b)	(c)	(d)
11.	(a)	(b)	(c)	(d)
12.	(a)	(b)	(c)	(d)
13.	(a)	(b)	(c)	(d)
14.	(a)	(b)	(c)	(d)
15.	(a)	(b)	(c)	(d)
16.	(a)	(b)	(c)	(d)
17.	(a)	(b)	(c)	(d)
18.	(a)	(b)	(c)	(d)
19.	(a)	(b)	(c)	(d)
20.	(a)	(b)	(c)	(d)
21.	(a)	(b)	(c)	(d)
22.	(a)	(b)	(c)	(d)
23.	(a)	(b)	(c)	(d)
24.	(a)	(b)	(c)	(d)
25.	(a)	(b)	(c)	(d)
26.	(a)	(b)	(c)	(d)
27.	(a)	(b)	(c)	(d)
28.	(a)	(b)	(c)	(d)
29.	(a)	(b)	(c)	(d)
30.	(a)	(b)	(c)	(d)
31.	(a)	(b)	(c)	(d)
32.	(a)	(b)	(c)	(d)
33.	(a)	(b)	(c)	(d)
34.	(a)	(b)	(c)	(d)
35.	(a)	(b)	(c)	(d)
36.	(a)	(b)	(c)	(d)
37.	(a)	(b)	(c)	(d)
38.	(a)	(b)	(c)	(d)
39.	(a)	(b)	(c)	(d)
40.	(a)	(b)	(c)	(d)

41.	(a)	(b)	(c)	(d)
42.	(a)	(b)	(c)	(d)
43.	(a)	(b)	(c)	(d)
44.	(a)	(b)	(c)	(d)
45.	(a)	(b)	(c)	(d)
46.	(a)	(b)	(c)	(d)
47.	(a)	(b)	(c)	(d)
48.	(a)	(b)	(c)	(d)
49.	(a)	(b)	(c)	(d)
50.	(a)	(b)	(c)	(d)
51.	(a)	(b)	(c)	(d)
52.	(a)	(b)	(c)	(d)
53.	(a)	(b)	(c)	(d)
54.	(a)	(b)	(c)	(d)
55.	(a)	(b)	(c)	(d)
56.	(a)	(b)	(c)	(d)
57.	(a)	(b)	(c)	(d)
58.	(a)	(b)	(c)	(d)
59.	(a)	(b)	(c)	(d)
60.	(a)	(b)	(c)	(d)
61.	(a)	(b)	(c)	(d)
62.	(a)	(b)	(c)	(d)
63.	(a)	(b)	(c)	(d)
64.	(a)	(b)	(c)	(d)
65.	(a)	(b)	(c)	(d)
66.	(a)	(b)	(c)	(d)
67.	(a)	(b)	(c)	(d)
68.	(a)	(b)	(c)	(d)
69.	(a)	(b)	(c)	(d)
70.	(a)	(b)	(c)	(d)
71.	(a)	(b)	(c)	(d)
72.	(a)	(b)	(c)	(d)
73.	(a)	(b)	(c)	(d)
74.	(a)	(b)	(c)	(d)
75.	(a)	(b)	(c)	(d)
76.	(a)	(b)	(c)	(d)
77.	(a)	(b)	(c)	(d)
78.	(a)	(b)	(c)	(d)
79.	(a)	(b)	(c)	(d)
80.	(a)	(b)	(c)	(d)

81.	(a)	(b)	(c)	(d)
82.	(a)	(b)	(c)	(d)
83.	(a)	(b)	(c)	(d)
84.	(a)	(b)	(c)	(d)
85.	(a)	(b)	(c)	(d)
86.	(a)	(b)	(c)	(d)
87.	(a)	(b)	(c)	(d)
88.	(a)	(b)	(c)	(d)
89.	(a)	(b)	(c)	(d)
90.	(a)	(b)	(c)	(d)
91.	(a)	(b)	(c)	(d)
92.	(a)	(b)	(c)	(d)
93.	(a)	(b)	(c)	(d)
94.	(a)	(b)	(c)	(d)
95.	(a)	(b)	(c)	(d)
96.	(a)	(b)	(c)	(d)
97.	(a)	(b)	(c)	(d)
98.	(a)	(b)	(c)	(d)
99.	(a)	(b)	(c)	(d)
100.	(a)	(b)	(c)	(d)
101.	(a)	(b)	(c)	(d)
102.	(a)	(b)	(c)	(d)
103.	(a)	(b)	(c)	(d)
104.	(a)	(b)	(c)	(d)
105.	(a)	(b)	(c)	(d)
106.	(a)	(b)	(c)	(d)
107.	(a)	(b)	(c)	(d)
108.	(a)	(b)	(c)	(d)
109.	(a)	(b)	(c)	(d)
110.	(a)	(b)	(c)	(d)
111.	(a)	(b)	(c)	(d)
112.	(a)	(b)	(c)	(d)
113.	(a)	(b)	(c)	(d)
114.	(a)	(b)	(c)	(d)
115.	(a)	(b)	(c)	(d)
116.	(a)	(b)	(c)	(d)
117.	(a)	(b)	(c)	(d)
118.	(a)	(b)	(c)	(d)
119.	(a)	(b)	(c)	(d)
120.	(a)	(b)	(c)	(d)

EMT Practice Exam 7

1. Exhaled air contains_____ oxygen.
   a. 16%
   b. 21%
   c. 5%
   d. 3% to 5%

2. When the level of carbon dioxide increases in the blood, the impulse to breathe
   a. increases.
   b. decreases.
   c. remains the same.
   d. increases and decreases.

3. What are the three primary characteristics that you must evaluate when assessing breath sounds?
   a. Presence, equality, and sounds
   b. Ease, rate, and rhythm
   c. Rate, rhythm, and sounds
   d. Sounds, ease, and depth

4. The scope of practice is most commonly defined by
   a. your medical director.
   b. your standard operating procedures.
   c. medical control.
   d. state law.

5. Upon arrival to the scene of a motor vehicle crash, you should be looking for
   a. hazardous and leaking materials from the vehicles.
   b. vehicle positions and stability.
   c. overhead hazards, such as power lines, trees, etc.
   d. all of the above.

6. When a patient is in anaphylaxis, the exaggerated immune response causes blood vessels to _____ and the airway passages to _____.
   a. constrict, dilate
   b. dilate, dilate
   c. constrict, constrict
   d. dilate, constrict

7. Your patient is a 19-year-old male with a severe nosebleed and no other signs of trauma. In which position should you place him?
   a. flat on his back, with lower extremities elevated
   b. sitting up and leaning forward
   c. prone
   d. supine

8. Using a reservoir with a bag-valve-mask system will allow oxygen levels to increase to nearly
   a. 70%.
   b. 90%.
   c. 80%
   d. 100%.

9. What should you assume when you hear wheezing during respiration?
   a. The small airways are constricted.
   b. The patient cannot keep the airway open.
   c. There is liquid in the airway.
   d. The patient is using accessory muscles.

10. Egg fertilization normally occurs in the
    a. uterus.
    b. fallopian tube.
    c. eustachian tube.
    d. ovary.

11. Another medical term for the womb is
   a. uterus.
   b. birth canal.
   c. cervix.
   d. amniotic sac.

12. As the infant moves through the birth canal during birth, what structure bulges significantly?
   a. perineum
   b. vagina
   c. fundus
   d. abdomen

13. Your patient has a large laceration to the top of his head. This area is best described as
   a. anterior.
   b. posterior.
   c. superior.
   d. proximal.

14. You are dispatched to a residence of a patient who has jumped into the shallow end of a pool headfirst. The scene is safe and the patient is breathing. Your first action should be to
   a. remove the patient from the water.
   b. stabilize the patient's c-spine while the patient is still in the water.
   c. insert an oropharyngeal airway.
   d. place the patient on a backboard.

15. You are dispatched to the scene of a gunshot wound to the abdomen. You would expect this patient's skin to be
   a. pale.
   b. pink.
   c. cyanotic.
   d. jaundiced.

16. Newton's _____ law states that for every action, there is an equal and opposite reaction.
   a. third
   b. first
   c. second
   d. fourth

17. The energy of a moving object is called
   a. velocity.
   b. potential energy.
   c. work.
   d. kinetic energy.

18. What blood vessels supply blood to the heart muscle and are located inferiorly to the aortic valve, starting at the first part of the aorta?
   a. plutonic arteries
   b. superior vena cava
   c. coronary arteries
   d. plutonic veins

19. The _____ deliver(s) blood to all the systemic arteries for transport to the tissues of the body.
   a. aorta
   b. pulmonic veins
   c. capillaries
   d. inferior vena cava

20. What has been the leading killer of Americans since the 1900s?
   a. head injury
   b. cardiovascular disease
   c. suicide
   d. trauma

21. The heart is divided down the middle into two sides (right and left) by a wall called the
  a. atrioventricular wall.
  b. septum.
  c. pericardium.
  d. transverse septal wall.

22. The _____ divides into two major branches, which supply blood to the left ventricle.
  a. left pulmonary vein
  b. left pulmonary artery
  c. right pulmonary artery
  d. left coronary artery

23. You have responded to the scene of a motor vehicle accident and suddenly feel overwhelmed. You should
  a. ask bystanders to call 911 and have them tell the dispatcher that you need more help.
  b. tell yourself it is not your emergency and you are there to help.
  c. not show outward signs of anxiety.
  d. take a step back and call for additional resources.

24. Your patient does not speak English and you do not speak his native language. You should
  a. do your best treating the patient without communicating.
  b. speak louder and slower.
  c. attempt to get a translator.
  d. ignore the patient's rambling and treat his injuries or illness the best that you can.

25. You have contacted the ED for medical direction. The physician has ordered you to assist the patient with the administration of his inhaler and administer two puffs. You should
  a. administer the medication.
  b. shake the inhaler prior to administration.
  c. ask the patient if he has any allergies.
  d. clearly and slowly repeat the orders back to the physician.

26. Decreased blood flow to the heart muscle, due to the narrowing or the partial or complete blockage of the coronary arteries, is referred to as
  a. infarction.
  b. ischemia.
  c. atherosclerosis.
  d. thromboembolism.

27. You are employed as an EMT in a tiered-response system. After assuring scene safety and BSI, your patient is found lying unconscious and unresponsive. Upon exiting the ambulance, you should first
  a. check his airway.
  b. check the patient for a pulse.
  c. apply oxygen.
  d. request paramedics to be dispatched to your location.

28. Your patient has suffered from an apparent heart attack. You should transport this patient to
  a. the closest hospital.
  b. a facility that has the capabilities for emergent angioplasty.
  c. the facility that is approved by and stated in your protocols.
  d. a level one cardiac center.

29. When a patient's breathing is reduced to the point where the oxygen intake is not enough to support life, the result is
   a. respiratory distress.
   b. agonal respirations.
   c. adventitious breath sounds.
   d. respiratory failure.

30. Which of the following is NOT a component of BVM?
   a. air chamber
   b. face mask
   c. one-way valve
   d. capnography

31. Which of the following is the best indicator for adequate ventilations when using a bag valve mask?
   a. skin color
   b. chest rise and fall
   c. O₂ saturation
   d. breath sounds

32. You are dispatched to a call for chest pain. The patient tells you the pain began approximately 20 minutes earlier while they were reading. The pain is crushing in nature and it has not gotten better after two nitroglycerin tablets. This patient is describing
   a. acute myocardial infarction.
   b. stable angina.
   c. unstable angina.
   d. spontaneous pneumothorax.

33. Which of the following carries sperm from the testicles to the urethra?
   a. ureter
   b. vas deferens
   c. seminal vesicle
   d. seminal ductus

34. The pancreas is located in the
   a. upper left quadrant.
   b. upper right quadrant.
   c. lower left quadrant.
   d. retroperitoneal space.

35. _____ is the bending of a joint.
   a. Extension
   b. Adduction
   c. Flexion
   d. Abduction

36. The bottom of the foot is referred to as the _____ surface.
   a. superior
   b. palmar
   c. plantar
   d. ventral

37. The coccyx is composed of _____ vertebrae fused together.
   a. two or three
   b. four or five
   c. seven
   d. three

38. The umbilical cord contains _____ blood vessel(s).
   a. two
   b. three
   c. one
   d. four

39. The placental barrier consists of _____ layers of cells and allows for nutrients and waste to be passed between the mother and the fetus.
   a. two
   b. four
   c. three
   d. five

40. The _____ carries oxygenated blood from the mother to the baby's heart.
a. placenta
b. umbilical vein
c. umbilical artery
d. amniotic sac

41. The _____ carries deoxygenated blood from the baby's heart to the mother.
a. umbilical artery
b. placenta
c. umbilical vein
d. bag of waters

42. In a frontal impact motor vehicle crash, there are typically three collisions that take place. The second collision is
a. the initial vehicle against another vehicle or object.
b. the organs against another structure or organ in the body.
c. the patient against the interior of the vehicle.
d. none of the above.

43. You are assessing a patient who was involved in a motor vehicle crash. He has injuries to his shoulder and temporal region. By this injury pattern, you would suspect a
a. frontal impact.
b. lateral impact.
c. rear impact.
d. rollover.

44. If the velocity of a bullet is doubled, the energy that is available to cause damage is
a. the same.
b. doubled.
c. tripled.
d. quadrupled.

45. Your concern for potentially serious underlying injuries is called
a. cause for concern.
b. index of suspicion.
c. nature of injury.
d. mechanism of injury.

46. When setting the tidal volume on an Automatic Transport Ventilator the EMT should increase the setting until
a. the peak inspiratory alarm sounds, then decrease by 10 ml.
b. the relief valve activates, then decrease by 10 ml.
c. the patient's chest rises and falls adequately.
d. none of the above.

47. The injury potential of a fall is directly related to the
a. patient's height.
b. patient's weight.
c. patient's age.
d. height from which the patient fell.

48. The electrical impulse is slowed to one- or two-tenths of a second to allow blood to pass into the ventricles at what part of the heart?
a. SA node
b. internodal pathway
c. AV node
d. left bundle branch

49. During physical exertion in the normal functioning heart, the increased need for blood supply is easily obtained by
a. dilation of the coronary arteries.
b. narrowing of the peripheral arteries.
c. dilation of the pulmonary arteries.
d. decreasing the pulse rate.

50. The _____ supply blood to the upper extremities.
  a. brachial arteries
  b. carotid arteries
  c. subclavian arteries
  d. radial arteries

51. The _____ arteries supply blood to the pelvis, groin, and legs.
  a. femoral
  b. iliac
  c. popliteal
  d. posterior tibial

52. _____ have the thickness of approximately one cell and connect arterioles to venules.
  a. Bronchioles
  b. Red blood cells
  c. Venule branches
  d. Capillaries

53. Because of the blockage (partial or complete) of blood flow through the coronary arteries, the heart muscle and other tissues fail to get enough oxygen. This insufficient amount of oxygen is also called
  a. cellular death.
  b. ischemia.
  c. narcosis.
  d. atherosclerosis.

54. _____ help(s) the blood to clot.
  a. Red blood cells
  b. Platelets
  c. White blood cells
  d. Plasma

55. You are assessing a 16 year-old male patient who is complaining of a sudden onset of dull, non-specific chest and upper abdominal pain. The patient also states that his arms feel heavy and numb. The patient denies recent injury, illness, or allergies. You notice a white powdery substance on the table, but the patient denies drug use. The EMT should recognize the patient may be suffering from?
  a. myocardial ischemia.
  b. abdominal aortic aneurysm.
  c. cerebral vascular accident.
  d. indigestion.

56. When lifting a patient who is in a sitting position and has no suspected spinal injury, the _____ should be used.
  a. extremity lift
  b. emergency move
  c. direct ground lift
  d. scoop stretcher

57. Which of the following is NOT an immunization recommended for EMS personnel?
  a. mumps
  b. tetanus
  c. varicella
  d. measles

58. A legal statement that states the patient's wishes regarding his or her own healthcare is called a(n)
  a. do not resuscitate order.
  b. statutory will.
  c. advance directive.
  d. testamentary trust will.

59. You are treating a patient for cardiac chest pain. Medical control has ordered you to administer 324 mg of ASA by mouth. What is a contraindication for the administration of aspirin?
   a. Blood pressure < 100 mmHg
   b. Patient has a recent history of GI bleeding
   c. Patient has recently taken erectile dysfunction medication
   d. Pulse rate is > 100 bpm

60. When transmitting a radio report to the receiving facility, you should not include the patient's
   a. medical history.
   b. age.
   c. mechanism of injury.
   d. name.

61. The *Ryan White Act* requires a hospital to notify your department's designated officer within _____ hours of the time a patient is identified with an infectious disease.
   a. 12
   b. 24
   c. 48
   d. 36

62. A bag valve mask that is not attached to oxygen delivers oxygen at what percentage?
   a. 100%
   b. 75%
   c. 21%
   d. 50%

63. How does the air pressure outside of the body normally compare with the pressure within the thorax?
   a. The pressures are the same.
   b. The pressure outside of the body is higher.
   c. The pressure outside of the body is lower.
   d. The pressure varies with the age of the patient.

64. After _____ minutes without oxygen, cells in the nervous system may die or be permanently damaged.
   a. four to six
   b. two to four
   c. zero to four
   d. one to three

65. Pink, frothy sputum is typically seen with a patient who has
   a. pulmonary edema.
   b. COPD.
   c. asthma.
   d. ARDS.

66. During exhalation, the diaphragm moves
   a. upward.
   b. downward.
   c. inward.
   d. side to side.

67. The passive process in which molecules from an area of higher concentration move to an area of lower concentration is
   a. osmosis.
   b. equalization.
   c. diffusion.
   d. metabolization.

68. The chemical that is inside alveoli and helps keep the alveoli open is called
   a. synovial fluid.
   b. surfactant.
   c. carbon dioxide.
   d. vitreous.

69. The _____ cavity contains the great vessels.
   a. abdominal
   b. chest (thorax)
   c. retroperitoneal
   d. vertebral

70. What separates the chest from the abdominal cavity?
   a. umbilicus
   b. costal arch
   c. diaphragm
   d. xiphoid process

71. What is the major artery that is located in the forearm and is palpable at the wrist along the thumb?
   a. ulnar artery
   b. brachial artery
   c. radial artery
   d. tibial artery

72. The gland that is responsible for metabolism regulation is the
   a. thyroid.
   b. pituitary.
   c. pancreas.
   d. adrenal.

73. Normal skin is _____ to the touch.
   a. cool
   b. diaphoretic
   c. dry
   d. moist

74. The amniotic sac normally contains _____ of fluid.
   a. 200–500 mL
   b. 500–1,000 mL
   c. 1,000–1,500 mL
   d. 1,000–2,000 mL

75. A full-term pregnancy is usually _____ weeks from the first day of the mother's last menstrual period.
   a. 30–36
   b. 32–38
   c. 36–38
   d. 36–40

76. Deliveries that occur before _____ weeks gestation are considered premature.
   a. 26
   b. 28
   c. 36
   d. 22

77. The fetus develops inside a membrane called the
   a. amniotic sac.
   b. placenta.
   c. uterine wall.
   d. fallopian tube.

78. Your first preparation for the delivery of an infant should be
   a. notifying the receiving facility.
   b. BSI precautions.
   c. applying oxygen to the mother.
   d. preparing a sterile environment.

79. The manner in which a traumatic injury occurs is the
   a. nature of illness.
   b. injury pattern.
   c. mechanism of injury.
   d. chief complaint.

80. Blood clots form in the body depending on the blood's ability to clot, blood stasis, and
   a. the amount of blood available.
   b. changes in the vessel wall.
   c. the amount of white blood cells in the blood.
   d. the amount of red blood cells in the blood.

81. During emergencies, the _____ redirects blood away from other organs and sends it to the brain, heart, lungs, and kidneys.
   a. cardiovascular system
   b. circulatory system
   c. somatic nervous system
   d. autonomic nervous system

82. The average-sized adult has approximately _____ of blood volume.
   a. six liters
   b. nine liters
   c. eight liters
   d. eight pints

83. A condition where a patient lacks one or more of the body's clotting factors is called
   a. anemia.
   b. hemophilia.
   c. leukemia.
   d. neutropenia.

84. When the aortic valve closes, blood flow
   a. stops.
   b. continues into the ventricles.
   c. slows to allow filling of the atria.
   d. increases in order to travel to the peripheral arteries.

85. _____ are found in all parts of the body and allow for the exchange of waste and nutrients at the cellular level.
   a. Arterioles
   b. Venules
   c. Alveoli
   d. Capillaries

86. Blood enters the system of veins starting with the
   a. capillaries.
   b. arterioles.
   c. venules.
   d. arteries.

87. A controllable risk factor for coronary artery disease is
   a. gender.
   b. elevated blood glucose levels.
   c. family history of atherosclerotic coronary artery disease.
   d. none of the above.

88. A danger zone is an area where individuals can be exposed to hazardous materials, toxic substances, sharp metals, etc. This zone is also referred to as a
   a. warm zone.
   b. cold zone.
   c. quarantine zone.
   d. hot zone.

89. You respond to a single-vehicle crash. Upon arrival at the scene, you see the car has impacted a power pole and there are downed power lines lying across the car. You should
   a. enter the area carefully and be aware of surrounding hazards.
   b. attempt to access the patient(s), while making sure that you are safely grounded.
   c. instruct the patient(s) to remain in the vehicle until the power is turned off or removed.
   d. approach the car carefully and do not touch the area of the car that the power lines are touching.

90. In which of the following situations should you NOT initiate CPR?
   a. The patient's spouse is adamant that you not perform CPR.
   b. The patient has a living will written in his own handwriting, which is signed by the patient but not witnessed.
   c. The patient's guardian has provided a valid DNR.
   d. Prior to becoming pulseless and apneic, the patient stated—in your presence—that he wanted to die and wants no measures performed to save him.

91. The removal of a motor vehicle from around a patient is called
   a. disentrapment.
   b. extrication.
   c. extraction.
   d. disentanglement.

92. If the reduction of blood flow and resultant hypoxia to the myocardium, due to a narrowing or blockage of the coronary arteries, is not restored in a timely manner a person may suffer from
   a. a thromboembolism.
   b. a pulmonary embolism.
   c. a myocardial ischemia.
   d. a myocardial infarction.

93. You are first on the scene of a patient who is unconscious and not breathing. The only equipment you have on your person is a pocket mask. You provide artificial ventilations with the pocket mask. What concentration of oxygen is the patient receiving with each breath?
   a. 16%
   b. 21%
   c. 3%
   d. 79%

94. You are dispatched to a patient who is complaining of shortness of breath. This is also called
   a. orthopnea.
   b. dysphagia.
   c. tachypnea.
   d. dyspnea.

95. When fluid accumulates in the lungs, it interferes with the gas exchange. This condition is called
   a. COPD.
   b. chronic bronchitis.
   c. pulmonary edema.
   d. asthma.

96. You are responding to a patient who has overdosed on sedatives. You would expect his respirations to be
   a. decreased and shallow.
   b. decreased and deep.
   c. increased and shallow.
   d. increased and deep.

97. When inserting a nasopharyngeal airway, the curvature of the device should follow the _____ of the nose.
   a. top
   b. side
   c. septum
   d. floor

98. You have inserted a nasopharyngeal airway, and the patient is not tolerant of it. You should
   a. insert the device in the other nostril.
   b. administer a sedative.
   c. try to calm the patient.
   d. remove the device.

99. A yellowish tint to the skin and conjunctiva is called
   a. flush.
   b. pallor.
   c. jaundice.
   d. cyanotic.

100. When determining if a patient has a behavioral emergency, you should first
   a. have law enforcement respond to place the person in custody.
   b. rule out any medical problems or emergencies.
   c. see what medications the patient is prescribed.
   d. interview bystanders.

101. Stable patients should be reevaluated at a minimum of every
   a. 5 minutes.
   b. 10 minutes.
   c. 15 minutes.
   d. None of the above.

102. A head bleed that is characterized by a loss of consciousness, a lucid period, then loss of consciousness again is a(n)
   a. epidural.
   b. subarachnoid.
   c. subdural.
   d. None of the above.

103. What kind of shock is caused by severe infections that abnormally dilate blood vessels?
   a. psychogenic
   b. hypovolemic
   c. neurogenic
   d. septic

104. To assist in the delivery of the placenta,
   a. massage the mother's abdomen in a circular motion.
   b. gently pull on the umbilical cord.
   c. tell the mother to push continuously after the infant is born.
   d. do not worry about the delivery of the placenta.

105. You are assessing a non-gravid female with profuse vaginal bleeding after an unknown injury. She has a tear noted just outside of the vagina. Treatment should include all the following EXCEPT to
   a. remove any foreign body.
   b. apply a sterile moist compress to the tear.
   c. perform ongoing assessments.
   d. apply local pressure.

106. You have just assisted in the delivery of an infant. He has no muscle tone, slow respirations, and a heart rate of 98. His hands and feet are blue. What is this infant's APGAR score?
   a. one
   b. two
   c. three
   d. four

107. In a breech presentation, which part of the infant presents first?
   a. lower limbs
   b. buttocks
   c. umbilical cord
   d. head

108. In a breech presentation, if the mother does not deliver within ten minutes of presentation, what should you do?
  a. Promptly transport the mother to the hospital.
  b. Gently massage the mother's abdomen in a circular motion.
  c. Gently pull on the presented part of the infant.
  d. Lay the mother left lateral recumbent and tell her to keep her knees together.

109. You are assessing a patient who has suffered from a significant fall. He begins to vomit bright, red blood. This is called
  a. melena.
  b. hemoptysis.
  c. hematuria.
  d. hematemesis.

110. You have been dispatched to a patient who has fallen through a pane of glass and has a possible arterial bleed. The minimum BSI precautions you should take are
  a. gloves.
  b. gloves and a gown.
  c. a gown and eye protection.
  d. gloves and eye protection.

111. You have applied the PASG to a patient. You should monitor the vital signs
  a. every 10 minutes.
  b. every 5 minutes.
  c. every 15 minutes.
  d. once before application and then again after application.

112. You would apply the PASG in which of the following conditions?
  a. a transport time of 30 minutes or less
  b. to control massive soft tissue bleeding in the lower extremities
  c. pulmonary edema
  d. a distal femur fracture

113. One of the earliest signs of cardiogenic shock is
  a. pale skin.
  b. increased pulse rate.
  c. rapid, shallow breathing.
  d. anxiety.

114. Complete cessation of cardiac activity is called
  a. cardiac arrest.
  b. asystole.
  c. ventricular cessation.
  d. sinus arrest.

115. A monitor/defibrillator that delivers a shock by sending energy in a flow from negative to positive is
  a. automated.
  b. biphasic.
  c. monophasic.
  d. triphasic.

116. During delivery, the mother will experience some bleeding. What amount of bleeding is considered to be excessive?
  a. greater than 275 mL
  b. greater than 300 mL
  c. greater than 375 mL
  d. greater than 500 mL

117. A developmental defect in which the infant's spinal cord or meninges protrudes outside of the vertebrae or body is called
   a. spinal meningitis.
   b. spina bifida.
   c. spinal scoliosis.
   d. spinal subluxation.

118. You are dispatched to a call of an infant with shortness of breath. Upon assessing the infant, you ascertain that the respiratory rate is 32. This finding is
   a. normal.
   b. agonal.
   c. tachypneic.
   d. shallow.

119. A proper-sized BVM for neonatal resuscitation would have a _____mL reservoir.
   a. 450
   b. 550
   c. 250
   d. 600

120. The individual who has overall command of the scene in the field is the
   a. battalion chief.
   b. incident commander.
   c. medical director.
   d. state officer.

Answers

1. a. Exhaled air contains 16% oxygen.

2. a. The brain stem contains nerves that act as sensors to monitor the level of carbon dioxide in blood. When the level of carbon dioxide becomes too high, impulses are sent from the brain stem and down the spinal cord, causing the diaphragm and abdominal muscles to contract. The higher the level of carbon dioxide, the stronger the impulse. This increases the respiratory rate.

3. a. The three primary characteristics that you must evaluate when assessing breath sounds are presence, equality, and sounds.

4. d. State law defines the scope of practice. Your medical director then further defines it by creating and writing your protocols and SOPs.

5. d. Upon arriving on the scene of a motor vehicle crash, you should perform the scene size-up before exiting your vehicle. This should include looking for overhead hazards, such as power lines and trees, looking at the stability of the vehicles involved, and observing for hazardous and leaking materials from the vehicles.

6. d. When a patient is in anaphylaxis, the exaggerated immune response causes blood vessels to dilate and the airway passages to constrict.

7. b. Have the patient sit up and lean forward so the blood does not enter the airway or stomach.

8. d. The use of a reservoir ensures that the patient receives the highest concentration of oxygen available.

9. a. Wheezing indicates that smaller airways and bronchioles are constricted, usually because of infection or allergy. Fluid is only one of the possible reasons; bronchial constriction is another cause.

10. b. Egg fertilization *normally* occurs in the fallopian tube.

11. a. A medical term for the womb is *uterus*.

12. a. As the infant moves through the birth canal during birth, the perineum will bulge significantly.

13. c. Superior is the part of the torso or any other part of the body that is close to the head.

14. b. Any patient who has a suspected spinal injury should have his c-spine immobilized while the EMT simultaneously assesses his airway. This includes stabilizing the c-spine prior to moving a patient out of water.

15. a. A patient who has sustained an open wound to the abdomen will usually have pale skin. This is due to the shunting of blood to the most vital organs.

16. a. Newton's third law states that for every action, there is an equal and opposite reaction.

17. d. Kinetic energy is the energy of a moving object.

18. c. Coronary arteries, which are located inferiorly to the aortic valve beginning at the first part of the aorta, supply blood to the heart muscle.

19. a. The aorta delivers blood to all the systemic arteries for transport to the tissues of the body.

20. b. Cardiovascular disease has been the leading killer of Americans since the 1900s.

21. b. The heart is divided down the middle into two sides (right and left) by the septum.

22. d. The left coronary artery divides into two major branches, which supply blood to the left ventricle.

23. d. If you are on a call and start feeling overwhelmed, the safest thing for you to do for yourself and your patient(s) is to take a step back and call for additional resources.

24. c. If there is a language barrier while assessing and treating a patient, make every attempt to get a translator.

25. d. When an order has been received by medical control, clearly and slowly repeat the orders as stated by the physician, prior to administering any treatment modality.

26. b. The reduction of blood flow to the heart muscle, myocardium, defines ischemia. An infarct is the death of tissue, atherosclerosis causes narrowing of the arteries, and a thromboembolism may cause a complete or partial blockage of the arteries.

27. d. Part of the scene size-up includes requesting additional units. In this situation, it is in the best interest of the patient to obtain care from an advanced life support unit.

28. c. Always follow your local protocols.

29. d. Respiratory failure is when a patient's breathing is reduced to the point where the oxygen intake is not enough to support life.

30. d. Capnography is not a component of BVM.

31. b. Although all the answers are correct in some way, the *best* answer that indicates adequate ventilations administered via BVM is by observing chest rise and fall.

32. c. This patient is describing unstable angina, which is characterized by chest pain that occurs at rest or wakes the patient from sleep, lasts 20 minutes or longer, and is not relieved by nitroglycerin. Unstable angina can lead to an AMI if not treated in a timely manner.

33. b. The vas deferens carry sperm from the testicles to the urethra.

34. d. The pancreas along with the kidneys is not part of the abdomen, but is located in the retroperitoneal space.

35. c. Flexion is the bending of a joint.

36. c. The bottom of the foot is referred to as the *plantar surface.*

37. b. The coccyx is composed of four or five vertebrae, which are fused together.

38. b. The umbilical cord contains three blood vessels.

39. a. The placental barrier consists of two layers of cells and allows for the exchange of nutrients and waste between the fetus and the mother.

40. b. The umbilical vein carries oxygenated blood from the mother to the baby's heart.

41. a. The umbilical artery carries deoxygenated blood from the baby's heart to the mother.

42. c. The second collision in a motor vehicle crash is when the patient collides against the interior of the vehicle.

43. b. Typically, injuries to the shoulder and temporal region occur during a lateral impact.

44. d. If the velocity of a bullet is doubled, the energy that is available to cause damage is quadrupled.

45. b. Your concern for potentially serious underlying injuries is called an *index of suspicion.*

46. c. The EMT should set the tidal volume based on the rise and fall of the patient's chest and physiologic response of the patient. The peak inspiratory alarm and relief valve help prevent barotraumas or other injuries, but do not indicate adequate tidal volume.

47. d. The injury potential of a fall is directly related to the height from which the patient fell.

48. c. The electrical impulse is slowed to one- or two-tenths of a second at the AV node to allow blood to pass into the ventricles.

49. a. In the normally functioning heart, the increased need for blood supply during physical exertion is obtained by the dilation of the coronary arteries.

50. c. The subclavian arteries supply blood to the upper extremities.

51. b. The iliac arteries supply blood to the pelvis, groin, and legs.

52. d. Capillaries have the thickness of approximately one cell and connect arterioles to venules.

53. b. Insufficient oxygen supply to the heart and tissues is called *ischemia.*

54. b. Platelets are responsible for helping the blood to clot.

55. a. Even though the patient denies drug use, the possibility of drug use, especially cocaine, coupled with the patient's chief complaint and history, should alert the EMT to a cardiac event in this young patient. An aortic aneurysm would present with a sharp and tearing pain and a CVA would not generally present with chest or abdominal pain. Although indigestion is possible, the EMT should always assume life threatening illnesses until they are ruled out.

56. a. The extremity lift should be used when lifting a patient who has no suspected spinal injury and is in a seated position.

57. c. Varicella is not a required immunization for EMS personnel.

58. c. An advance directive is a legal statement that states the patient's wishes regarding his or her own healthcare.

59. b. The contraindications for the administration of ASA to a patient with suspected cardiac chest pain include the patient being allergic to ASA, the patient having a recent history of GI bleeding, or the patient is unable to chew and swallow the medication.

60. d. When transmitting a radio report to the receiving facility, the patient's name should *not* be included.

61. c. The *Ryan White Act* requires a hospital to notify the responding unit's designated department officer within 48 hours of the time a patient is identified with an infectious disease.

62. c. A bag valve mask that is not attached to oxygen delivers oxygen at 21%.

63. b. The air pressure outside of the body is normally higher than the pressure within the thorax.

64. a. After four to six minutes without oxygen, cells in the nervous system may die or be permanently damaged.

65. a. Pink, frothy sputum is typically seen in a patient who is suffering from pulmonary edema.

66. a. During exhalation, the diaphragm moves upward.

67. c. Diffusion is the process in which molecules from an area of higher concentration move to an area of lower concentration.

68. b. Alveoli contain a chemical called *surfactant* that helps keep them from collapsing.

69. b. The chest cavity (thorax) contains the great vessels.

70. c. The diaphragm separates the chest from the abdominal cavity.

71. c. The radial artery is palpable in the forearm along the thumb side of the wrist.

72. a. The thyroid gland is responsible for metabolism regulation.

73. c. Normal skin is dry to the touch.

74. b. The amniotic sac normally contains 500 mL to 1,000 mL of fluid.

75. d. A full-term pregnancy is usually 36–40 weeks from the first day of the mother's last menstrual period.

76. c. Deliveries that occur before 36 weeks gestation are considered premature.

77. a. The fetus develops inside a membrane called the *amniotic sac.*

78. b. Your *first* preparation for the delivery of an infant is BSI precautions. At a minimum, gloves and eye shielding should be used.

79. c. The manner in which a traumatic injury occurs is the mechanism of injury.

80. b. Blood clots form in the body depending on the blood's ability to clot, blood stasis, and changes in the vessel wall.

81. d. During emergencies, the autonomic nervous system redirects blood away from the other organs, sending it to the brain, heart, lungs, and kidneys.

82. a. The average-sized adult has approximately six liters of blood volume.

83. b. Hemophilia is a condition where a patient lacks one or more of the body's clotting factors.

84. a. When the aortic valve closes, blood flow stops.

85. d. Capillaries are found in all parts of the body and allow for the exchange of wastes and nutrients at the cellular level.

86. c. Blood enters the system of veins starting with the venules.

87. b. Elevated blood glucose levels are a controllable risk factor for coronary artery disease.

88. d. A hot zone, also called a danger zone, is an area where individuals can be exposed to hazardous materials, toxic substances, sharp metals, etc.

89. c. If power lines are lying across a car, you must instruct the individuals to remain in the vehicle until the power is turned off or removed. Do not approach the car until you are directed to by the power company.

90. c. When a valid DNR is presented, CPR should *not* be initiated.

91. d. Disentanglement is the removal of a motor vehicle from around a patient.

92. d. If blood flow to the myocardium is not returned to normal in a timely manner, then the myocardium will begin to die. This is the definition of an acute myocardial infarction (AMI). Myocardial ischemia is the decreased blood flow to the heart tissue. A thrombo-embolism may cause the blockage resulting in reduced blood flow and a pulmonary embolism may cause a reduced blood flow to the lungs/ischemia to the lung tissue.

93. a. Artificial ventilations that are administered with a pocket mask deliver 16% oxygen with each breath given.

94. d. *Dyspnea* is another term for shortness of breath.

95. c. The accumulation of fluid in the lungs is called *pulmonary edema*. This condition interferes with the gas exchange in the alveoli.

96. a. Sedatives will cause respirations to be decreased and shallow.

97. d. When inserting a nasopharyngeal airway, the curvature of the device should follow the floor of the nose.

98. d. If a patient does not tolerate a nasopharyngeal airway, remove it.

99. c. A yellow tint to the skin and conjunctiva is called *jaundice*.

100. b. When determining if a patient has a behavioral emergency, you should first rule out any medical problems or emergencies.

101. c. Stable patients should be reevaluated at a minimum of every 15 minutes.

102. a. An epidural bleed is characterized by a loss of consciousness, a lucid period, and the loss of consciousness again.

103. d. Septic shock is caused by severe infections that abnormally dilate blood vessels.

104. a. To assist in the delivery of the placenta, massage the mother's abdomen over the fundus in a circular motion.

105. a. Foreign bodies or impaled objects should be left in place and stabilized with bulky dressings.

106. c. This infant's APGAR score is three. A = 1, P = 1, G = 0, A = 0, and R = 1.

107. b. In a breech presentation, the buttocks present first.

108. a. In a breech presentation, if the mother does not deliver within ten minutes of the presentation, promptly transport the mother to the hospital.

109. d. Hematemesis is the vomiting of bright red or dark blood.

110. d. When there is a suspicion of severe bleeding, gloves and eye protection should be applied at a minimum.

111. b. When the PASG has been applied to a patient, recheck the patient's vital signs every five minutes.

112. b. The PASG can be applied on a patient to control massive soft tissue bleeding in the lower extremities.

113. d. Anxiety is one of the earliest signs of cardiogenic shock.

114. a. Complete cessation of cardiac activity is called *cardiac arrest*.

115. c. A monophasic defibrillator delivers a shock by sending energy in a flow from negative to positive.

116. d. Postdelivery, a mother will experience some vaginal bleeding. This bleeding is considered excessive if it is greater than 500 mL.

117. b. Spina bifida is a developmental defect in which the infant's spinal cord or meninges protrudes outside of the vertebrae or body.

118. a. A respiratory rate of 32 is normal in an infant.

119. a. A proper-sized BVM for neonatal resuscitation has a reservoir of 450 mL.

120. b. The incident commander has overall command of the scene in the field.

10 ▶ EMT PRACTICE EXAM 8

CHAPTER SUMMARY
This is the eighth of ten practice exams in this book based on the National Registry's EMT cognitive exam. Use this test to continue your study and practice. Notice how knowing what to expect on the exam makes you feel better prepared!

Like the other practice exams you've completed, this exam is based on the National Registry's cognitive exam for EMT Exams, which is outlined in Chapter 1.

An answer sheet for recording your responses appears next. Following the exam is an answer key, with all detailed explanations. These explanations will help you see where you need to concentrate your studies. When you've finished the exam and scored it, examine your weak areas so that you'll know which parts of your textbook to concentrate on before you take the next practice exam.

1.	a	b	c	d	41.	a	b	c	d	81.	a	b	c	d
2.	a	b	c	d	42.	a	b	c	d	82.	a	b	c	d
3.	a	b	c	d	43.	a	b	c	d	83.	a	b	c	d
4.	a	b	c	d	44.	a	b	c	d	84.	a	b	c	d
5.	a	b	c	d	45.	a	b	c	d	85.	a	b	c	d
6.	a	b	c	d	46.	a	b	c	d	86.	a	b	c	d
7.	a	b	c	d	47.	a	b	c	d	87.	a	b	c	d
8.	a	b	c	d	48.	a	b	c	d	88.	a	b	c	d
9.	a	b	c	d	49.	a	b	c	d	89.	a	b	c	d
10.	a	b	c	d	50.	a	b	c	d	90.	a	b	c	d
11.	a	b	c	d	51.	a	b	c	d	91.	a	b	c	d
12.	a	b	c	d	52.	a	b	c	d	92.	a	b	c	d
13.	a	b	c	d	53.	a	b	c	d	93.	a	b	c	d
14.	a	b	c	d	54.	a	b	c	d	94.	a	b	c	d
15.	a	b	c	d	55.	a	b	c	d	95.	a	b	c	d
16.	a	b	c	d	56.	a	b	c	d	96.	a	b	c	d
17.	a	b	c	d	57.	a	b	c	d	97.	a	b	c	d
18.	a	b	c	d	58.	a	b	c	d	98.	a	b	c	d
19.	a	b	c	d	59.	a	b	c	d	99.	a	b	c	d
20.	a	b	c	d	60.	a	b	c	d	100.	a	b	c	d
21.	a	b	c	d	61.	a	b	c	d	101.	a	b	c	d
22.	a	b	c	d	62.	a	b	c	d	102.	a	b	c	d
23.	a	b	c	d	63.	a	b	c	d	103.	a	b	c	d
24.	a	b	c	d	64.	a	b	c	d	104.	a	b	c	d
25.	a	b	c	d	65.	a	b	c	d	105.	a	b	c	d
26.	a	b	c	d	66.	a	b	c	d	106.	a	b	c	d
27.	a	b	c	d	67.	a	b	c	d	107.	a	b	c	d
28.	a	b	c	d	68.	a	b	c	d	108.	a	b	c	d
29.	a	b	c	d	69.	a	b	c	d	109.	a	b	c	d
30.	a	b	c	d	70.	a	b	c	d	110.	a	b	c	d
31.	a	b	c	d	71.	a	b	c	d	111.	a	b	c	d
32.	a	b	c	d	72.	a	b	c	d	112.	a	b	c	d
33.	a	b	c	d	73.	a	b	c	d	113.	a	b	c	d
34.	a	b	c	d	74.	a	b	c	d	114.	a	b	c	d
35.	a	b	c	d	75.	a	b	c	d	115.	a	b	c	d
36.	a	b	c	d	76.	a	b	c	d	116.	a	b	c	d
37.	a	b	c	d	77.	a	b	c	d	117.	a	b	c	d
38.	a	b	c	d	78.	a	b	c	d	118.	a	b	c	d
39.	a	b	c	d	79.	a	b	c	d	119.	a	b	c	d
40.	a	b	c	d	80.	a	b	c	d	120.	a	b	c	d

EMT Practice Exam 8

1. You are assessing a patient who is complaining of weakness and syncope. His pulse rate is 42 and his blood pressure is 108/60. His wife states that he has a pacemaker. You should initially suspect that
a. he is having an acute myocardial infarction.
b. he is hypoglycemic.
c. his pacemaker is malfunctioning.
d. he is dehydrated.

2. You have responded to a patient who has had a sudden onset of unconsciousness and unresponsiveness. His family states that he has an automated implantable cardiac defibrillator (AICD). He has no pulse and the AED has advised there is a shockable rhythm. The EMT should
a. ensure the pads are clear of the AICD and defibrillate.
b. use the pediatric pads to reduce the energy level.
c. not defibrillate a patient with an AICD.
d. start CPR, but withhold defibrillation.

3. What carries blood from the body to the right atrium?
a. vena cava
b. aorta
c. pulmonary vein
d. pulmonary artery

4. What carries blood from the right ventricle to the lungs for gas exchange?
a. aorta
b. vena cava
c. pulmonary artery
d. pulmonary vein

5. Arteries become smaller and smaller until they develop into
a. arterioles.
b. capillaries.
c. venules.
d. alveoli.

6. You are treating a patient complaining of chest pain who suddenly collapses and becomes unresponsive. You immediately assess the patient's airway, breathing, and circulation and determine the patient is unresponsive, apneic, and pulseless. The reason you determine the patient does not have a pulse prior to applying the AED is most likely which of the following?
a. The AED will not analyze if it senses a pulse
b. You must begin CPR prior to applying the AED
c. The AED will shock ventricular tachydcardia with a pulse
d. The AED will not shock a patient with a pulse

7. Select the correct order of treatment for the traumatic injury patient.
    1. control significant bleeding
    2. body substance isolation (BSI)
    3. airway and breathing
    4. transport decision
a. 2, 3, 1, 4
b. 2, 1, 3, 4
c. 2, 3, 4, 1
d. 4, 2, 3, 1

8. You suspect hypovolemic shock in your trauma patient. What can you do to treat this condition?
a. Administer dopamine.
b. Control obvious bleeding.
c. Administer vasoconstrictors (epinephrine).
d. Give fluids *per os* (P.O.).

9. You are assessing a patient who has bruising and blue-and-black discoloration to the skin. This is also called a(n)
   a. erythema.
   b. hematoma.
   c. eczema.
   d. contusion.

10. A patient who has a compression injury may develop a serious condition in which fluid can leak in the spaces between cells. Blood vessels also become compressed, inhibiting blood flow to the surrounding tissues. This condition is called
    a. compression syndrome.
    b. compartment syndrome.
    c. decompression syndrome.
    d. a hematoma.

11. To determine the responsiveness in a child, you should
    a. shake the child.
    b. speak loudly and shake the child.
    c. tap the child on the shoulder while speaking loudly.
    d. administer two breaths.

12. You are assessing a patient who is approximately 24-hours postpartum and is complaining of a sudden onset of severe chest pain and shortness of breath. You suspect
    a. postpartum hemorrhage.
    b. eclampsia.
    c. pulmonary embolism.
    d. myocardial infarction.

13. Painless, bright red blood is usually present with
    a. spontaneous abortion.
    b. cervical rupture.
    c. placenta previa.
    d. abruption placenta.

14. The umbilical cord normally contains
    a. one artery and one vein.
    b. two arteries and one vein.
    c. two veins and one artery.
    d. two veins and two arteries.

15. Which of the following is NOT a cause for fetal bradycardia?
    a. epidural medications
    b. hypoxia
    c. narcotics
    d. maternal anxiety

16. If a diabetic patient takes his insulin but does not eat, the condition that he may develop is called
    a. diabetic ketoacidosis.
    b. hyperglycemia.
    c. hypoglycemia.
    d. diabetic coma.

17. In the early stage of hypothermia, respirations will be
    a. rapid.
    b. slow.
    c. normal.
    d. deep.

18. Which of the following is the membrane that lies directly over the brain tissue?
    a. dura mater
    b. pia mater
    c. arachnoid membrane
    d. cranial membrane

19. What part of the brain is responsible for coordination?
    a. brain stem
    b. cerebrum
    c. cerebellum
    d. medulla oblongata

20. Your patient has been stung by a bee. You notice that the stinger is still visible. How would you remove the stinger?
   a. You would stick a piece of tape on the area, then quickly pull it off.
   b. Using a gloved hand, you would attempt to pull the stinger out with your fingers.
   c. You would scrape it out, using a plastic card.
   d. You would not attempt to remove the stinger.

21. When testing your suction equipment prior to use, you should turn it on and make sure that it is able to generate a vacuum of more than _____mmHg.
   a. 100
   b. 550
   c. 1,000
   d. 300

22. You are suctioning a patient and are unable to clear the debris from her airway. You should
   a. do a blind sweep of the mouth using your fingers.
   b. keep attempting to suction the airway.
   c. roll the patient onto her side and attempt to clear her mouth with your gloved hand.
   d. attempt to ventilate the patient.

23. While suctioning an adult patient, he continuously produces pink, frothy sputum, and his airway fills as fast as you are able to suction it. In this circumstance, you should suction the patient for _____ seconds and ventilate him for _____ minute(s), continuing this pattern until the secretions have been cleared from the airway.
   a. 10, 1
   b. 10, 2
   c. 15, 2
   d. 30, 1

24. To maintain a patent airway in a uninjured patient who is breathing on his own, the patient should be placed in the _____ position.
   a. Trendelenburg
   b. recovery
   c. supine
   d. prone

25. What is the name of the safety system for large, compressed gas cylinders, such as those with medical oxygen?
   a. American Standard Safety System
   b. Pin Index Safety System
   c. Oxygen Safety System
   d. Compressed Gas Safety System

26. You are assisting a paramedic with an intubation attempt of an unresponsive and apneic 6-year-old child. The paramedic has asked you to gather the supplies and they prepare to visualize the vocal cords. When selecting an endotracheal tube you should
   a. use a commercial sizing.
   b. match the inner diameter of the tube to the patient's little finger.
   c. bring a tube ½ size smaller and ½ size larger than the tube you have selected.
   d. All of the above.

27. You are on the scene of a cardiac arrest involving a 4-year-old child. After determining the patient is unresponsive, apneic, and pulseless and performing two minutes of CPR you should do which of the following?
   a. Check for a pulse and place the patient in the recovery position.
   b. Apply the AED with a dose-attenuating system and follow the prompts.
   c. Continue CPR without the AED as children suffer respiratory failure first.
   d. Request ALS assistance as only paramedics can defibrillate pediatric patients.

28. You have arrived on the scene of a 55-year-old female patient who is complaining of diffuse abdominal pain that is dull and aching. She also states she is having the same pain between her shoulder blades and she is lightheaded. Your physical exam reveals a pulse of 96, BP is 130/90, respirations are 20, breath sounds are clear and equal, skin is cool and clammy, and her pupils are equal and reactive. She states the pain began 30 minutes ago without provocation and she has a history of high cholesterol. You suspect
  a. cholecystitis.
  b. peptic ulcer.
  c. ectopic pregnancy.
  d. unstable angina.

29. You are assessing a minor who has fallen off her bike and has obvious deformity to her upper extremity. She needs to be evaluated at the hospital, but her parents are not available. You are able to treat and transport this patient under
  a. implied consent.
  b. informed consent.
  c. the Good Samaritan law.
  d. expressed consent.

30. The best treatment for ventricular fibrillation is
  a. high flow O_2.
  b. early defibrillation.
  c. early CPR.
  d. early administration of antiarrhythmic medications.

31. The initial cardiac electrical impulse in the normal functioning heart originates in the
  a. left atrium.
  b. sinoatrial node.
  c. Perkinje fibers.
  d. atrioventricular node.

32. The apex of the heart is located in the
  a. middle of the chest.
  b. right side of the chest.
  c. left side of the chest.
  d. lower left quadrant.

33. Red blood cells are also called
  a. leukocytes.
  b. monocytes.
  c. erythrocytes.
  d. platelets.

34. You are assessing a patient who is complaining of chest pain by obtaining a set of vital signs. The top number of the blood pressure is caused by
  a. atrial kick.
  b. contraction of the atria.
  c. filling of the ventricles.
  d. contraction of the left ventricle.

35. What should be your primary concern on the scene with a burn patient?
  a. the golden hour
  b. volume loss
  c. scene safety
  d. percentage of the body surface area that is burned

36. In a patient with an arterial bleed, what is the order in which you should attempt to stop the severe bleeding, from first to last?
  1. Tourniquet
  2. Direct pressure
  3. Elevation
  4. Pressure point
  a. 4, 3, 2, 1
  b. 2, 3, 1
  c. 2, 3, 4
  d. 2 and 3 only

37. Your patient has fallen off a bike and has abrasions to his right knee. Which type of bleeding corresponds to this injury?
   a. capillary
   b. venous
   c. arterial
   d. internal

38. Which of the following is NOT a function of the skin?
   a. fluid balance
   b. temperature regulation
   c. protection
   d. none of the above

39. What layer of the skin is comprised mostly of fatty tissue?
   a. dermis
   b. epidermis
   c. subcutaneous
   d. fascia

40. The APGAR score after one minute should be
   a. seven or greater.
   b. five.
   c. between one and five.
   d. three or greater.

41. A woman's gestation is
   a. 25 weeks.
   b. 40 weeks.
   c. 36 weeks.
   d. 28 weeks.

42. The disc-shaped, temporary organ that delivers nutrients and oxygen from the mother to the fetus is the
   a. umbilical cord.
   b. placenta.
   c. amniotic sac.
   d. uterus.

43. When birth is imminent, the mother should be placed
   a. in a position of comfort.
   b. left lateral recumbent.
   c. in a seated position.
   d. supine with her knees up and spread apart.

44. After week eight, the embryo is now called a
   a. zygote.
   b. fetus.
   c. neonate.
   d. zygoma.

45. The spitting up of blood is called
   a. epistaxis.
   b. hemolysis.
   c. hematuria.
   d. hemoptysis.

46. The heel bone is also called the
   a. calcaneus.
   b. malleolus.
   c. carpal.
   d. patella.

47. To check for a carotid pulse, place your fingers _____ to the larynx.
   a. lateral
   b. superiorly
   c. distal
   d. proximal

48. Your medical director has authorized EMTs in your area to use blind insertion airway devices (BIAD). These devices are meant to be inserted into the
   a. nasopharynx.
   b. trachea.
   c. esophagus.
   d. larynx.

49. How many bones are in the vertebral column?
   a. 35
   b. 22
   c. 26
   d. 33

50. The pressure of gas in a full oxygen cylinder is approximately _____ psi.
   a. 2,000
   b. 1,700
   c. 1,500
   d. 2,500

51. Your patient is an infant who is apneic with a pulse. This patient should be ventilated with _____ breath(s) every _____ seconds.
   a. two, five to six
   b. one, five to six
   c. two, three
   d. one, three

52. Which of the following is NOT a component of a BVM?
   a. a transparent face mask
   b. a rebreathing valve
   c. a self-refilling bag
   d. an oxygen reservoir

53. Which of the following is true regarding the Sellick's maneuver?
   a. The Sellick's maneuver should be used to keep the gastric contents from entering the trachea in a patient who is actively vomiting.
   b. The Sellick's maneuver is used to prevent gastric distention.
   c. Effective ventilation can occur when one rescuer ventilates using a BVM with one hand and applies the cricoid pressure with the other hand.
   d. The Sellick's maneuver is performed by placing the thumb and index finger on either side of the cricoid cartilage at the superior border of the larynx.

54. Which of the following is an indication that the artificial ventilation is inadequate?
   a. The heart rate does not return to the normal range.
   b. There is adequate chest rise and fall.
   c. The heart rate returns to the normal range.
   d. The ventilations are administered at a proper rate for the patient's age.

55. The movement of air in and out of the lungs is called _____ and the amount of air moved in and out of the lungs in one breath is called _____.
   a. ventilation, tidal volume
   b. respiration, tidal volume
   c. ventilation, minute volume
   d. perfusion, stroke volume

56. Every patient encounter should be considered
   a. critical.
   b. medical.
   c. potentially dangerous.
   d. potentially life threatening.

57. If you see the potential for a possible violent encounter during a scene size-up, you should
 a. call for additional resources.
 b. find something to use as a weapon.
 c. enter the scene carefully.
 d. lock the ambulance.

58. The amount of blood pumped by the heart in one minute is called
 a. Minute volume
 b. Stroke volume
 c. Cardiac output
 d. Minute circulation

59. Before you obtain a signature from a patient for refusal of care, you should
 a. contact your supervisor.
 b. be sure that the patient is mentally competent.
 c. contact medical control.
 d. take at least three sets of vital signs.

60. Nitroglycerine is a(n)
 a. vasodilator.
 b. antiarrhythmic.
 c. antispasmodic.
 d. vasoconstrictor.

61. When performing CPR on an adult patient, how deeply should the chest be depressed?
 a. $1\frac{1}{2}$ to 2 inches
 b. $\frac{1}{2}$ to 1 inch
 c. 1 to $1\frac{1}{2}$ inches
 d. 2 to 3 inches

62. You have responded to a residence and find that the spouse is doing CPR. She tells you that she has been doing CPR for approximately five minutes. You should first
 a. apply an AED.
 b. stop compressions and check for a pulse.
 c. apply high flow O_2.
 d. ask if the patient has a DNR.

63. You are dispatched to the park basketball courts for a patient who is complaining of severe, crushing chest pain. Upon arrival, you find the patient unresponsive. Your first action should be to
 a. interview bystanders.
 b. check for a pulse.
 c. apply an AED.
 d. open and assess his airway.

64. Myocardium is muscle that is only found in the _____ and has the ability to _____.
 a. brain, stimulate nerves
 b. heart, generate electrical impulses
 c. stomach, produce digestive juices
 d. lungs, stimulate breathing

65. The type of injury that is characterized by the underlying tissues being forcibly torn away is called a(n)
 a. amputation.
 b. avulsion.
 c. penetration.
 d. laceration.

66. The type of injury that is caused when a part of the body is trapped between two surfaces is a(n)
 a. blunt force trauma.
 b. hematoma.
 c. crush injury.
 d. abrasion.

67. The most serious concern with an electrical burn is
   a. electrolyte imbalance.
   b. destruction of limbs involved.
   c. the amount of electricity the patient came in contact with.
   d. cardiac arrest or dysrhythmia.

68. You are treating a patient with severe arterial bleeding to the right forearm, which has not slowed with direct pressure and elevation. After applying a pressure dressing what would you do next?
   a. brachial artery
   b. radial artery
   c. carotid artery
   d. subclavian artery

69. You are treating a patient with severe arterial bleeding to the right forearm, which has not slowed with direct pressure and elevation. After applying a pressure dressing what would you do next?
   a. Apply a tourniquet proximal to the wound.
   b. Apply pressure to the brachial artery.
   c. Apply pressure to the radial artery.
   d. Apply a tourniquet distal to the wound.

70. When a baby is born, it can take up to _____ for him or her to begin to breathe on his or her own.
   a. 30 seconds
   b. 1 minute
   c. 2 minutes
   d. 3 minutes

71. You are dispatched to the local park for a pregnant female who is complaining of severe shortness of breath after being stung by a bee. She tells you that she carries an EpiPen and has a history of allergies to bee stings. You should
   a. transport the patient rapidly.
   b. administer the EpiPen.
   c. contact medical control prior to assisting with the EpiPen.
   d. none of the above.

72. You respond to the elementary school for an 8-year-old girl with an altered LOC. The school nurse tells you that the patient has been acting strangely and may have a behavioral emergency. You should first suspect
   a. that she is most likely having a diabetic emergency.
   b. that she has not taken her psychiatric meds regularly.
   c. that she is faking it and wants to get out of taking a test.
   d. a possible head injury.

73. Pediatric patients are able to maintain a normal blood pressure until they lose approximately _____ of their blood volume.
   a. one-third
   b. one-quarter
   c. one-half
   d. three-quarters

74. Another name for the shoulder blade is the
   a. scapula.
   b. sternum.
   c. clavicle.
   d. ischium.

75. The gallbladder is located in the
   a. upper right quadrant.
   b. upper left quadrant.
   c. lower right quadrant.
   d. lower left quadrant.

76. The elbow is _____ to the shoulder.
   a. distal
   b. proximal
   c. medial
   d. lateral

77. A patient who weighs 130 pounds weighs approximately _____ kilograms.
   a. 100
   b. 59
   c. 120
   d. 70

78. The central nervous system consists of the
   a. brain.
   b. brain and spinal cord.
   c. brain and sensory nerves.
   d. spinal cord.

79. Which of the following is true regarding gastric distention?
   a. Gastric distention most commonly affects children.
   b. Gastric distention can significantly reduce lung volume.
   c. Fast, gentle breaths should be administered to avoid gastric distention.
   d. In all patients, if you notice that gastric distention is occurring while administering ventilations, reposition the head and apply cricoid pressure.

80. You may encounter patients who have had their larynx removed. This procedure is called a
   a. stoma.
   b. tracheostomy.
   c. cricothyroidotomy.
   d. laryngectomy.

81. You have responded to a patient who has choked on an unknown object. He is awake and alert but is not moving air. The most effective way to dislodge the foreign body from his airway is to
   a. slap him on the back.
   b. lay the patient on the floor and perform chest thrusts.
   c. perform abdominal thrusts.
   d. use Magill forceps to remove the object.

82. Which of the following statements is true?
   a. It is easier to provide ventilations when using a bag-valve-mask device or the mouth-to-mask technique when dentures are left in place.
   b. Dentures should be removed when providing ventilations.
   c. Tight-fitting dentures make it more difficult to obtain a proper face-to-mask seal.
   d. Dentures will cause an inadequate tidal volume to be administered when ventilating a patient.

83. The most difficult aspect of providing artificial ventilations with a BVM is
   a. administering the proper tidal volume for the patient.
   b. maintaining a seal on the patient's face.
   c. squeezing the bag.
   d. refilling the bag.

84. Once your ambulance has responded to a call,
  a. only dispatch can cancel you.
  b. you must transport the patient.
  c. you have a duty to act.
  d. you can cancel only if another responder is on the scene.

85. Threatening to forcibly restrain a mentally competent patient in order to transport him could be considered
  a. battery.
  b. slander.
  c. kidnapping.
  d. assault.

86. When you are in doubt of the validity of a living will or DNR,
  a. follow the family's wishes.
  b. contact your supervisor.
  c. you have an obligation to resuscitate.
  d. call the patient's physician.

87. Which of the following is a presumptive sign of death?
  a. no systolic blood pressure
  b. lividity
  c. rigor mortis
  d. putrefaction

88. Which of the following is NOT a criterion for proving negligence?
  a. breach of duty
  b. cause
  c. abandonment
  d. damages

89. Which of the following indicates the need for immediate defibrillation?
  a. asystole
  b. PEA
  c. pulseless ventricular tachycardia
  d. atrial fibrillation

90. You are on the scene with a patient who is complaining of chest pain. Nitroglycerine is contraindicated because
  a. he states that he has taken Viagra four days ago.
  b. his blood pressure is 108/68.
  c. his pain has increased from three to five on a one to ten scale.
  d. none of the above.

91. The heart is covered by a fibrous sac called the
  a. pericardium.
  b. epicardium.
  c. visceral pleura.
  d. parietal pleura.

92. You and your partner have responded to a call for a newborn who is having difficulty breathing. Upon your arrival you find a 3-week-old infant with inadequate respiratory effort, cyanosis, and limp body tone. You have begun bag-valve mask ventilations with 100% oxygen and you have found the patient has a brachial pulse of 52. You should
  a. continue bag-valve mask ventilations and transport rapidly.
  b. immediately apply the AED with a dose-attenuating system.
  c. perform 5 back blows to stimulate the patient.
  d. immediately begin chest compressions.

93. The medical term for a heart attack is
  a. ischemia.
  b. cardiac arrest.
  c. myocardial infarction.
  d. cardiac standstill.

94. Normal skin should feel
  a. cool.
  b. hot.
  c. warm.
  d. diaphoretic.

95. A patient in a postictal state is one who has
  a. stopped breathing but not yet died.
  b. demonstrated the early signs of shock.
  c. had a seizure and is now unresponsive.
  d. just given birth but not yet delivered the placenta.

96. You are assessing a patient who has been involved in a single vehicle accident. The patient was unrestrained and you notice starring of the windshield. When assessing his pupils, you shine a light into his right eye. Normally, the pupil in the other eye will
  a. dilate.
  b. not react.
  c. constrict.
  d. have the opposite reaction of the right eye.

97. Your patient has an impaled object in the thigh. You should
  a. stabilize the object with a bulky dressing.
  b. remove the object, then apply direct pressure.
  c. remove the object, apply direct pressure, and then apply a pressure dressing.
  d. leave the object alone.

98. You are treating a 24-year-old male patient who is complaining of severe dyspnea and cannot speak in full sentences. You have found wheezing in all lobes upon auscultating breath sounds and the patient states he has a history of asthma and is prescribed an MDI. Medical control has given you an order to assist the patient with his prescribed MDI. When assisting the patient you should
  a. place the MDI in his hand and tell him to take a puff.
  b. instruct the patient to exhale deeply, press the MDI, and inhale the mist.
  c. instruct the patient to avoid touching the MDI with his mouth, depress the MDI, inhale deeply, and then exhale fully.
  d. instruct the patient to place his lips around the MDI, inhale deeply, and hold his breath as long as possible, then exhale gently.

99. A blood loss of _____ in an infant can be life threatening.
  a. 50–75 cc
  b. 100–200 cc
  c. 75–100 cc
  d. 50 cc

100. In an infant, what may bulging fontanels indicate?
  a. increased intracranial pressure
  b. increased blood pressure
  c. dehydration
  d. abuse

101. Infants primarily breathe through
  a. their noses.
  b. their mouths.
  c. their noses and their mouths.
  d. none of the above.

102. Which of the following is true regarding intercostals muscles of children?
   a. They are used frequently in normal breathing.
   b. The muscles are immature, causing fatigue rather quickly.
   c. They are rarely used in respiratory distress.
   d. None of the above.

103. Since blood pressures are difficult to obtain in an infant or child less than 3 years old, your assessment of circulation must rely on and include the capillary refill, quality of pulses, and
   a. breathing quality.
   b. respiratory rate.
   c. mental status.
   d. O_2 saturation.

104. A normal blood glucose level for an adult is
   a. 100–180 mg/dL
   b. 60–80 mg/dL
   c. 80–120 mg/dL
   d. 120–180 mg/dL

105. Reddened skin is called
   a. cyanosis.
   b. ecchymosis.
   c. erythema.
   d. cellulitis.

106. When referring to a medication, the _____ name is the name that a pharmaceutical company gives to the medication.
   a. trade
   b. generic
   c. chemical
   d. proper

107. Which of the following medications is supplied as a suspension?
   a. albuterol
   b. oral glucose
   c. activated charcoal
   d. nitroglycerine

108. What is the lowest possible score given on the Glasgow Coma Scale?
   a. one
   b. five
   c. three
   d. zero

109. Once oxygen-poor blood passes through the capillaries, it moves to the
   a. skin.
   b. arterioles.
   c. veins.
   d. venules.

110. Breathing concentrations of carbon dioxide greater than _____ will result in death within minutes.
   a. 5%
   b. 10%
   c. 2%
   d. 7%

111. Another term for whooping cough is
   a. stridor.
   b. pertussis.
   c. pneumonia.
   d. SARS.

112. The space between the base of the tongue and the epiglottis is known as the
   a. uvula.
   b. vallecula.
   c. larynx.
   d. glottic foramen.

113. The last portion of tracheal cartilage that separates the opening into the right and left mainstem bronchi is the
   a. epiglottis.
   b. vallecula.
   c. larynx.
   d. carina.

114. Which of the following is NOT an aim of HIPAA?
   a. improving the continuity of health insurance coverage
   b. preventing healthcare workers from sharing patient information
   c. safeguarding patient confidentiality
   d. strengthening laws for the protection of the privacy of health information

115. You are dispatched to respond to a patient who has burns to his chest. Your top priority should be
   a. to ascertain the source of the burn.
   b. the patient's airway compromise.
   c. if there is a need for additional units.
   d. your safety.

116. You are assessing a patient who has been ejected from a car. He is breathing four times per minute and has an open fracture to his right femur. What should you do first?
   a. Stop the bleeding from the femur fracture and apply a splint.
   b. Apply high flow O_2 via a nonrebreathing mask.
   c. Assess distal pulses.
   d. Assist ventilations with a bag-valve-mask.

117. If the scene is NOT safe,
   a. enter slowly and cautiously.
   b. call for additional units.
   c. contact medical control.
   d. do not enter.

118. The agency that develops the National Education Standards for various levels of providers is the
   a. National Registry of Emergency Medical Technicians.
   b. National Highway Traffic Safety Administration.
   c. National Association of Emergency Medical Technicians.
   d. National Association of Prehospital Medical Providers.

119. The orbit (eye socket) is made up of what bones?
   a. frontal, maxillae, and sphenoid
   b. frontal, mandible, and zygoma
   c. zygoma, temporal, and frontal
   d. frontal, zygoma, and maxillae

120. The strongest bone in the body is the
   a. femur.
   b. skull.
   c. pelvis.
   d. humerus.

Answers

1. c. A patient who has a pacemaker will have a normal pulse rate if the pacemaker is functioning properly.

2. a. If a patient is in a shockable rhythm with an AICD, then the AICD has failed and the patient should be defibrillated. If the AICD can be located, ensure the pads are not over the AICD prior to defibrillation. If it cannot be seen, then place the pads as usual and defibrillate.

3. a. The vena cava carries blood from the body to the right atrium.

4. c. The pulmonary artery carries blood from the right ventricle to the lungs for gas exchange.

5. a. Arteries become smaller and smaller until they become arterioles.

6. c. AEDs are designed to detect electrical activity in the heart and will shock ventricular tachycardia and ventricular fibrillation even if the patient has a pulse. If this happens, the shock may terminate all electrical activity and be lethal for the patient. AEDs do not have the ability to sense a pulse, immediate defibrillation is called for in a witnessed cardiac arrest, and AEDs will shock a patient with a pulse.

7. a. The correct order of treatment for the traumatic injury patient is BSI, airway and breathing, controlling significant bleeding, and then the transport decision.

8. b. To treat hypovolemic shock in the trauma patient, control obvious bleeding.

9. d. Bruising and a black-and-blue discoloration on the skin is also called a *contusion*.

10. b. Compartment syndrome is a serious condition in which fluid can leak into the spaces between cells. Blood vessels also become compressed, inhibiting blood flow to the surrounding tissues.

11. c. To determine the responsiveness in a child, gently tap the child on the shoulder while speaking loudly.

12. c. Pulmonary embolism can occur during pregnancy, especially after childbirth. If a female who is postpartum complains of acute chest pain and shortness of breath, suspect a pulmonary embolism.

13. c. Painless, bright red blood is usually present with placenta previa.

14. b. The umbilical cord normally contains two arteries and one vein.

15. d. An epidural, hypoxia, and narcotic medications are all causes for fetal bradycardia. Maternal anxiety does not lower the infant's heart rate.

16. c. If a diabetic patient does not eat and takes his insulin, hypoglycemia may develop.

17. a. In the early stages of hypothermia, respirations will be rapid.

18. b. The membrane that lies directly over the brain tissue is the pia mater.

19. c. The cerebellum is responsible for coordination.

20. c. To remove a bee's stinger, use a plastic card, scraping over the stinger in a downward motion.

21. d. When testing suction equipment, the unit must generate a vacuum of more than 300 mmHg.

22. c. If you are unable to clear debris out of the airway while suctioning, roll the patient onto her side and attempt to clear her mouth with your gloved hand.

23. c. In this situation, suction the patient for 15 seconds and ventilate him for 2 minutes, continuing the pattern until the secretions have been cleared from the airway.

24. b. To maintain a patent airway in a patient who is breathing on his own and is uninjured, the patient should be in the recovery position.

25. a. The name of the safety system for large, compressed gas cylinders is the American Standard Safety System.

26. d. All of the answers are adequate for obtaining the proper sized ET tube for a child. The best method is to have a commercial sizing chart like the Broselow tape. If a sizing chart is unavailable then you can measure the inner diameter of the tube to the diameter of the patients little finger. Either way, you should always have prepared a tube a half size smaller and larger than the one selected.

27. b. Once you have performed two minutes of CPR the AED should be applied. An AED with pediatric pads and a dose-attenuating system is preferred, but if one is not available, then adult pads should be used.

28. d. Many women have atypical complaints when suffering from unstable angina. The fact that the pain was dull and radiating coupled with lightheadedness, a history of high cholesterol, and sudden onset without provocation should have made you suspicious of unstable angina.

29. a. A minor patient who needs emergency care but has no parent or guardian present can be treated under implied consent.

30. b. The best treatment for ventricular fibrillation is early defibrillation.

31. b. The initial electrical impulse in the normal functioning heart originates in the sinoatrial node.

32. c. The apex of the heart is located in the left side of the chest.

33. c. Red blood cells are also called *erythrocytes*.

34. d. The top number of the blood pressure, the systolic pressure, is caused by the contraction of the left ventricle.

35. c. The primary concern on the scene with a burn patient is scene safety.

36. b. The new guidelines for bleeding control indicate the EMT should attempt bleeding control by direct pressure, then add elevation, and then move to a tourniquet. In severe cases the attempts at direct pressure may be short lived and a tourniquet may have to be rapidly placed to prevent life-threatening exsanguinations. Pressure points are no longer recommended.

37. a. Bleeding from an abrasion is usually from the capillaries.

38. d. Fluid balance, temperature regulation, and protection are all functions of the skin.

39. c. The subcutaneous layer is comprised mostly of fatty tissue.

40. a. The APGAR score after one minute should be seven or greater.

41. b. A woman's gestation is 40 weeks.

42. b. The disc-shaped, temporary organ that delivers nutrients and oxygen from the mother to the fetus is the placenta.

43. d. When birth is imminent, the mother should be placed supine or in semi-Fowler's with her knees up and spread apart.

44. b. After week eight, the embryo is called a *fetus*.

45. d. The spitting up of blood is called *hemoptysis*.

46. a. The heel bone is also called the *calcaneus*.

47. a. To check for a carotid pulse, place your fingers lateral to the larynx.

48. c. BIADs are intended to be inserted into the esophagus. Some are designed (multi-lumen) to allow ventilations if the device is inserted into the trachea.

49. d. There are 33 bones in the vertebral column.

50. a. The pressure of gas in a full oxygen cylinder is approximately 2,000 psi.

51. d. An infant that is apneic should be ventilated with one breath every three seconds.

52. b. A rebreathing valve is *not* a component of a BVM.

53. b. The Sellick's maneuver is used to prevent gastric distention.

54. a. If the heart rate of a patient who is receiving artificial ventilation does not return to the normal range, the ventilations are inadequate.

55. a. The simple movement of air in and out of the lungs is called ventilation and the amount of air moved in one breath is called tidal volume. Respiration is the exchange of gases, nutrients, and wastes at the alveolar level. Minute volume is the amount of air moved in one minute and equals respiratory rate times tidal volume. Perfusion is the exchange of gases, nutrients, and wastes at the cellular level. Strike volume is the amount of blood ejected from the heart in one contraction.

56. c. Every patient encounter should be considered potentially dangerous.

57. a. If you see the potential for a possibly violent encounter during a scene size-up, call for additional resources.

58. c. The amount of blood pumped by the heart in one minute defines cardiac output, which is calculated by multiplying the heart rate by stroke volume.

59. b. Before obtaining a signature from a patient who is refusing care, be sure that the patient is mentally competent.

60. a. Nitroglycerine is a vasodilator.

61. a. When performing CPR on an adult patient, compress the chest $1\frac{1}{2}$ to 2 inches.

62. b. When arriving on the scene to find a patient who has CPR in progress, stop the compressions and check for a pulse.

63. d. When assessing an unresponsive patient, open and assess the airway first.

64. b. Myocardium is muscle found only in the heart and is the only muscle that can generate its own electrical impulse.

65. b. The type of injury that is characterized by the underlying tissues being forcibly torn away is called an *avulsion*.

66. c. A crush injury is an injury that is caused when a part of the body is trapped between two surfaces.

67. d. The most serious concern with an electrical burn is cardiac arrest or dysrhythmia.

68. a. Hemorrhage control guidelines now recommend placing a tourniquet proximal to the wound if direct pressure and elevation fail to control the hemorrhage. Pressure points are no longer recommended.

69. c. If an infant is not breathing after warming, drying, and tactile stimulation, administer bag valve mask ventilations.

70. a. When a baby is born, it can take up to 30 seconds for him or her to begin to breathe on his or her own.

71. c. In this situation, contact medical control prior to the administration of the medication. This may include standing orders.

72. a. Suspect and rule out medical conditions in a patient who is behaving strangely.

73. c. Pediatric patients are able to maintain a normal blood pressure until they lose approximately one-half of their blood volume.

74. a. Another name for the shoulder blade is the *scapula*.

75. a. The gallbladder is located in the upper right quadrant.

76. a. The elbow is distal to the shoulder.

77. b. A patient who weighs 130 pounds weighs approximately 59 kilograms.

78. b. The central nervous system consists of the brain and spinal cord.

79. b. Gastric distention can significantly reduce lung volume.

80. d. A surgical procedure that removes the larynx is a laryngectomy.

81. c. The most effective way to dislodge a foreign body in a choking patient who is conscious, awake, and alert is to perform abdominal thrusts.

82. a. It is easier to provide ventilations and maintain a good seal when using a bag-valve-mask device or the mouth-to-mask technique when dentures are left in place.

83. b. The most difficult aspect of providing artificial ventilations with a bag-valve-mask device is maintaining a seal on the patient's face.

84. c. Once your ambulance has responded to a call, a duty to act has been established.

85. d. Threatening to forcibly restrain a mentally competent patient in order to transport him could be considered assault.

86. c. If any doubt exists to the validity of a DNR, CPR must be initiated.

87. a. The lack of a systolic blood pressure is a presumptive sign of death.

88. c. Abandonment is not a criterion for proving negligence.

89. c. Pulseless ventricular tachycardia is an indication for immediate defibrillation.

90. d. None of the answers listed are contraindications for the administration of nitroglycerine. Each choice is an indication for the administration of nitroglycerine.

91. a. The heart is covered by a fibrous sac called the *pericardium*.

92. d. In an infant that is in respiratory distress or failure and who has a bradycardic heart rate (< 60 bpm), cardiac compressions should be started along with positive pressure ventilations. An AED is not indicated as the patient has a pulse.

93. c. The medical term for a heart attack is *myocardial infarction*.

94. c. Normal skin should feel warm to the touch.

95. c. A patient who is in a postictal state has just had a seizure and appears to be asleep.

96. c. When a light is shined into one pupil, normally the other pupil should have the same reaction.

97. a. Impaled objects should be stabilized with bulky dressings.

98. d. When assisting a patient with his MDI you should instruct him to close his lips around the MDI, inhale as deeply as possible, and hold his breath to allow the medication to settle deep in his lungs.

99. b. A blood loss of 100 cc to 200 cc can be life threatening in an infant.

100. a. Bulging fontanels in an infant can mean an increase in intracranial pressure.

101. a. Infants primarily breathe through their noses.

102. b. Children can get respiratory fatigue rather quickly because their intercostals muscles are immature.

103. c. Since blood pressures are difficult to obtain in infants and children younger than three years old, you must rely on the capillary refill, quality of pulses, and mental status to assess their circulation.

104. c. A normal blood glucose level for an adult is 80 mg/dL to 120 mg/dL.

105. c. Reddened skin is called *erythema*.

106. a. The trade name of a medication is the name that the pharmaceutical company gives to it.

107. c. Activated charcoal is supplied as a suspension.

108. c. The lowest possible score given on the Glasgow Coma Scale is three.

109. d. Once oxygen-poor blood passes through the capillaries, it moves to the venules.

110. b. Breathing concentrations of carbon dioxide greater than 10% will result in death within minutes.

111. b. Another term for whooping cough is *pertussis*.

112. b. The space between the base of the tongue and the epiglottis is known as the *vallecula*.

113. d. The carina is the last portion of the tracheal cartilage that separates the opening into the right and left mainstem bronchi.

114. b. HIPAA aims to improve the continuity of health insurance coverage, safeguard patient confidentiality, and strengthen laws for the protection of the privacy of health information.

115. d. The top priority when responding to a call is safety.

116. d. Assisting ventilations with a bag-valve-mask is your first priority with this patient.

117. d. If the scene is not safe, do *not* enter it.

118. b. The National Highway Traffic Safety Administration develops the National Education Standard for various levels of providers.

119. d. The orbit is made up of the frontal, zygomatic, and maxillae bones.

120. a. The strongest bone in the body is the femur.

11 ▶ EMT PRACTICE EXAM 9

CHAPTER SUMMARY

This is the ninth of ten practice exams in this book based on the National Registry's EMT cognitive exam. Use this test to continue your study and practice. Notice how knowing what to expect on the exam makes you feel better prepared!

Like the previous practice exams, this exam is based on the National Registry's cognitive exam for EMT Exams. This is the final multiple-choice practice exam.

As before, the answer sheet you should use appears next. Following the exam is an answer key, with all the answers explained. These explanations will help you see where you need to concentrate further study. When you've finished the exam and scored it, note your weaknesses so that you'll know which parts of your textbook to concentrate on before you take the next exam.

1.	ⓐ	ⓑ	ⓒ	ⓓ	41.	ⓐ	ⓑ	ⓒ	ⓓ	81.	ⓐ	ⓑ	ⓒ	ⓓ
2.	ⓐ	ⓑ	ⓒ	ⓓ	42.	ⓐ	ⓑ	ⓒ	ⓓ	82.	ⓐ	ⓑ	ⓒ	ⓓ
3.	ⓐ	ⓑ	ⓒ	ⓓ	43.	ⓐ	ⓑ	ⓒ	ⓓ	83.	ⓐ	ⓑ	ⓒ	ⓓ
4.	ⓐ	ⓑ	ⓒ	ⓓ	44.	ⓐ	ⓑ	ⓒ	ⓓ	84.	ⓐ	ⓑ	ⓒ	ⓓ
5.	ⓐ	ⓑ	ⓒ	ⓓ	45.	ⓐ	ⓑ	ⓒ	ⓓ	85.	ⓐ	ⓑ	ⓒ	ⓓ
6.	ⓐ	ⓑ	ⓒ	ⓓ	46.	ⓐ	ⓑ	ⓒ	ⓓ	86.	ⓐ	ⓑ	ⓒ	ⓓ
7.	ⓐ	ⓑ	ⓒ	ⓓ	47.	ⓐ	ⓑ	ⓒ	ⓓ	87.	ⓐ	ⓑ	ⓒ	ⓓ
8.	ⓐ	ⓑ	ⓒ	ⓓ	48.	ⓐ	ⓑ	ⓒ	ⓓ	88.	ⓐ	ⓑ	ⓒ	ⓓ
9.	ⓐ	ⓑ	ⓒ	ⓓ	49.	ⓐ	ⓑ	ⓒ	ⓓ	89.	ⓐ	ⓑ	ⓒ	ⓓ
10.	ⓐ	ⓑ	ⓒ	ⓓ	50.	ⓐ	ⓑ	ⓒ	ⓓ	90.	ⓐ	ⓑ	ⓒ	ⓓ
11.	ⓐ	ⓑ	ⓒ	ⓓ	51.	ⓐ	ⓑ	ⓒ	ⓓ	91.	ⓐ	ⓑ	ⓒ	ⓓ
12.	ⓐ	ⓑ	ⓒ	ⓓ	52.	ⓐ	ⓑ	ⓒ	ⓓ	92.	ⓐ	ⓑ	ⓒ	ⓓ
13.	ⓐ	ⓑ	ⓒ	ⓓ	53.	ⓐ	ⓑ	ⓒ	ⓓ	93.	ⓐ	ⓑ	ⓒ	ⓓ
14.	ⓐ	ⓑ	ⓒ	ⓓ	54.	ⓐ	ⓑ	ⓒ	ⓓ	94.	ⓐ	ⓑ	ⓒ	ⓓ
15.	ⓐ	ⓑ	ⓒ	ⓓ	55.	ⓐ	ⓑ	ⓒ	ⓓ	95.	ⓐ	ⓑ	ⓒ	ⓓ
16.	ⓐ	ⓑ	ⓒ	ⓓ	56.	ⓐ	ⓑ	ⓒ	ⓓ	96.	ⓐ	ⓑ	ⓒ	ⓓ
17.	ⓐ	ⓑ	ⓒ	ⓓ	57.	ⓐ	ⓑ	ⓒ	ⓓ	97.	ⓐ	ⓑ	ⓒ	ⓓ
18.	ⓐ	ⓑ	ⓒ	ⓓ	58.	ⓐ	ⓑ	ⓒ	ⓓ	98.	ⓐ	ⓑ	ⓒ	ⓓ
19.	ⓐ	ⓑ	ⓒ	ⓓ	59.	ⓐ	ⓑ	ⓒ	ⓓ	99.	ⓐ	ⓑ	ⓒ	ⓓ
20.	ⓐ	ⓑ	ⓒ	ⓓ	60.	ⓐ	ⓑ	ⓒ	ⓓ	100.	ⓐ	ⓑ	ⓒ	ⓓ
21.	ⓐ	ⓑ	ⓒ	ⓓ	61.	ⓐ	ⓑ	ⓒ	ⓓ	101.	ⓐ	ⓑ	ⓒ	ⓓ
22.	ⓐ	ⓑ	ⓒ	ⓓ	62.	ⓐ	ⓑ	ⓒ	ⓓ	102.	ⓐ	ⓑ	ⓒ	ⓓ
23.	ⓐ	ⓑ	ⓒ	ⓓ	63.	ⓐ	ⓑ	ⓒ	ⓓ	103.	ⓐ	ⓑ	ⓒ	ⓓ
24.	ⓐ	ⓑ	ⓒ	ⓓ	64.	ⓐ	ⓑ	ⓒ	ⓓ	104.	ⓐ	ⓑ	ⓒ	ⓓ
25.	ⓐ	ⓑ	ⓒ	ⓓ	65.	ⓐ	ⓑ	ⓒ	ⓓ	105.	ⓐ	ⓑ	ⓒ	ⓓ
26.	ⓐ	ⓑ	ⓒ	ⓓ	66.	ⓐ	ⓑ	ⓒ	ⓓ	106.	ⓐ	ⓑ	ⓒ	ⓓ
27.	ⓐ	ⓑ	ⓒ	ⓓ	67.	ⓐ	ⓑ	ⓒ	ⓓ	107.	ⓐ	ⓑ	ⓒ	ⓓ
28.	ⓐ	ⓑ	ⓒ	ⓓ	68.	ⓐ	ⓑ	ⓒ	ⓓ	108.	ⓐ	ⓑ	ⓒ	ⓓ
29.	ⓐ	ⓑ	ⓒ	ⓓ	69.	ⓐ	ⓑ	ⓒ	ⓓ	109.	ⓐ	ⓑ	ⓒ	ⓓ
30.	ⓐ	ⓑ	ⓒ	ⓓ	70.	ⓐ	ⓑ	ⓒ	ⓓ	110.	ⓐ	ⓑ	ⓒ	ⓓ
31.	ⓐ	ⓑ	ⓒ	ⓓ	71.	ⓐ	ⓑ	ⓒ	ⓓ	111.	ⓐ	ⓑ	ⓒ	ⓓ
32.	ⓐ	ⓑ	ⓒ	ⓓ	72.	ⓐ	ⓑ	ⓒ	ⓓ	112.	ⓐ	ⓑ	ⓒ	ⓓ
33.	ⓐ	ⓑ	ⓒ	ⓓ	73.	ⓐ	ⓑ	ⓒ	ⓓ	113.	ⓐ	ⓑ	ⓒ	ⓓ
34.	ⓐ	ⓑ	ⓒ	ⓓ	74.	ⓐ	ⓑ	ⓒ	ⓓ	114.	ⓐ	ⓑ	ⓒ	ⓓ
35.	ⓐ	ⓑ	ⓒ	ⓓ	75.	ⓐ	ⓑ	ⓒ	ⓓ	115.	ⓐ	ⓑ	ⓒ	ⓓ
36.	ⓐ	ⓑ	ⓒ	ⓓ	76.	ⓐ	ⓑ	ⓒ	ⓓ	116.	ⓐ	ⓑ	ⓒ	ⓓ
37.	ⓐ	ⓑ	ⓒ	ⓓ	77.	ⓐ	ⓑ	ⓒ	ⓓ	117.	ⓐ	ⓑ	ⓒ	ⓓ
38.	ⓐ	ⓑ	ⓒ	ⓓ	78.	ⓐ	ⓑ	ⓒ	ⓓ	118.	ⓐ	ⓑ	ⓒ	ⓓ
39.	ⓐ	ⓑ	ⓒ	ⓓ	79.	ⓐ	ⓑ	ⓒ	ⓓ	119.	ⓐ	ⓑ	ⓒ	ⓓ
40.	ⓐ	ⓑ	ⓒ	ⓓ	80.	ⓐ	ⓑ	ⓒ	ⓓ	120.	ⓐ	ⓑ	ⓒ	ⓓ

EMT Practice Exam 9

1. The assessment of the airway should take no longer than
   a. 15 seconds.
   b. 5 seconds.
   c. 10 seconds.
   d. 30 seconds.

2. You are assessing a patient who is unconscious and unresponsive. You notice that he has agonal respirations. You have determined this because agonal respirations are characterized by
   a. deep, slow breaths.
   b. occasional gasping breaths.
   c. rapid, shallow breaths.
   d. slow, shallow breaths.

3. Normal breathing has which of the following characteristics?
   a. regular chest rise and fall
   b. movement of the abdomen
   c. a normal rate and rhythm
   d. all of the above

4. In compensated shock, the respirations will be
   a. normal.
   b. increased.
   c. decreased.
   d. agonal.

5. Which of the following is the narrowest part of the airway in an adult?
   a. the glottis opening
   b. the carina
   c. the epiglottis
   d. the bronchus

6. You are providing positive pressure ventilations via an automatic transport ventilator (ATV) and you notice inadequate chest rise and fall and an alarm on the unit is sounding. You should
   a. increase the tidal volume.
   b. increase the respiratory rate.
   c. decrease the tidal volume.
   d. discontinue the ATV and begin bag-valve mask ventilations.

7. You are treating a 65-year-old female patient who is experiencing a dull ache in her chest and numbness in her left arm and jaw. Her skin is diaphoretic and her vital signs are: P – 96, BP – 124/86, R – 24, and breath sounds are clear and equal bilaterally. You have placed the patient on oxygen and medical control has ordered 324 mg of ASA by mouth. You recognize the benefit of ASA administration, as
   a. aspirin prevents clots from getting bigger.
   b. aspirin breaks up clots.
   c. aspirin dilates coronary arteries.
   d. aspirin increases the contractility of the myocardium.

8. The muscle cells of the heart have a unique characteristic that allows them to contract/ generate their own impulses without an external stimulus. This characteristic is known as
   a. contractility.
   b. automaticity.
   c. conductivity.
   d. autonomic pacemaker.

9. What structure is also called the Adam's apple?
   a. hyoid bone
   b. thyroid cartilage
   c. cricoid cartilage
   d. larynx

10. You are assessing a patient who has overdosed on cocaine. You would expect his pupils to be
   a. dilated.
   b. pinpoint.
   c. normal.
   d. unequal.

11. Which of the following is more emergent?
   a. a child who is not crying and has poor muscle tone and pale skin
   b. a screaming child with a laceration to the back of the head
   c. a child with a humeral fracture and bruising to the face
   d. a whimpering child who is afraid of you

12. In infants, most of their body heat is lost through their
   a. hands.
   b. feet.
   c. head.
   d. torso.

13. You are dispatched to a residence for a pediatric patient in respiratory distress. The patient's father states that the child had fallen into the pool earlier that day but was released from the hospital after a brief evaluation. He is most likely suffering from
   a. pulmonary edema.
   b. secondary drowning syndrome.
   c. pneumonia.
   d. asthma.

14. You are assessing a pediatric patient with special needs. His caregiver states that he has a history of hydrocephalus. You notice a bulge to the side of his head and feel something hard under the surface of the scalp. This is probably due to the presence of a
   a. gastrostomy tube.
   b. central venous line.
   c. ventriculoperitoneal shunt.
   d. intraventricular tube.

15. The birth of the infant indicates what stage of labor?
   a. end of the first
   b. beginning of the second
   c. end of the second
   d. end of the third

16. Which is NOT a required element for an accusation of negligence to hold up in the court of law?
   a. damages
   b. duty to act
   c. breach of duty
   d. none of the above

17. On a hazardous materials call, park your ambulance
   a. uphill and downwind.
   b. downhill and upwind.
   c. uphill and upwind.
   d. downhill and downwind.

18. A competent adult patient who gives permission to treat does so with
   a. implied consent.
   b. expressed consent.
   c. informed consent.
   d. alert consent.

19. The first incident management system was known as the
   a. national incident management system.
   b. incident command system.
   c. incident management system.
   d. none of the above.

20. Which of the following is considered a member of the incident management system's command staff?
   a. operations officer
   b. incident commander
   c. section chief
   d. safety officer

21. A significant finding in head trauma that indicates a skull fracture is
   a. bruising to the sphenoid bone.
   b. the presence of cerebrospinal fluid.
   c. altered LOC.
   d. a full thickness laceration with bone exposure.

22. You are dispatched to a minor MVC. The patient, sitting on the curb side, tells you that he was just bitten by ants and has severe allergies to many insect bites. His skin is currently warm and dry, and he doesn't appear to be in distress. You should
   a. administer benadryl.
   b. administer an EpiPen.
   c. apply high flow O_2.
   d. continue with your physical exam.

23. You are assessing a patient who was struck by a car. He has pain and swelling over his upper right quadrant and appears to be developing symptoms of shock. You suspect
   a. a lacerated liver.
   b. splenetic rupture.
   c. injuries to the right kidney.
   d. traumatic injury to the large bowel.

24. The areas for greatest concern of internal blood loss are the chest, abdomen, and
   a. thighs.
   b. pelvis.
   c. brain.
   d. lower extremities.

25. The condition characterized by the separation of the inner layers of the aorta, which allows blood to flow between theses layers, is called
   a. aortic aneurysm.
   b. arteriosclerosis.
   c. aortic dissection.
   d. atherosclerosis.

26. Which of the following are the correct four links in the chain of survival, which is recommended by the American Heart Association for successful care of prehospital cardiac arrest victims?
   a. early access to emergency care, early ventilations, early defibrillation, and early advanced care
   b. early access to the hospital, early ventilations, early defibrillation, and early evacuation
   c. early access to emergency care, early cardiac monitoring, early defibrillation, and early advanced care
   d. early access to emergency care, early CPR, early defibrillation, and early advanced care

27. A condition that is caused by the heart's inability to pump and leads to an overload of fluid in the tissues is
   a. COPD.
   b. CHF.
   c. chronic bronchitis.
   d. asthma.

28. Which of the following is an indication of cardiac compromise?
   a. increased pulse rate
   b. altered mental status
   c. agitation
   d. all of the above

29. When assessing a patient with chest pain, asking the patient to rate the pain on a scale from one to ten would fall under what part of the acronym OPQRST?
   a. quality
   b. severity
   c. provocation
   d. radiate

30. In order to assist in the administration of nitroglycerine to a patient, his or her systolic blood pressure should be above
   a. 100 mmHg.
   b. 90 mmHg.
   c. 110 mmHg.
   d. 120 mmHg.

31. The Sellick's maneuver is performed by applying _____ pressure on the cricoid cartilage.
   a. downward
   b. upward
   c. backward
   d. frontward

32. The CombiTube is a
   a. single lumen device.
   b. blind insertion device.
   c. triple lumen device.
   d. device to be used under direct laryngoscopy.

33. When inserted, the CombiTube will enter the trachea approximately _____ of the time.
   a. 90%
   b. 60% to 80%
   c. 10% to 20%
   d. 50%

34. The laryngeal mask airway was initially designed
   a. for the use of EMTs in the field.
   b. for use in a controlled environment, such as the operating room.
   c. for use by the military.
   d. to allow the patient to step down from a more invasive device when healing.

35. The mechanical device that uses negative pressure to differentiate tracheal from esophageal intubation is a(n)
   a. capnographer.
   b. capnometer.
   c. end-tidal carbon dioxide ($ETCO_2$) detector.
   d. esophageal detector device (EDD).

36. The side or part of the body that is farthest from the midline is described as
   a. distal.
   b. dorsal.
   c. lateral.
   d. medial.

37. The largest organ of the body is part of the
   a. circulatory system.
   b. integumentary system.
   c. endocrine system.
   d. respiratory system.

38. You respond to a patient who has a behavioral emergency. The patient states that he hears voices talking to him, and the voices are telling him to kill. You should
   a. believe him and be alert to possible violence.
   b. try to talk sense into him.
   c. tell him that the voices are not real.
   d. restrain him until law enforcement arrives for assistance.

39. A common symptom seen with a diabetic patient is excessive drinking to satisfy extreme thirst. This is also called
   a. polyuria.
   b. polydipsia.
   c. polyphagia.
   d. dysphagia.

40. Patients who do not produce insulin at all
   a. have type 2 diabetes.
   b. are hypoglycemic.
   c. have normal blood sugar levels.
   d. have type 1 diabetes.

41. The leading cause of maternal death in the first trimester of pregnancy is
   a. placenta abruption.
   b. eclampsia.
   c. internal hemorrhage, secondary to an ectopic pregnancy.
   d. bleeding associated with a miscarriage.

42. A multipara woman is one who
   a. is experiencing her first pregnancy.
   b. has had more than one baby born alive.
   c. has had one live birth.
   d. None of the above.

43. You arrive on the scene to find a patient in the beginning of the second stage of labor. You should
   a. stay on the scene and deliver the baby.
   b. transport immediately.
   c. contact medical control for orders.
   d. all of the above.

44. The presence of meconium
   a. is an indicator of fetal distress.
   b. is a normal finding.
   c. is only emergent if the baby is in respiratory distress.
   d. occurs in 80% of births.

45. Preeclampsia typically develops after the_____ week of pregnancy.
   a. 20th
   b. 30th
   c. 28th
   d. 36th

46. When resources and personnel are provided by other jurisdictions, this is called
   a. an MCI.
   b. a unity of command.
   c. mutual aid.
   d. supporting material.

47. Prior to the establishment of National Incident Management Sysstem, the incident command system was developed and designed for
   a. the 9/11 terrorist attack.
   b. wildfires in California.
   c. flooding disasters.
   d. a chemical warfare attack.

48. Which of the following is a component of the MSDS?
a. reactivity data
b. health hazard data
c. the boiling point
d. all of the above

49. A DOT Hazard Class 1 indicates
a. explosives.
b. combustible liquids.
c. gases.
d. infectious substances.

50. Radioactive material can kill or injure by
a. Interrupting cardiac rhythms.
b. Disrupting cellular functions.
c. Increasing blood clot formation.
d. Acting as a corrosive.

51. When applying a bandage or a dressing to a hand, you should put the hand in what position?
a. position of function
b. slightly flexed
c. slightly extended
d. flat

52. You are treating a 52-year-old female patient who has been complaining of substernal chest pain radiating into her left arm. The pain began as she was playing tennis and has lasted approximately ten minutes. You apply oxygen and medical control authorized you to assist the patient with her nitroglycerin. The patient states she feels relief from the chest pain within five minutes of the nitroglycerin administration. You understand the reason the nitroglycerin may have relieved her pain is by increasing oxygenation by
a. reducing the clot.
b. dilating bronchioles.
c. preventing the clot from getting bigger.
d. dilating blood vessels.

53. Using the rule of nines, the posterior trunk accounts for what percentage of body surface area on an adult?
a. 18
b. 9
c. 36
d. 14

54. Using the rule of nines, each lower extremity in a pediatric patient accounts for what percentage of body surface area?
a. 14
b. 7
c. 9
d. 18

55. Which of the following is a high priority (severe) burn injury?
a. full thickness burns affecting less than 2%
b. partial thickness burns affecting 12%
c. burns complicated by an extremity fracture
d. superficial burns affecting 55%

56. In which instance is the placement of an AED indicated?
a. a pulseless patient
b. an unresponsive patient
c. a choking patient who is losing consciousness
d. a patient with apnea

57. Early advanced care is the _____ link in the chain of survival.
a. third
b. first
c. second
d. fourth

58. Besides ventricular fibrillation, the second rhythm that the AED considers shockable is
a. rapid ventricular tachycardia.
b. asystole.
c. atrial fibrillation.
d. pulseless electrical activity.

59. *Infarction* means
   a. the death of tissue.
   b. inadequate tissue perfusion.
   c. decreased blood flow.
   d. none of the above.

60. Another term for an abnormal cardiac rhythm is
   a. cardiomyopathy.
   b. arrhythmia.
   c. asystole.
   d. tachypnea.

61. Which of the following is an indicator of correct endotracheal tube placement?
   a. abdominal rise and fall
   b. gastric sounds
   c. positive waveform capnography
   d. your partner's assurance that he saw the tube pass through the vocal cords

62. What is the best indicator of correct tube placement?
   a. direct visualization
   b. chest rise and fall
   c. O_2 sat monitoring
   d. $ETCO_2$ monitoring

63. The most common complication from the use of a flow-restricted, oxygen-powered ventilation device is
   a. a tension pneumothorax.
   b. hyperventilation.
   c. decreased O_2 sat.
   d. gastric distention.

64. The medical term for shortness of breath is
   a. orthopnea.
   b. orthodontalgia.
   c. dyspnea.
   d. apnea.

65. Patients who have severe difficulty breathing are usually found in what position?
   a. high-Fowler's
   b. Trendelenburg
   c. semi-Fowler's
   d. tripod

66. You are assessing a patient who has inhaled a poisonous substance and has no signs of trauma. You should initially
   a. apply high flow O_2.
   b. identify the substance.
   c. call poison control.
   d. move the patient into the fresh air.

67. Approximately 80% of all poisonings are by
   a. ingestion.
   b. inhalation.
   c. surface contact.
   d. injection.

68. You are assessing a patient who has a history of behavioral emergencies and hostile tendencies. What should be a major clue for the possibility of danger?
   a. the patient's violent history
   b. the patient's posture
   c. the level of the patient's distress
   d. all of the above

69. The two categories in which the underlying causes of behavioral emergencies fall under are
   a. psychogenic brain disorders and neural dysfunctions.
   b. behavioral disorders and environmental influences.
   c. organic brain syndrome and functional disorders.
   d. none of the above.

70. The topographic anatomical term for the front side of the body is
   a. anterior.
   b. dorsal.
   c. inferior.
   d. medial.

71. Bleeding after labor should NOT be managed by
   a. administering high flow O_2 via an NRB mask.
   b. applying a sanitary napkin into the vagina.
   c. placing the mother left laterally recumbent.
   d. placing the infant on the mother's chest and allowing him or her to nurse.

72. Which of the following is NOT a sign of respiratory distress in children?
   a. crying
   b. head bobbing
   c. retractions
   d. grunting

73. A carcinogenic effect is
   a. an increase in the risk of an individual developing cancer.
   b. an increase in the risk of a developing embryo having physical effects.
   c. a permanent change in the individual's DNA.
   d. none of the above.

74. Secondary decontamination is performed
   a. in the cold zone.
   b. in the warm zone.
   c. in a shower area.
   d. at the hospital.

75. A combustible liquid is considered a DOT Hazard Class
   a. 2.
   b. 3.
   c. 9.
   d. 6.

76. When at a landing zone, how should the aircraft be approached?
   a. from the rear
   b. from the side
   c. depends on the make and model of the aircraft
   d. only when accompanied by a flight crew member

77. The optimal landing zone should be established on level ground, free of debris, and measure
   a. 60 feet by 60 feet.
   b. 100 feet by 100 feet.
   c. 50 feet by 50 feet.
   d. None of the above.

78. You are conducting primary triage during an MCI. Which of the following patients would be tagged yellow?
   a. A patient breathing 24 times per minute without a radial pulse
   b. A patient breathing 14 times per minute, without a radial pulse present, who obeys simple commands and has an arterial bleed controlled by a tourniquet
   c. A patient who begins spontaneous respirations after you open the airway, has a radial pulse, and is unresponsive
   d. A patient walking to the treatment area with an amputated right arm

79. You have been dispatched to a patient with an altered mental status. Upon your arrival you find a male patient who is speaking with slurred speech and confused words. His skin is diaphoretic and bystanders state the patient was fine a few moments ago and then suddenly began acting disoriented. The patient has no facial droop and equal hand grips. He has a medic alert tag that indicates he has a history of diabetes. Your treatment should include
   a. oxygen and requesting ALS for a normal saline IV bolus.
   b. placing the patient in soft restraints and request law enforcement assistance.
   c. oxygen, oral glucose, and requesting ALS.
   d. assisting the patient with his insulin and request ALS.

80. What is the term that identifies the three signs that are indicative of increased intracranial pressure?
   a. Cullen's sign
   b. Beck's triad
   c. Battle's sign
   d. Cushing's triad

81. Bleeding from a subdural hematoma is
   a. arterial.
   b. venous.
   c. a collection of blood between the dura mater and the skull.
   d. more rare than epidural hematomas.

82. Which of the following is NOT a component of the Glasgow Coma Scale?
   a. motor response
   b. respirations
   c. eye opening
   d. verbal response

83. The electrode that is placed either on the right arm or just below the right clavicle is what color?
   a. red
   b. black
   c. yellow
   d. white

84. Common signs and symptoms of myocardial infarction include
   a. chest discomfort lasting less than 20 minutes, dyspnea, and pain relieved by rest.
   b. sharp tearing chest pain lasting more than 30 minutes, dyspnea, and pain unrelieved by rest or nitroglycerin.
   c. chest pressure lasting more than 30 minutes, nausea, dyspnea, and pain unrelieved by rest or nitroglycerin.
   d. chest tightness, dyspnea, wheezing breath sounds, and pain unrelieved by rest.

85. You are assessing a hypertensive patient with epistaxis. After scene safety and BSI precautions have been taken, you should first
   a. apply direct pressure, squeezing both nostrils.
   b. lay the patient flat.
   c. apply supplemental O_2.
   d. attempt to calm and reassure the patient.

86. There are _____ cranial nerves.
   a. 7
   b. 12
   c. 9
   d. 10

87. The term describing structures that are located closer to the trunk is
   a. superficial.
   b. proximal.
   c. lateral.
   d. distal.

88. A normal pupil reaction to shining a bright light into an eye would be the _____ of the pupil.
  a. constriction
  b. dilation
  c. unequal reaction
  d. unresponsiveness

89. Which of the following is a method of indirect disease transmission?
  a. mosquito
  b. water
  c. coughing
  d. sexual contact

90. A _____ is a microorganism that is capable of causing a disease in a host.
  a. vector
  b. spore
  c. droplet
  d. pathogen

91. Which of the following statements is true?
  a. Only some infectious diseases are contagious, but all contagious diseases are infectious.
  b. All infectious diseases are contagious.
  c. Some contagious diseases are infectious.
  d. None of the above.

92. What is the incubation period for Hepatitis B?
  a. 1–2 weeks
  b. 2–10 weeks
  c. 4–12 weeks
  d. 2–6 weeks

93. Cirrhosis of the liver develops in _____ of patients with chronic Hepatitis C.
  a. 100%
  b. 20%
  c. 50%
  d. 30%

94. Tuberculosis is a _____ organism.
  a. viral
  b. bacterial
  c. dormant
  d. genetic

95. The term *power lift* refers to using muscle groups in your
  a. back.
  b. legs.
  c. arms.
  d. abdomen.

96. Rapid extrication should be used for which of the following?
  a. A patient who is bleeding profusely from the back of the head
  b. A patient who is screaming and stating that she is unable to breathe
  c. An accident where the airbag was not deployed
  d. None of the above

97. What is the ventilation rate for children who are experiencing brain herniation?
  a. 20 breaths per minute
  b. 30 breaths per minute
  c. 40 breaths per minute
  d. 12 breaths per minute

98. Injuries to the spine that cause the individual vertebrae to pull apart and separate from one another are called
   a. distraction injuries.
   b. extension injuries.
   c. compression injuries.
   d. displaced injuries.

99. Aniscoria is
   a. explosive diarrhea.
   b. posturing.
   c. unequal pupils.
   d. dilation of the blood vessels.

100. The best way to treat a patient who has a large, spurting laceration on the head is to
   a. apply pressure to the carotid artery.
   b. place a gloved hand over gauze while holding constant, firm pressure.
   c. apply a bandage and dressing to the head.
   d. all of the above.

101. You are assessing a child who has sustained burns to his entire anterior legs bilaterally and to his anterior right arm. He has a burned body surface area of _____.
   a. 22.5%.
   b. 27%.
   c. 23%.
   d. 18.5%.

102. Which of the following is a curved forcep that can be used to remove a foreign body from a patient's mouth?
   a. McWhirter prongs
   b. Magill forceps
   c. Miller blades
   d. Magoo prongs

103. Which of the following is true regarding laryngeal mask airways?
   a. They can be used in morbidly obese patients.
   b. They are a single lumen, blind insertion airway device.
   c. They are classified as a high-pressure airway device.
   d. They decrease the risk of aspiration in patients who have a full stomach.

104. What does the *P* stand for in SAMPLE?
   a. pain
   b. provocation
   c. past medical history
   d. past meal eaten

105. You are evaluating a patient who you believe is having a stroke. You decide to use the Cincinnati Prehospital Stroke scale as part of your patient assessment. The three components of the Cincinnati Stroke Scale are
   a. facial droop, arm drift, and abnormal speech.
   b. facial grimace, arm strength, and abnormal speech.
   c. facial droop, arm drift, and altered mental status.
   d. facial droop, arm strength, and altered mental status.

106. Which of the following is the medical term for double vision?
   a. dysplopia
   b. diplopia
   c. photophobia
   d. conjunctival vision

107. What is another name for the mitral valve in the heart?
   a. biscuspid valve
   b. aortic knob
   c. tricuspid valve
   d. pulmonic valve

108. You are treating a 58-year-old male patient for a possible AMI. During your assessment you noted the patient is extremely diaphoretic with sweat soaking through his shirt. You have the patient on oxygen and have administered 324 mg ASA and .12 mg nitroglycerin per medical control. The patient suddenly collapses and is unresponsive, pulseless, and apneic. As you expose his chest you notice a medication patch at midclavicular line and distal to the right clavicle. How do you proceed?
   a. Immediately place the AED pads and defibrillate if indicated
   b. Quickly dry the chest, place the pads anterior/posterior, and defibrillate if indicated
   c. Quickly remove the medication patch, wipe off the excess medication, dry the chest, apply pads in the standard position, and defibrillate if indicated
   d. Begin CPR and contact medical control for instructions

109. During your assessment of a patient, you note that her skin is very pale. Which of the following would be the most likely cause?
   a. fever
   b. hypertension
   c. carbon monoxide poisoning
   d. blood loss

110. Which of the following is NOT one of the classic signs seen in Cushing's triad?
   a. rise in blood pressure
   b. slowing pulse
   c. irregular pupils
   d. erratic respirations

111. What does the *S* stand for in the charting mnemonic SOAP?
   a. signs and symptoms
   b. subjective
   c. scene description
   d. skin color

112. The AED will prompt you to defibrillate which two cardiac rhythms?
   a. pulseless electrical activity and ventricular fibrillation
   b. premature ventricular beats and ventricular tachycardia
   c. sinus bradycardia and supraventricular tachycardia
   d. ventricular tachycardia and ventricular fibrillation

113. An explosion has occurred, and your patient sustained injuries when they were thrown into a brick wall. This type of injury is classified as a
   a. primary blast injury
   b. secondary blast injury
   c. tertiary blast injury
   d. quaternary blast injury

114. What is the medical term for the passage of dark, tarry stools that is indicative of lower gastrointestinal bleeding?
   a. Melena
   b. Hematochezia
   c. Epistaxis
   d. Hemoptysis

115. Which of the following would cause obstructive shock?
   a. tension pneumothorax
   b. massive myocardial infarction
   c. severe blood loss
   d. anaphylactic shock

116. What type of burn involves the epidermis and varying layers of the dermis?
   a. superficial burn
   b. partial thickness burn
   c. full thickness burn
   d. combination burn

117. Your patient has had battery acid splashed in his eyes and now has no vision. Which of the following treatments would be most appropriate?
   a. Immediately neutralize the acid with a base, such as baking soda.
   b. Cover both his eyes with a sterile dressing.
   c. Flush the affected eye with normal saline for ten minutes.
   d. Flush both eyes with eyewash or normal saline for ten minutes.

118. Which one of the following is a contraindication for the administration of nitroglycerin?
   a. Cardiac related chest pain
   b. Diastolic blood pressure < 100 mmHg
   c. Headache
   d. Systolic blood pressure < 100 mmHg

119. Which one of the meninges is closest to the skull?
   a. pia mater
   b. dura mater
   c. arachnoid membrane
   d. corpus callosum

120. What part of the spinal cord innervates the diaphragm?
   a. cervical spine
   b. thoracic spine
   c. lumbar spine
   d. all the spine innervates the diaphragm

Answers

1. a. The assessment of the airway should be done rapidly and completed within 15 seconds.

2. b. Agonal respirations are considered *dying gasps* and are characterized by irregular, occasional gasps for air.

3. d. Normal breathing will have a regular rise and fall of the chest, movement of the abdomen, and a normal rate and rhythm.

4. b. During compensated shock, respirations will increase to compensate for the decrease in perfusion.

5. a. The glottis opening is the narrowest portion of the adult airway.

6. d. If the ATV goes into alarm or you notice a sudden change in the adequacy of the chest rise and fall, it is best to begin bag-valve mask ventilations to ensure adequate ventilations as you troubleshoot the issue with the ATV..

7. a. Aspirin makes the platelets in the blood less likely to stick together and, therefore, prevents clots from getting any bigger. Aspirin cannot break up clots and nitroglycerin causes vasodilation of the coronary arteries..

8. b. Automaticity is the unique characteristic possessed by cardiac muscle. Contractility is the ability of the muscle to contract when stimulated by an electrical impulse. Conductivity is the ability of the muscle to rapidly conduct electrical impulses to other parts of the muscle.

9. b. The thyroid cartilage makes up what is known as the *Adam's apple*.

10. a. Cocaine overdoses will present with dilated pupils, unless other drugs have been taken along with cocaine.

11. a. A child who is not crying and has poor muscle tone and pale skin is presenting in an emergent condition. The child should immediately be evaluated for life-threatening problems.

12. c. Infants lose the majority of their body heat through their heads.

13. b. Secondary drowning syndrome can occur within 24 hours after a drowning incident.

14. c. A ventriculoperitoneal shunt is placed in the brain to help drain excess CSF and would be common in a child with hydrocephalus.

15. c. The birth of an infant occurs in the end of the second stage of labor.

16. d. All the answers listed are required elements for a negligence lawsuit to hold up in court.

17. c. At the scene of a hazardous material call, park the ambulance uphill and upwind in order to lessen the exposure to toxic fumes.

18. b. A competent adult gives permission to treat with expressed consent.

19. b. The first incident management system was originally known as the incident command system (ICS).

20. d. The safety officer reports directly to the incident commander and is considered a member of the command staff.

21. b. The presence of cerebrospinal fluid should always raise suspicion for a skull fracture.

22. d. At present, the patient is not currently displaying any signs or symptoms of a severe allergic reaction, so you should continue with your physical exam.

23. a. Blunt trauma with pain and swelling over the upper right quadrant should raise a high index of suspicion for a lacerated liver.

24. b. A patient can lose all his or her blood volume through an open pelvic fracture.

25. c. When the inner layers of the aorta become separated and blood, many times under high pressure, flows in between those layers an aortic dissection or dissecting aneurysm has occurred. These are many times characterized by a sharp or tearing pain. An aneurysm is a weakening in the vessel wall that allows it to balloon out.

26. d. The American Heart Association has recognized four links in the chain of survival, including early access to emergency care, early CPR, early defibrillation, and early advanced care.

27. b. Congestive heart failure (CHF) is a condition in which the heart loses the ability to adequately pump, allowing fluid to overload in the tissues.

28. d. Cardiac compromise will present signs of shock, including increased pulse rate, altered mental status, and agitation.

29. b. When asking a patient to rate their pain on a one to ten scale, you are attempting to quantify the severity of the pain.

30. a. The systolic blood pressure should be above 100 mmHg in order to give nitroglycerin.

31. a. The Sellick's maneuver is performed by applying downward pressure on the cricoid cartilage.

32. b. The CombiTube is a dual lumen, blind insertion airway device.

33. c. When inserted, the CombiTube will go into the esophagus approximately 80% to 90% of the time and into the trachea 10% to 20% of the time.

34. b. The laryngeal mask airway (LMA) was originally designed to be used in the operating room.

35. d. The esophageal detector device (EDD) uses negative pressure to differentiate from intubations in the trachea versus in the esophagus.

36. c. The part of the body farthest from the midline is said to be lateral.

37. b. The integumentary system (skin) is the largest organ in the body.

38. a. Always be alert for the potential of violence on behavioral emergency calls.

39. b. *Polydipsia* is the medical term for excessive thirst and is frequently seen in patients with high blood sugar.

40. d. Patients who do not produce insulin have type 1 diabetes.

41. c. The leading cause of maternal death in the first trimester of pregnancy is internal bleeding, secondary to an ectopic pregnancy.

42. b. *Multipara* means that the patient has had more than one baby born alive.

43. a. If the patient is beginning the second stage of labor, then birth is imminent. As long as there are no complications suspected, you should remain on the scene and deliver the baby.

44. a. The presence of meconium is an indicator of fetal distress.

45. a. Preeclampsia typically develops after the twentieth week of pregnancy.

46. c. Mutual aid occurs when resources and personnel are provided by other jurisdictions.

47. b. The incident command system was originally developed for the wildfires in California.

48. d. Reactivity data, health hazard data, and the product boiling point are all components of the MSDS.

49. a. A DOT Hazard Class 1 is an explosive.

50. b. Radioactive material can cause injury and death through the disruption of cellular function (i.e., depleting the immune system or instigating cancers). Radioactive material can also cause severe burns.

51. a. When applying a bandage or dressing to a hand, place the hand in the position of function.

52. d. Nitroglycerin improves blood flow and, therefore, improves perfusion of the myocardium by dilating the blood vessels.

53. a. Using the rule of nines, the posterior trunk accounts for 18% of body surface area of the adult.

54. a. Using the rule of nines, each lower extremity in a pediatric patient accounts for 14% of body surface area.

55. c. Any burn that is complicated by an extremity fracture is classified as a severe burn.

56. a. The AED should only be applied to patients who are pulseless. All other patients listed may still have a pulse, which is a contraindication for applying the AED.

57. d. Early advanced care is the fourth link in the chain of survival.

58. a. An AED will shock ventricular fibrillation and rapid ventricular tachycardia.

59. a. *Infarction* means tissue death.

60. b. An arrhythmia is an abnormal cardiac rhythm.

61. c. Positive waveform capnography is an indicator of correct endotracheal tube placement.

62. d. End-tidal CO_2 monitoring is optimal for indicating correct tube placement.

63. d. Gastric distention is the most common complication when using flow-restricted, oxygen-powered ventilation devices.

64. c. *Dyspnea* is the medical term for shortness of breath.

65. d. Patients who have severe shortness of breath are usually in the tripod position because this helps to maximize air exchange in the lungs.

66. d. Any patients that have inhaled a toxic substance should be immediately moved to fresh air.

67. a. Approximately 80% of poisonings are by ingestion.

68. d. The patient's history, posture, and level of distress are all indicators of the possibility of danger to the EMTs.

69. c. The two classifications of behavioral emergencies are organic brain syndrome and functional disorders.

70. a. The anatomical term for the front of the body is *anterior*.

71. b. Never place anything inside the vagina in an attempt to control vaginal bleeding.

72. a. Crying is not a sign of respiratory distress in children; it is usually a good indicator of airway patency.

73. a. A carcinogenic effect is one that will increase an individual's risk of developing cancer.

74. d. Secondary decontamination is typically performed at the hospital.

75. b. A combustible liquid is a DOT Hazard Class 3.

76. d. An aircraft should never be approached unless you are accompanied by a member of the flight team.

77. b. The optimal landing zone measures 100 feet by 100 feet and is free of obstacles and debris.

78. b. The patient breathing less than 30 times per minute, having a radial pulse, and having the ability to obey simple commands, but cannot walk is categorized as yellow regardless of other injuries. Patients breathing faster than 30 times per minute or who were not breathing before you opened their airways are tagged red, as are patients without a radial pulse or who cannot obey simple commands. Any patient who can walk to the treatment area is initially tagged green until further assessed in the treatment area.

79. c. This patient is exhibiting signs and symptoms of hypoglycemia and can protect his airway.

80. d. Cushing's triad consists of increased blood pressure, decreased heart rate, and irregular respirations. In addition, it is a sign of increased intracranial pressure.

81. b. Bleeding from a subdural hematoma is venous in nature.

82. b. Respirations are not included in the Glasgow Coma Scale.

83. d. The white electrode is placed either on the right arm or just below the right clavicle.

84. c. These are all common signs and symptoms of a myocardial infarction. The others could be angina, dissecting aorta, or asthma.

85. a. Control of an epistaxis includes applying direct pressure and squeezing both nostrils.

86. d. There are 10 cranial nerves.

87. b. The term *proximal* describes a structure that is located closer to the trunk.

88. a. A normal pupil reaction is to constrict when exposed to a bright light.

89. b. Water is an example of an indirect vehicle-borne method for disease transmission.

90. d. A pathogen is a microorganism that is capable of causing a disease in a host.

91. a. Only some infectious diseases are contagious, but all contagious diseases are infectious.

92. c. The normal incubation period for Hepatitis B is 4 to 12 weeks.

93. c. Cirrhosis of the liver will develop in about one-half of patients with chronic Hepatitis C.

94. b. Tuberculosis is a bacterial organism.

95. b. The term *power lift* refers to lifting while using muscles in your legs.

96. d. None of the answer choices is an emergency life threatening situation and, therefore, does not warrant the risk to the spine and neck that rapid extrication presents. Many head injuries bleed profusely due to the large amount of capillaries in the head, but the bleeding is rarely uncontrollable or life threatening. A patient screaming she can't breathe generally can breathe and clearly has a patent airway. An undeployed airbag is a risk to the patient and EMT, but can be minimized by moving the seat back or using a commercial airbag restraint device and cutting power to the vehicle..

97. b. Children should be ventilated at a rate of 30 breaths per minute when brain herniation is suspected.

98. a. Distraction injuries are injuries to the spine in which the individual vertebrae pull apart and separate from each other.

99. c. The term *aniscoria* means unequal pupils.

100. b. The best way to treat a patient who has a large, spurting laceration on the head is to place a gloved hand over gauze while holding constant, firm pressure.

101. d. Burns to a child's anterior legs bilaterally and his anterior right arm cover a body surface area of 18.5%.

102. b. Magill forceps are used to remove foreign objects from a patient's mouth.

103. b. Laryngeal mask airways are single lumen, blind insertion airway devices. They are not to be used in morbidly obese patients. These patients cannot tolerate high airway pressures, and using this device on them can increase the risk of aspiration of gastric contents.

104. c. The *P* in SAMPLE stands for past medical history.

105. a. The Cincinnati Prehospital Stroke Scale involves an assessment of the symmetry of the face's "facial droop" by having the patient smile. Arm drift can be assessed by asking the patient to hold her arms out with her eyes closed and see if one drifts downwards, and abnormal speech can be assessed to see if the patient slurs her words or uses the wrong words.

106. b. *Diplopia* is the medical term for double vision.

107. c. The tricuspid valve is also called the mitral valve.

108. c. You should remove the medication patch and wipe the chest dry and free of excess medication. You should then apply the AED as normal and follow the prompts.

109. d. Blood loss would cause pale skin. Fever, hypertension, and carbon monoxide poisoning would typically present with red skin.

110. c. Pupillary response is *not* one of the three classic signs seen with Cushing's response.

111. b. The *S* in SOAP stands for subjective.

112. d. The two rhythms an AED will prompt the EMT to shock are ventricular tachycardia and ventricular fibrillation.

113. c. Tertiary blast injuries occur when a person is thrown into an object from an explosion.

114. a. *Melena* is the medical term for the passage of dark, tarry stools and is indicative of lower gastrointestinal bleeding.

115. a. A tension pneumothorax would cause obstructive shock.

116. b. A partial thickness burn (second degree) involves the epidermis and varying layers of the dermis.

117. d. If a patient has any chemical in his or her eyes, immediately flush both eyes with eyewash or normal saline for at least ten minutes. Never attempt to neutralize a chemical burn.

118. d. Systolic blood pressure < 100 mmHg is a contraindication. Cardiac chest pain is an indication. Headache is a side effect of nitroglycerin. Diastolic blood pressure has no relation to the administration of nitroglycerin.

119. b. The dura mater is the layer of the meninges that is closest to the skull.

120. a. The cervical spine innervates the diaphragm.

12 ▶ EMT PRACTICE EXAM 10

CHAPTER SUMMARY
This is the final practice exam in this book based on the National Registry's EMT cognitive exam. Use this test to continue your study and practice.

L ike Chapter 6, this chapter contains questions in free-response format. The questions in this exam represent each of the modules found in the U.S. Department of Transportation's Emergency Medical Technician National Education Standards. The results can be used to guide your study. If necessary, use the open-book technique and refer to your EMT training text as you go. Take your time—there is more to this exam than simply getting the answer correct; you must also understand the concept.

EMT Practice Exam 10

1. Which lung has three lobes?

_____

_____

_____

_____

2. What are the five stages of the grieving process?

_____

_____

_____

3. Name six physiologic signs of stress.

_____

_____

_____

_____

4. Explain how the hypoxic drive works.

_____

_____

_____

5. Describe *automaticity*.

_____

_____

_____

_____

6. You were called to the residence of an adult female in labor. After delivery, you assess that the newborn has a pink body and blue hands. He has a pulse of 110 beats per minute, resists your attempts to straighten his hips and knees, cries when his foot is flicked, and has slow respirations. What is the APGAR score of the infant?

_____

_____

_____

_____

7. Explain the electrical conduction system of a normal functioning heart and state the normal electrical current pathway.

_____

_____

_____

_____

8. Explain what the SAMPLE history is used for and state what each letter in the acronym stands for.

_____

_____

_____

_____

9. How would you recognize labored breathing in a pediatric patient? Explain.

_____

_____

_____

_____

10. Name a situation in which a healthy patient may have a delayed capillary refill.

_____

_____

_____

_____

11. Name the components of blood.

_____

_____

_____

_____

12. Describe what happens in the heart during diastole.

_____

_____

_____

_____

13. What is peristalsis?

_____

_____

_____

_____

14. Why is good nutrition important to the performance of an EMT?

_____

_____

_____

_____

15. What is the definition of a *vector-borne disease*?

_____

_____

_____

_____

16. What is diabetic ketoacidosis?

_____

_____

_____

_____

17. What is the APGAR score used for, and what does each letter in the acronym stand for?

_____

_____

_____

_____

18. Name two instances in which the pulse oximeter may provide a false reading.

_____

_____

_____

19. Why is it important to select the proper-sized blood pressure cuff for your patient?

_____

_____

_____

_____

20. What method should be used to carry a patient on a backboard or cot? How many rescuers are used in this method, and where are the rescuers positioned?

_____

_____

_____

_____

21. Name three contraindications for the application of a traction splint.

_____

_____

_____

_____

22. Define _shock_.

_____

_____

_____

_____

23. How should you treat a patient who presents a flail chest?

_____

_____

_____

_____

24. List the steps in applying a tourniquet.

_____

_____

_____

25. Why should you closely monitor glucose levels after a diabetic patient has a seizure?

_____

_____

_____

26. What is the difference between ventilation and respiration?

_____

_____

_____

27. What are the three elements of the Pediatric Assessment Triangle (PAT)?

_____

_____

_____

28. What should raise your index of suspicion for child abuse when you are treating a pediatric patient?

_____

_____

_____

29. Besides urinary output, how else would you determine that your infant patient may be dehydrated?

_____

_____

_____

30. What should you suspect when you discover ecchymosis behind your patient's ear over the mastoid process? What is this ecchymosis called?

_____

_____

_____

_____

31. Name four situations in which it is appropriate to remove a patient's helmet.

_____

_____

_____

_____

32. Define _retrograde amnesia._

_____

_____

_____

_____

33. Why are head injuries more common in children?

_____

_____

_____

_____

34. What is blood pressure?

_____

_____

_____

_____

35. What other devices can be used to immobilize a pediatric patient other than the long spine board?

_____

_____

_____

_____

36. What are the blood vessels that carry blood to the heart?

_____

_____

_____

_____

37. List the types of shock.

_____

_____

_____

_____

38. What are the three layers of the skin?

_____

_____

_____

39. What is a low angle rescue?

_____

_____

_____

40. What is the difference between a sprain and a strain?

_____

_____

_____

41. In an incident command system, what does the _span of control_ refer to?

_____

_____

_____

42. Where is the _popliteal region_?

_____

_____

_____

_____

43. You have arrived at a hospital and waited several minutes for a nurse to arrive in order to give your report. A call comes through dispatch for a traffic accident with injuries, and you know that you are the closest unit. How should you handle this situation?

_____

_____

_____

_____

44. List the steps taken for attaching a regulator to an oxygen cylinder.

_____

_____

_____

_____

45. When should you suspect that delivery of an infant is imminent?

_____

_____

_____

_____

46. What is the purpose of a liter flow device on oxygen?

_____

_____

_____

47. How is the Sellick's maneuver performed?

_____

_____

_____

48. Why are the elderly more at risk for c-spine injuries?

_____

_____

_____

49. What is an ectopic pregnancy?

_____

_____

_____

_____

50. What is meconium?

_____

_____

_____

51. What is supine hypotensive syndrome?

_____

_____

_____

52. Why is suction an immediate priority when there is presence of meconium?

_____

_____

_____

53. Why is it important to place gentle pressure on the baby's head as soon as crowning occurs?

_____

_____

_____

_____

54. Why should you wear gloves when administering nitroglycerine?

_____

_____

_____

_____

55. In what ways can poisons or medications enter the body?

_____

_____

_____

_____

56. How will you know if the application of the PASG has worked?

_____

_____

_____

_____

57. List the signs and symptoms of a severe allergic reaction (anaphylaxis).

_____

_____

_____

_____

58. What is a behavioral emergency?

_____

_____

_____

_____

59. What are some conditions that can mimic the signs and symptoms of a heart attack?

_____

_____

_____

_____

60. What are some changes that take place in the mother during pregnancy that may affect your assessment and care?

_____

_____

_____

_____

61. What are the two methods for performing chest compressions on an infant?

_____

_____

_____

_____

62. You have been dispatched to the scene of a possible shooting. When is it okay to leave the staging area and enter the scene?

_____

_____

_____

_____

63. You have been requested to enter a crime scene for an injured patient. How do you handle this situation?

_____

_____

_____

_____

64. List some strategies that will help you manage and decrease stress in your life.

_____

_____

_____

_____

65. What are some signs that can help you determine when a patient may become violent with you or others on scene?

_____

_____

_____

_____

66. List some scene hazards that may be dangerous to you and your partner.

_____

_____

_____

_____

67. What are some common hazards in a fire?

_____

_____

_____

_____

68. What is meant by *duty to act*?

_____

_____

_____

69. When does a patient have the right to refuse medical care?

_____

_____

_____

70. What does the acronym HIPAA stand for, what is its purpose, and how does it apply to you?

_____

_____

_____

71. Your patient has sustained a superficial injury to the arm. What does this mean?

_____

_____

_____

72. What is meant by the term *retroperitoneal*?

_____

_____

_____

73. How is the respiratory system in a pediatric patient different from that in an adult patient?

_____

_____

_____

74. What are the three main functions of the skin?

_____

_____

_____

75. What is preeclampsia?

_____

_____

_____

76. How does eclampsia differ from preeclampsia?

_____

_____

_____

_____

77. How do you treat eclampsia?

_____

_____

_____

_____

78. What are the characteristics of an increased work of breathing in pediatric patients?

_____

_____

_____

_____

79. Why might blood pressure determination and interpretation be difficult in pediatric patients?

_____

_____

_____

_____

80. Retractions may be present in a patient with an increased work of breathing. Where would you see this accessory muscle use?

_____

_____

_____

_____

81. What is the function of the pancreas?

_____

_____

_____

_____

82. When is it appropriate to use a Reeves stretcher?

_____

_____

_____

_____

83. When oral suctioning, how far should the tip of the catheter be placed?

_____

_____

_____

_____

84. A compressed gas cylinder that is color-coded yellow contains what type of gas?

_____

_____

_____

_____

85. In a head-on collision, what injuries could you expect to see in an unrestrained driver?

_____

_____

_____

86. There are two pathways that the body can travel along in a frontal collision when not restrained. What are these two pathways?

_____

_____

_____

87. What is *cavitation*?

_____

_____

_____

88. What are some common factors to take into consideration when assessing for significant mechanism of injury in a motor vehicle crash?

_____

_____

_____

_____

89. List the steps that are taken when palpating a blood pressure.

_____

_____

_____

_____

90. Where can skin color be assessed to determine good perfusion in your patient?

_____

_____

_____

91. Without a thermometer, how would you check the skin temperature of your patient?

_____

_____

_____

_____

92. In the acronym PERRL, what do the two *R*s stand for?

_____

_____

_____

_____

93. What is the condition suspected when orthostatic vital signs are positive?

_____

_____

_____

_____

94. In the acronym OPQRST, what does the *P* stand for and what does it mean?

_____

_____

_____

_____

95. When assessing pulses, what should you assess?

_____

_____

_____

_____

96. A person who is A&O ×4 is oriented to what four things?

_____

_____

_____

_____

97. What factors may have you place a patient into a high-priority category?

_____

_____

_____

_____

98. What is a multi-system trauma?

_____

_____

_____

_____

99. When assessing the abdomen of a patient who has a traumatic injury, besides DCAP-BTLS, what are you looking for?

_____

_____

_____

_____

100. What is crepitus?

_____

_____

_____

101. During a detailed physical exam of a trauma patient, what are you checking the ears for?

_____

_____

_____

102. When giving a report to the hospital staff via radio, what is pertinent information that should be included in the report?

_____

_____

_____

_____

103. Why is aspirin given to a patient complaining of chest pain?

_____

_____

_____

_____

104. What items should your OB kit contain?

_____

_____

_____

105. What is the rule of palm?

_____

_____

_____

_____

106. What are signs and symptoms that you may see associated with rib fractures?

_____

_____

_____

_____

107. What are some advantages of an AED?

_____

_____

_____

_____

108. What is _dead space_ in the lung?

_____

_____

_____

_____

109. What are some common causes for seizures?

_____

_____

_____

110. What are some medications that should make you suspect that your patient is a diabetic?

_____

_____

_____

111. At what point should compressions be interrupted when using an AED?

_____

_____

_____

_____

112. What is a TIA?

_____

_____

_____

_____

113. What is status epilepticus?

_____

_____

_____

_____

114. Why are elderly patients more susceptible to heat loss than non-elderly patients?

_____

_____

_____

_____

115. If able to do so, what position should you place a patient with an evisceration? Why?

_____

_____

_____

_____

116. What is a prolapsed cord?

_____

_____

_____

_____

117. What are the criteria for the use of an AED?

_____

_____

_____

_____

118. What should be placed directly over an open wound to control bleeding and protect from infection?

_____

_____

_____

_____

119. Why is a prolapsed cord dangerous to the baby?

_____

_____

_____

_____

120. In an unwitnessed cardiac arrest, why should defibrillation be delayed until at least two minutes of CPR have been administered?

_____

_____

_____

_____

121. What is the difference between stable and unstable angina?

_____

_____

_____

122. What is positional asphyxia?

_____

_____

_____

123. What are some important questions that you should ask a pregnant patient that will help you to determine if birth is imminent?

_____

_____

_____

124. What is another term that a pregnant female may use instead of _amniotic sac_?

_____

_____

_____

125. Your patient has suffered a penetrating wound to his chest wall. What is another term for this wound? What type of dressing should be applied?

_____

_____

_____

_____

126. If signs and symptoms of a tension pneumothorax occur after you have sealed the open chest wound, what should you do?

_____

_____

_____

_____

127. Who establishes command on scene?

_____

_____

_____

128. What do end-tidal carbon dioxide detectors do?

_____

_____

_____

129. The paramedic on scene has established an IV. The solution is not flowing properly. What can you do to troubleshoot this problem?

_____

_____

_____

130. On a conscious, pregnant female with a foreign body obstruction, where should you place your hands to provide thrusts to expel the object?

_____

_____

_____

131. What does the anatomical term _medial_ refer to?

_____

_____

_____

_____

132. What does the term _proper body mechanics_ refer to?

_____

_____

_____

_____

133. What are the types of suction units that you may need to know how to use?

_____

_____

_____

_____

134. Why is the insertion of a nasopharyngeal airway contraindicated in patients with significant facial trauma?

_____

_____

_____

_____

135. Where should you auscultate breath sounds?

_____

_____

_____

136. When assessing the skin, what do you assess?

_____

_____

_____

137. In a dark-skinned patient, how would you be able to see if the patient is pale?

_____

_____

_____

_____

138. In a patient with a hip fracture, what might you notice in the lower extremity?

_____

_____

_____

_____

139. When assessing the neck after a traumatic injury, what are you looking for besides DCAP-BTLS?

_____

_____

_____

_____

140. What is subcutaneous emphysema?

_____

_____

_____

_____

141. Why should ongoing assessments be performed on all patients?

_____

_____

_____

142. What are the contraindications for oral glucose?

_____

_____

_____

143. What is a febrile seizure?

_____

_____

_____

144. How should you care for a patient who is having an active seizure?

_____

_____

_____

145. What is the phase that immediately follows a seizure where the patient may remain unresponsive, have an altered level of consciousness, become agitated, or appear sleepy?

_____

_____

_____

_____

146. What are some symptoms associated with an envenomation?

_____

_____

_____

_____

147. What are the six things that you must know when considering what medication to administer to a patient?

_____

_____

_____

_____

148. What are some medications that an EMT may be called upon to assist administering?

_____

_____

_____

_____

149. What are some common causes of shock in a pediatric patient?

_____

_____

_____

150. What is an epistaxis?

_____

_____

_____

_____

Answers

1. The right lung has three lobes: upper, middle, and lower lobes.
2. The five stages of the grieving process include denial, anger and hostility, bargaining, depression, and acceptance.
3. Physiologic signs of stress include increased blood pressure, dilated pupils, increased heart rate, perspiration, tense muscles, dilated blood vessels, decreased blood flow to the GI tract, increased respirations, and increased blood glucose levels.
4. Considered the backup plan to control respiration, the hypoxic drive will stimulate breathing when the body cannot rely on the carbon dioxide receptors. When the carbon dioxide receptors fail, the oxygen receptors in the brain, carotid arteries, and the walls of the aorta will sense when oxygen levels are low, thus stimulating breathing.
5. Automaticity is the ability of the heart (cardiac cells) to contract at its own rate independently from the influence of the brain.
6. The APGAR score of this newborn is 8: A = 1, P = 2, G = 2, A = 2, R = 1.
7. The electrical conduction system is a network of specialized cardiac tissue that carries the electrical impulses throughout the heart. In a normal functioning heart, the electrical impulse begins in the right atria at the sinoatrial (SA) node. It then travels to the atrioventricular (AV) node located in the interatrial septum, then moves along the Purkinje fibers located along the walls of the ventricles.
8. The SAMPLE history is an acronym that is used for guidance when performing further assessment and obtaining a portion of the patient's history after immediate life threats have been stabilized. S = signs and symptoms; A = allergies to medications, food, or other

substances; M = medications (what medications the patient is currently taking, including prescribed, over-the-counter, and herbal medications); P = pertinent past history; L = last oral intake; and E = events leading up to the injury or illness.

9. You can recognize labored breathing in a pediatric patient by intercostal retractions, nasal flaring, gasping, and/or grunting.

10. A healthy patient may have a delayed capillary refill in a few situations. Certain medications, positions, body temperatures, and ages (elderly) can all affect the capillary refill time.

11. The components of blood include plasma, red blood cells, white blood cells, and platelets.

12. During diastole, the ventricles relax and fill with blood.

13. Peristalsis is the wave-like contractions that propel the contents of tubular organs.

14. The physical exertion and stress that are part of the EMT's job require an extremely high output of energy. Certain foods can affect energy levels and knowing which foods provide the highest amount of fuel is paramount.

15. A vector-borne disease is a disease that is caused by an infectious microbe and is transmitted to people through a blood-sucking arthropod (either an insect or arachnid).

16. Diabetic ketoacidosis is a condition in which there is an abnormally high accumulation of acids in the bloodstream, resulting from prolonged and very high hyperglycemia. Insulin is not available in the body to lower the sugar concentration.

17. The APGAR score is a scoring system used to assess the status of a newborn. A = Appearance, P = Pulse, G = Grimace, A = Activity, and R = Respirations.

18. Sickle cell disease, anemia, carbon monoxide poisoning, COPD, bright light, nail polish, and hypovolemia may all cause a false reading on the pulse oximeter.

19. A blood pressure cuff that fits too loosely on the patient may result in a falsely low blood pressure reading. A cuff that fits too tightly may result in a blood pressure reading that is falsely high.

20. The diamond-carry method should be used if a patient needs to be carried on a backboard or cot. This method uses four rescue personnel. One rescuer stands at the head, another at the feet, and one at each side of the patient.

21. Contraindications for applying a traction splint are injuries occurring close to or involving the knee, additional fractures in the affected limb, injuries of the pelvis, and partial amputations or avulsions with bone separation.

22. *Shock* is defined as inadequate tissue perfusion.

23. A patient with a flail chest should be treated by maintaining his or her airway, providing respiratory support as needed, administering supplemental oxygen, performing ongoing assessments, and possible splinting/immobilizing the flail segment.

24. Have someone continue to hold direct pressure and elevation to the extremity. Apply a commercial tourniquet per the manufacturer's specification proximal to the wound. If you do not have a commercial tourniquet a blood pressure cuff may be used. Place the cuff proximal to the wound and inflate the cuff until the bleeding stops. Continuously reassess the cuff to ensure it does not become deflated and allows bleeding to begin again. If you have neither a commercial tourniquet nor a blood pressure cuff you can make a tourniquet out of cloth/triangular bandage and a stick. Make a 4" wide strip out of the cloth and wrap the cloth twice around the extremity proximal to the wound. Tie a knot and place a stick or similar object on top of the knot. Tie a square knot over the stick. Start twisting the stick until the bleeding stops and then secure the stick so it will not unwind. Once a tourniquet is placed you

need to clearly mark, either on a piece of tape placed on the forehead or directly on the forehead, the fact that a tourniquet has been applied, where, and at what time. You also must document the same information in your run report and you must notify those assuming care of your patient that the tourniquet is in place.

25. You should closely monitor the glucose levels of a diabetic post-seizure because the glucose levels may drop significantly due to the excessive muscular contractions that take place during seizure activity.

26. Ventilation is the body's ability to move air in and out of the lungs, and respiration is the exchange of gasses in the alveoli of the lung tissue.

27. The three elements of the Pediatric Assessment Triangle (PAT) are work of breathing, circulation to skin, and appearance.

28. Injuries that are not consistent with the mechanism of injury given, conflicting stories from the parents or caregivers, and abnormal reaction from the child toward the parents or caregivers should all raise your index of suspicion for child abuse.

29. An infant who is dehydrated may have flat or sunken fontanels, dry oral mucosa, or may not produce tears while crying.

30. When ecchymosis is found behind a patient's ear, you should immediately suspect that they may have a skull fracture. Typically, the type of skull fracture with this sign is a basilar skull fracture. This sign is called Battle's sign.

31. You may remove a patient's helmet if you are unable to assess a patient's airway, you are unable to immobilize the patient's spine properly, the helmet causes excessive movement of the head, or if the patient is in cardiac arrest.

32. Retrograde amnesia is a type of amnesia where the patient is unable to recall the events that occurred just prior to the traumatic event or brain injury.

33. Head injuries are more common in children because of the size of their heads in proportion to their bodies.

34. Blood pressure is the pressure that is exerted on the walls of an artery.

35. A child may also be immobilized by using a short spine board or Kendrick Extrication Device.

36. Veins are blood vessels that carry blood to the heart.

37. The types of shock that the body may suffer are anaphylactic shock, neurogenic shock, hemorrhagic shock, cardiogenic shock, hypovolemic shock, septic shock, and psychogenic shock.

38. The three layers of the skin are the epidermis, the dermis, and the subcutaneous layer.

39. A low angle rescue is a rope rescue that involves terrain at a less than 40-degree angle.

40. A sprain is caused by the stretching and/or tearing of tendons and ligaments. A strain is when a muscle is pulled or torn.

41. The *span of control* refers to the amount of people or elements that can be directly managed by another person.

42. The *popliteal region* refers to the area that is posterior (behind) to the knee.

43. A medical call is not completed until a formal transfer of care has taken place. Leaving the patient prior to proper transfer is abandonment. Prior to taking another call, regardless of the location, the patient must be transferred properly.

44. To attach a regulator to an oxygen cylinder, first remove the seal. Then, inspect the valve for cleanliness and any defects. Purge the valve to express debris or dust particles that may have gotten into the valve. Confirm the presence of an O ring and inspect it for damage. Replace the O ring, if needed. Slip the yoke of the regulator over the cylinder valve. Line up the pins with the holes on the valve and tighten the thumb screw.

Turning the pressure gauge away from you, open the valve one full turn. Confirm the pressure in the cylinder by reading the gauge.

45. You should suspect that delivery of the infant is imminent when the baby is crowning, the mother feels a strong urge to move her bowels, and the mother's contractions become less than two minutes apart.

46. Liter flow devices increase the amount of oxygen available to the patient.

47. The Sellick's maneuver is performed by compressing the patient's neck just below the thyroid cartilage (Adam's apple), placing the thumb and forefinger on each side of the cricoid cartilage.

48. The elderly are at increased risk for cervical spine injuries because they may have decreased vision, be arthritic, or be on medications that make them dizzy or weak.

49. An ectopic pregnancy occurs when a fertilized egg implants itself and begins to develop in an area outside of the uterus.

50. Meconium is fecal matter that is excreted by the baby while it is still in the uterus.

51. Supine hypotensive syndrome is a condition that occurs when the fetus compresses the mother's vena cava as the mother is lying supine. The compression of the vena cava reduces blood return to the heart, causing significantly low blood pressure.

52. If suctioning is delayed, the infant can aspirate the meconium. Aspiration of meconium can cause serious damage to the newborn's lungs and even death.

53. Placing pressure on the baby's scalp when it becomes visible is done to prevent an explosive birth. This pressure helps to prevent injury to both the mother and the baby.

54. Gloves should be worn when administering nitroglycerin because it can be absorbed through the skin and enter the bloodstream.

55. Medications and poisons can enter the body through ingestion, injection, absorption, and inhalation.

56. The PASG are generally limited to use as a splint. You can tell when the PASG are successful when they have immobilized the injury and there is still a pulse, sensation, and motor function distal to the injury. If your local protocol allows the use of PASG to treat for hypoperfusion, then you know the PASG are successful if there is an increase in the patient's blood pressure.

57. Signs and symptoms of a severe allergic reaction include tightness in the chest, severe wheezing, rapid and labored breathing, stridorous respirations, hypotension, altered level of consciousness, and an increased heart rate.

58. A behavioral emergency occurs when a patient's behavior is dangerous, abnormal, or intolerable and causes concern for family, bystanders, caregivers, or the patient.

59. There are many conditions that can mimic the signs and symptoms of a heart attack. Some of these conditions include a panic attack, angina, pericarditis, anxiety, and a pulmonary embolism.

60. Some changes that occur in a mother during pregnancy that may affect your assessment and care are an increase in cardiac output, 50% increase in blood volume, and blood pressure decrease by as much as 10 mmHg. Her pulse rate may also increase, and her respirations may be shallow and difficult.

61. The two methods for performing chest compressions on an infant are the two-finger technique and the two-thumb encircling hands technique.

62. Regardless of the chief complaint, you must only enter the scene when law enforcement has requested you to do so and stated that the scene is safe for you to enter.

63. After ensuring the scene is safe, enter the scene carefully, as to not disturb possible evidence. The patient is your top priority; however, try not to disturb anything around you unless things must be moved in order to properly treat the patient. If you do move objects, be sure to let law enforcement know what you did. Never take anything from a scene of a crime. Enter and exit the scene in the same manner.

64. It is important to be able to manage the amount of stress in your life. You can do this by reducing the amount of hours that you work, changing your attitude, changing work partners to avoid negativity, implementing a workout or exercise program, maintaining friendships outside of the work environment, and focusing on the quality of care that you provide.

65. Always pay attention to certain behaviors of individuals on scene. Their behavior may signal that they may become violent. Pay attention to their past history, vocal activity, physical activity, substance abuse, and posture.

66. Some scene hazards that can be harmful to you and your partner are fires, electricity, hazardous materials, unstable vehicles, and bystanders.

67. Toxic gases, structural collapse, elevated temperatures, smoke, and oxygen deficiencies are all common hazards associated with fires.

68. Duty to act is the individual's responsibility to provide patient care.

69. A patient who is a competent adult and has been advised of all the risks, alternative treatments, and benefits may refuse treatment at any time.

70. The acronym HIPAA stands for the Health Insurance Portability and Accountability Act. HIPAA not only aims to combat fraud in health insurance, but one of its main purposes is to also safeguard a patient's confidentiality.

71. A superficial injury is an injury that is close to or directly on the skin.

72. Structures that lie retroperitoneal are those that lie behind the abdominal cavity.

73. The respiratory system of a pediatric patient is smaller proportionally and is less rigid than the respiratory system in an adult.

74. The three main functions of the skin are temperature regulation of the body, protection, and the transmission of information from the environment to the brain.

75. Preeclampsia, also known as pregnancy-induced hypertension, is a condition that is characterized by swelling in the hands and feet, high blood pressure, headache, and visual disturbances.

76. Eclampsia has the same signs and symptoms as preeclampsia; however, in the eclamptic mother there will be seizure activity.

77. To treat eclampsia, lay the mother left lateral recumbent and apply oxygen. Maintain the patient's airway and suction vomitus as needed. As with every other call, perform scene size-up and BSI, do initial assessments, obtain history, and perform a physical exam. Obtain baseline vital signs and treat the patient as needed. Transport the patient rapidly and do ongoing assessments.

78. Characteristics of an increased work of breathing in pediatric patients are nasal flaring, abnormal positioning, abnormal airway sounds, head bobbing, and accessory muscle use (retractions).

79. Obtaining blood pressures in pediatric patients may be difficult due to an EMT having difficulty remembering the normal values for the patient's age, lack of cooperation from the patient, loud crying, and confusion as to the proper blood pressure cuff size.

80. Retractions (accessory muscle use) may be seen above the clavicles, under the sternum, and between the ribs.

81. The pancreas produces and secretes insulin and also produces and secretes fluids that aid in digestion.

82. A Reeves stretcher is used for supine patients that need to be carried through tight spaces or down stairs.

83. When oral suctioning, the tip of the catheter should be placed into the mouth only as far as you can see.

84. A compressed gas cylinder that is color-coded yellow indicates that the contents are medical grade air.

85. During a head-on collision, the rescuer may see injuries to the head, neck, chest, abdomen, hip, knee, leg, and internal organs.

86. When not restrained, the body can travel in two pathways: down-and-under or up-and-over.

87. When a medium- to high-velocity projectile enters the body, the energy of the projectile can cause the surrounding tissues to expand greater than the actual size of the projectile. This expansion is called *cavitation*.

88. Some common factors to take into consideration when determining whether there has been a significant mechanism of injury in a motor vehicle crash are intrusion into the passenger compartment, airbag deployment, bent steering wheel, usage of restraints, windshield starring, death of an occupant inside the vehicle, and the speed of the vehicles involved.

89. Assessing a blood pressure by palpation is done by first taking proper BSI precautions. Then, choose an appropriately sized cuff and place it on the upper arm, ensuring that the gauge is visible. Locate and palpate the radial pulse in the arm on which you placed the blood pressure cuff. With the valve closed, inflate the cuff at least 30 mmHg above where you last felt the radial pulse. Gently and slowly open the valve and deflate the cuff slowly, waiting for the return of the radial pulse. Note where the needle on the gauge is located when you felt the first beat return to the radial artery. This

number will be the systolic blood pressure. Document the pressure.

90. Skin color can be assessed for adequate perfusion in the face, oral mucosa, conjunctiva, and nail beds.

91. The back of an ungloved hand can be used to assess a patient's skin temperature.

92. The two *R*s in PERRL stand for round and reactive.

93. When orthostatic vital signs are positive, hypovolemia should be suspected.

94. The P in OPQRST stands for provocation/palliation. When assessing a patient, provocation/palliation should lead you to ask questions about what makes the patient's symptoms or pain better or worse.

95. When assessing pulses, rhythm, strength, and rate should be assessed.

96. A person who is A&O ×4 is oriented to person, place, time, and event.

97. Factors that may indicate that a patient should be placed into a high-priority category include unresponsiveness, difficulty breathing, signs and symptoms of shock, chest pain, altered level of consciousness, poor general appearance or impression, complicated childbirth, and uncontrolled breathing.

98. A multi-system trauma is a traumatic injury that involves more than one organ system.

99. After assessing DCAP-BTLS on the abdomen of a patient who sustained a traumatic injury, palpate and look for distention, rigidity, or guarding.

100. Crepitus is a grinding sound or feeling when broken bones rub together.

101. When checking the ears of a trauma patient during a detailed physical exam, the ears are checked for DCAP-BTLS and drainage of blood and cerebrospinal fluid.

102. When giving a report to a hospital via the radio, the information that should be included in the transmission is your unit ID number, the patient's age and gender, the patient's chief complaint, a brief history of the present illness or complaint, relevant medical history (if any), vital signs, results of your examination, care that was provided to the patient, any changes in the patient's condition, and your ETA to the hospital.

103. Aspirin is given to patients with chest pain due to its prevention of blood clotting.

104. An OB kit should contain a bulb syringe, umbilical clamps, surgical scissors or scalpel, 4x4 gauze, towel drapes, baby blanket or foil baby bunting, sanitary napkins, infant cap, and biohazard bags.

105. The rule of palm is a method for assessing the total body surface area of a burn patient using his or her own palm. The patient's own palmar surface is equal to approximately 1% of his or her total body surface area.

106. Signs and symptoms associated with rib fractures are painful respirations, crepitus, and deformity.

107. Speed of operation, continuous monitoring, and ease of operation are all advantages of an AED.

108. Dead space in the lung refers to any area outside of the alveoli where gas exchange does not take place.

109. Common causes for seizures are hypoxia, head injuries, intracranial bleeding, brain tumors, alcohol withdrawal, metabolic changes, and infections.

110. Some of the medications found at a patient's residence that should make you suspect that your patient is a diabetic are insulin, glucophage, Avandia™, Amaryl™, Actos™, and glucagon.

111. When using an AED, compressions should only be interrupted when the AED is in either analyze or shock mode.

112. TIA stands for transient ischemic attack. Although it has similar signs and symptoms of a stroke, it typically resolves within 24 hours.

113. Status epilepticus can be a seizure that lasts approximately ten minutes or longer, or several seizures that occur back-to-back with no period of consciousness in between seizures.

114. Elderly patients are more susceptible to heat loss because of their reduced circulation and compensatory mechanisms.

115. If possible, a patient with an evisceration should be placed supine with his or her knees bent to reduce pressure on the abdominal muscles.

116. A prolapsed cord is when the umbilical cord enters the birth canal before the baby's head.

117. To use an AED on a patient, the patient must be unconscious, unresponsive, apneic, have a clear airway, and be at least one year old.

118. A bandage should be placed directly over an open wound to control bleeding and protect from infection.

119. With a prolapsed cord, the blood flow may become occluded, depriving the baby of oxygen and nutrients.

120. Two minutes of CPR should be administered prior to administering a shock to ensure that the heart is adequately perfused.

121. Stable angina is characterized by chest pain that is of coronary origin that is usually relieved by sitting down, resting, and administering nitroglycerine. Unstable angina is characterized by similar chest pain of coronary origin that is produced by fewer stimuli than that of stable angina. The pain is not relieved by rest, nitroglycerine, etc.

122. Positional asphyxia is suffocation that occurs when a patient is restrained improperly, restricting the neck, chest wall, or diaphragm.

123. When interviewing a pregnant patient, it is important to ask the patient's previous birth history, including the number of live births. Typically, the more live births, the faster the labor process will occur. Other questions should include (1) time between contractions, (2) length of contractions, (3) presence of a mucous or watery discharge, and (4) if the patient has an urge to bear down or feels like they need to make a bowel movement.

124. Lay people frequently refer to the amniotic sac as the "bag of waters."

125. Penetrating trauma to the chest wall is frequently referred to as an "open pneumothorax." This should be treated with an occlusive dressing to prevent air from entering the chest cavity. If there is evidence that it is a sucking chest wound, then a three-side dressing should be applied.

126. If signs and symptoms of a tension pneumothorax develop after you have sealed the open chest, ensure that a three-sided dressing is in place to assist with relieving the pressure. One can also lift up a side of the dressing in a process known as "burping the dressing."

127. The first emergency person to arrive on scene should establish command. If needed, command can then be passed to more qualified responders as they arrive on scene.

128. End-tidal carbon dioxide detectors measure the amount of exhaled carbon dioxide from a patient.

129. If an IV is not flowing properly, perform the following steps: (1) Ensure that there are no signs of infiltration at the site of the IV; (2) Check to make sure that all clamps are open; (3) Check to see if any of the IV tubing is kinked; (4) Check to see if the IV is positional; (5) Drop the IV bag below the site of the IV and assess for blood return in the tubing; and (6) If there are any doubts as to the functionality of the IV, turn off the fluid and remove the IV.

130. If a conscious pregnant patient is choking, place two hands in the center of the chest and compress inward. The patient should not receive compressions to the abdomen.

131. The anatomical term *medial* refers to placement toward the midline of the body.

132. *Proper body mechanics* refers to the proper use of your body when lifting or moving objects so that injury will not occur.

133. Three types of suction units that may be used in the field are electric, manually operated, and oxygen powered.

134. Nasopharyngeal airways are contraindicated in patients with significant facial trauma because the airway may pass into the cranium or a sinus cavity if fractures are present.

135. Breath sounds should be auscultated on the upper and lower chest and back and at the midaxillary line.

136. When assessing skin, assess moisture, temperature, and color.

137. In a dark-skinned patient, the oral mucosa and nail bed are good places to assess normal skin color.

138. When a patient presents a hip fracture, you may notice shortening and rotation of the lower extremity of the affected hip.

139. When assessing the neck of a patient who has sustained a traumatic injury, inspection should include looking for tracheal deviation, jugular vein distension, and crepitus.

140. Subcutaneous emphysema is a crackling sound or sensation that is caused by air trapped underneath the skin.

141. Ongoing assessments should be performed on all patients to determine if the treatments have been effective, find any changes that may occur in the patients' conditions, and identify any other injuries or illnesses that may have been overlooked during the initial assessments.

142. If a patient is unconscious or unable to swallow, oral glucose must not be administered.

143. A febrile seizure is a seizure caused by a rapid increase in body temperature. It is usually associated with an infection.

144. When a patient is experiencing a seizure, perform a scene size-up, take body substance isolation precautions, protect the patient from injuring him- or herself by moving objects that he or she may strike or objects that pose a threat to his or her safety, and place something soft beneath the patient's head, if able to do so. Apply oxygen via non-rebreather mask, have suction readily available, and prepare to transport.

145. The phase that immediately follows a seizure in which the patient may continue to be unresponsive or have an altered level of consciousness is called the *postictal phase.*

146. Signs and symptoms of an envenomation include swelling, pain, bite marks, chills, weakness, nausea, vomiting, fever, dizziness, tightness in the chest, and shortness of breath.

147. When considering what medication to administer to a patient, the six things that you must know include the correct patient, the actions, the dose, the indications, the contraindications, and the route of the drug.

148. Some medications that an EMT may assist administering include aspirin, albuterol inhaler or nebulizer, epinephrine auto injector, nitroglycerine, oral glucose, and oxygen.

149. Common causes of shock in a pediatric patient are vomiting, trauma, diarrhea, blood loss, and infection.

150. Epistaxis is a nosebleed.

13 ▶ EMT PRACTICAL SKILLS EXAM

CHAPTER SUMMARY

This chapter presents the National Registry's EMT practical skills examination, which is used by many states and forms the basis for the practical exam in many other states. Being familiar with what will be expected of you—and knowing how the practical exam is scored—will help your self-confidence when you take the practical exam.

During your EMT training, you practiced various techniques and skills under a variety of conditions. But during a practical examination for certification, conditions have to be standardized as much as possible. The procedural guidelines that your examiners will be following will be sequential and often stringent. You have to do things in a particular order, just as you are told. This means that testing can be stressful. Proper preparation can help you overcome this stress.

The National Registry of Emergency Medical Technicians (NREMT) requires successful completion of a state-approved practical examination that meets the NREMT's minimum standards. The following ten skills are tested because they are directly related to the potential loss of life or limb.

1. Patient Assessment/Management—Trauma
2. Patient Assessment/Management—Medical
3. Bag-Valve-Mask Ventilation of an Apneic Adult Patient
4. Oxygen Administration by Non-rebreather Mask
5. Cardiac Arrest Management/AED
6. Spinal Immobilization (Supine Patient)
7. Spinal Immobilization (Seated Patient)
8. Bleeding Control/Shock Management
9. Long Bone Immobilization
10. Joint Immobilizationt

The National Registry developed a sample practical examination to help states develop their EMT practical exam. Many states have adopted this sample exam as their skills certification examination. Whether your state uses the NREMT exam or has developed its own EMT skills exam, the NREMT exam that follows will help you prepare for your practical examination. *However, you should become familiar with your state's examination, local scope of practice, and treatment protocols before you take the exam.*

The skills examination consists of six stations. Five of these stations are mandatory stations, and one is a random skill station. The stations and time limits are listed in the table on this page.

NREMT PRACTICAL SKILLS EXAM		
STATION	**SKILLS TESTED**	**TIME**
Station 1	Patient Assessment/Management—Trauma	10 minutes
Station 2	Patient Assessment/Management—Medical	15 minutes
Station 3	Bag-Valve-Mask Ventilation of an Apneic Adult Patient	5 minutes
Station 4	Oxygen Administration by Non-rebreather Mask	5 minutes
Station 5	Cardiac Arrest Management/AED	10 minutes
Station 6	Spinal Immobilization – Supine Patient	10 minutes
Station 7	Random Skill:	10 minutes
	Spinal Immobilization – Seated Patient	10 minutes
	Bleeding Control/Shock Management	10 minutes
	Long Bone Immobilization	5 minutes
	Joint Immobilization	5 minutes

You will not be told which random skill you will be tested on before the examination. Many examiners will have you blindly select from skills listed on separate cards, or the coordinator may select one skill to administer to all candidates.

This chapter contains the NREMT sample practical examination and the instruction to the candidates. Generally, you can fail up to three skills and retest those skills on the same day. Retests are proctored by a different examiner. Please refer to Candidate General Instructions starting on page 278 for more detailed information.

It may be helpful to the examiner during the examination process if you talk aloud while performing each skill. The examiner can then not only see what you are doing, but he or she can also hear what you are thinking as you go through the process. This might also help you stay on track during the skills exam, as it might jog your memory of a missing or out-of-sequence step.

Instructions for each station are listed, along with the minimum score for each station. In addition,

failure to perform critical criteria, listed at the bottom of each skill-assessment sheet, constitutes failure of that station. All the necessary equipment will be provided for you at each station. You must follow proper body substance isolation procedures for every skill.

To access and download the actual NREMT Skill Sheets for the purposes of administering or practicing an NREMT equivalent psychomotor exam, visit www.nremt.org/nremt/about/psychomotor_exam_emt.asp.

Before you begin each station, ask any questions that you have; you will not be permitted to ask questions during the assessment. Remember, good communication and critical-thinking skills are vital to successfully completing any practical examination.

Remember this: "Practice makes perfect" applies perfectly to the skills exam portion of any EMT testing process. The more times you can rehearse these skills, the more comfortable you will be when performing them in front of an examiner. This translates directly to the field setting, where you can be confident that your skills will be competent when the patient needs them the most!

EMT
Practical Examination

Candidate General Instructions

Welcome to the EMT practical examination. I'm *name and title*. By successfully completing this examination process and receiving subsequent certification, you will have proven to yourself and the medical community that you have achieved the level of competency assuring the public receives quality prehospital care.

I will now read the roster, for attendance purposes, before we begin the orientation. Please identify yourself when your name is called.

The skill station examiners utilized today were selected because of their expertise in the particular skill station. Skill station examiners observe and record your expected appropriate actions. They record your performance in relationship to the criteria listed on the evaluation instrument.

The skill station examiner will call you into the station when it is prepared for testing. No candidate, at any time, is permitted to remain in the testing area while waiting for his or her next station. You must wait outside the testing area until the station is open and you are called. You are not permitted to take any books, pamphlets, brochures, or other study materials into the station. You are not permitted to make any copies or recordings of any station. The skill station examiner will greet you as you enter the skill station. The examiner will ask your name. Please assist him or her in spelling your name so that your results may be reported accurately. Each skill station examiner will then read aloud "Instructions to the Candidate" exactly as printed on the instruction provided to him or her by the examination coordinator. The information is read to each candidate in the same manner to ensure consistency and fairness.

Please pay close attention to the instructions, as they correspond to dispatch information you might receive on a similar emergency call and give you valuable information on what will be expected of you during the skill station. The skill station examiner will offer to repeat the instructions and will ask you if the instructions were understood. Do not ask for additional information. Candidates sometimes complain that skill station examiners are abrupt, cold, or appear unfriendly. No one is here to add to the stress and anxiety you may already feel. It is important to understand that the examiners have been told they must avoid casual conversation with candidates. This is necessary to assure fair and equal treatment of all candidates throughout the examination. We have instructed the skill station examiners not to indicate to you, in any way, a judgment regarding your performance in the skill station. Do not interpret any of the examiner's remarks as an indication of your overall performance. Please recognize the skill station examiner's attitude as professional and objective, and simply perform the skills to the best of your ability.

Each skill station is supplied with several types of equipment for your selection. You will be given time at the beginning of the skill station to survey and select the equipment necessary for the appropriate management of the patient. Do not feel obligated to use all the equipment. If you brought any of your own equipment, I must inspect and approve it before you can enter the skill station.

As you progress through the practical examination, each skill station examiner will be observing and recording your performance. Do not let his or her documentation practices influence your performance in the station.

If the station has an overall time limit, the examiner will inform you of this when reading the instructions. When you reach the time limit, the skill station examiner will instruct you to stop your performance. However, if you complete the station before the allotted time, inform the examiner that you are finished. You may be asked to remove equipment from the patient before leaving the skill station.

You are not permitted to discuss any specific details of any station with each other at any time. Please be courteous to the candidates who are testing by keeping all excess noise to a minimum. Be prompt in reporting to each station so that we may complete this examination within a reasonable time period.

Failure of three or fewer skill stations entitles you to a same-day retest of those skills failed. Failure of four or more skill stations constitutes a failure of the entire practical examination, requiring a retest of the entire practical examination. Failure of a same-day retest entitles you to a retest of those skills failed. This retest must be accomplished at a different site with a different examiner. Failure of the retest at the different site constitutes a complete failure of the practical examination, and you will be required to retest the entire practical examination.

The results of the examination are reported as pass/fail of the skill station. You will not receive a detailed critique of your performance on any skill. Please remember that today's examination is a formal verification process and was not designed to assist with teaching or learning. The purpose of this examination is to verify achievement of the minimal DOT competencies after the educational component has been completed. Identifying errors would be contrary to the principle of this type of examination and could result in the candidate "learning" the examination while still not being competent in the necessary skill. It is recommended that you contact your teaching institution for remedial training if you are unsuccessful in a skill station.

If you feel you have a complaint concerning the practical examination, a formal complaint procedure does exist. You must initiate any complaint with me today. Complaints will not be valid after today and will not be accepted if they are issued after you learn of your results or leave this site. You may file a complaint for only two reasons:

1. You feel you have been discriminated against. Any situation that can be documented in which you feel an unfair evaluation of your abilities occurred may be considered discriminatory.
2. There was an equipment problem or malfunction in your station.

If you feel either occurred, you must contact me immediately to initiate the complaint process. You must submit the complaint in writing. The examination coordinator and the medical director will review your concerns.

I am here today to assure you that fair, objective, and impartial evaluations occur in accordance with the guidelines contained in this guide. If you have any concerns, notify me immediately to discuss your concerns. I will be visiting all skill stations throughout the examination to verify adherence to these guidelines. Please remember that if you do not voice your concerns or complaints today before you leave this site or before I inform you of your results, your complaints will not be accepted.

The skill station examiner does not know or play a role in the establishment of pass/fail criteria, but he or she is merely an observer and recorder of your actions in the skill station. This is an examination experience, not a teaching or learning experience.

Does anyone have any questions concerning the practical examination at this time?

Points to Remember

1. Follow instructions from the staff.
2. During the examination, move only to areas directed by the staff.
3. Give your name as you arrive at each station.
4. Listen carefully as the testing scenario is explained at each station.
5. Ask questions if the instructions are not clear.
6. During the examination, do not talk about the examination with anyone other than the skill station examiner, programmed patient, and when applicable, the EMT assistant.
7. Be aware of the time limit, but do not sacrifice quality performance for speed.
8. Equipment will be provided. Select and use only what is necessary to care for your patient adequately.

Patient Assessment/Management—Trauma

Instructions to the Candidate

Minimum Score: 33

This station is designed to test your ability to perform a patient assessment of a victim of multisystems trauma and "voice" treat all conditions and injuries discovered. You must conduct your assessment as you would in the field, including communicating with your patient. You may remove the patient's clothing down to shorts or swimsuit if you feel it is necessary. As you conduct your assessment, you should state everything you are assessing. Clinical information not obtainable by visual or physical inspection will be given to you after you demonstrate how you would normally gain that information. You may assume that you have two EMTs working with you and that they are correctly carrying out the verbal treatments you indicate. You have ten minutes to complete this skill station. Do you have any questions?

Sample Trauma Scenario

The following is an example of an acceptable scenario for this station. It is not intended to be the only possible scenario for this station. Variations of the scenario are possible and should be used to reduce the possibility of future candidates knowing the scenario before entering the station. If the scenario is changed, the following four guidelines must be used.

1. A clearly defined mechanism of injury must be included. The mechanism of injury must indicate the need for the candidate to perform a rapid trauma assessment.
2. There must be a minimum of an airway, breathing, and circulatory problem.
3. There must be an additional associated soft-tissue or musculoskeletal injury.
4. Vital signs must be given for the initial check and one recheck.

Trauma Situation #1: Patient Assessment/Management

Mechanism of Injury

You are called to the scene of a motor vehicle crash, where you find a victim who was thrown from a car. You find severe damage to the front end of the car. The victim is found lying in a field 30 feet from the upright car.

Injuries

The patient will present with the following injuries. All injuries will be moulaged. Each examiner should program the patient to respond appropriately throughout the assessment and assure the victim has read the "Instructions to Simulated Trauma Victim" that have been provided.

1. unresponsive
2. left side flail chest
3. decreased breath sounds, left side
4. cool, clammy skin; no distal pulses
5. distended abdomen
6. pupils equal
7. neck veins flat
8. pelvis stable
9. open injury of the left femur with capillary bleeding

Vital Signs

1. Initial vital signs—BP, 72/60; P, 140; RR, 28
2. Upon recheck—if appropriate treatment: BP, 86/74; P, 120; RR, 22
3. Upon recheck—if inappropriate treatment: BP, 64/48; P, 138; RR, 44

Patient Assessment/ Management—Medical

Instructions to the Candidate

Minimum Score: 33

This station is designed to test your ability to perform a patient assessment of a patient with a chief complaint of a medical nature and "voice" treat all conditions discovered. You must conduct your assessment as you would in the field, including communicating with your patient. You may remove the patient's clothing down to shorts or swimsuit if you feel it is necessary. As you conduct your assessment, you should state everything you are assessing. Clinical information not obtainable by visual or physical inspection will be given to you after you demonstrate how you would normally gain that information. You may assume that you have two EMTs working with you and that they are correctly carrying out the verbal treatments you indicate. You have 15 minutes to complete this skill station. Do you have any questions?

When assessing the signs and symptoms of the patient, the candidate must gather the appropriate information by asking the questions listed on the skill sheet.

Each candidate is required to complete a full patient assessment. The candidate choosing to transport the victim immediately after the initial assessment must be instructed to continue the focused history, physical examination, and ongoing assessment en route to the hospital.

NOTE: The preferred method to evaluate a candidate is to write the exact sequence the candidate follows during the station as it is performed. You may then use this documentation to fill out the evaluation instrument after the candidate completes the station. This documentation may then be used to validate the score on the evaluation instrument if questions arise later.

Sample Medical Scenarios

ALTERED MENTAL STATUS

When you arrive on the scene, you meet a 37-year-old male who says his wife is a diabetic and isn't acting normally.

Initial Assessment

Chief Complaint:	"My wife just isn't acting right. I can't get her to stay awake. She only opens her eyes, then goes right back to sleep."
Apparent Life Threats:	Depressed central nervous system, respiratory compromise
Level of Responsiveness:	Opens eyes in response to being shaken
Airway:	Patent
Breathing:	14 and shallow
Circulation:	120 and weak
Transport Decision:	Immediate

Focused History and Physical Examination

Description of Episode:	"My wife took her insulin this morning like any other morning, but she has had the flu and has been vomiting."
Onset:	"It happened so quickly. She was just talking to me and then she just went to sleep. I haven't really been able to wake her up since."
Duration:	"She's been this way for about 15 minutes now. I called you right away. I was really scared."
Associated Symptoms:	"The only thing that I can think of is that she was vomiting last night and this morning."
Evidence of Trauma:	"She didn't fall. She was just sitting on the couch and fell asleep. I haven't tried to move her."

Interventions:	"I haven't done anything but call you guys. I know she took her insulin this morning."
Seizures:	None
Fever:	Low-grade fever
Allergies:	Penicillin
Medications:	Insulin
Past Medical History:	Insulin-dependent diabetic since 21 years of age
Last Meal:	"My wife ate breakfast this morning."
Events Leading to Illness:	"My wife has had the flu and been vomiting for the past 24 hours."
Focused Physical Examination:	Complete a rapid assessment to rule out trauma.
Vitals:	RR, 14; P, 120; BP, 110/72

ALLERGIC REACTION

You arrive to find a 37-year-old male who reports eating cookies he purchased at a bake sale. He has audible wheezing and is scratching red, blotchy areas on his abdomen, chest, and arms.

Initial Assessment

Chief Complaint:	"I'm having an allergic reaction to those cookies I ate."
Apparent Life Threats:	Respiratory and circulatory compromise
Level of Responsiveness:	Awake, very anxious, and restless
Airway:	Patent
Breathing:	26, wheezing, and deep
Circulation:	No bleeding, pulse 120 and weak, cold and clammy skin
Transport Decision:	Immediate

Focused History and Physical Examination

History of Allergies: "Yes. I'm allergic to peanuts."

When Ingested: "I ate cookies about 20 minutes ago and began itching all over about five minutes later."

How Much Ingested: "I ate only two cookies."

Effects: "I'm having trouble breathing, and I feel lightheaded and dizzy."

Progression: "My wheezing is worse. Now I'm sweating really badly."

Interventions: "I have my epi-pen upstairs, but I'm afraid to stick myself."

Allergies: Peanuts and penicillin

Medications: None

Past Medical History: "I had to spend two days in the hospital the last time this happened."

Last Meal: "The last thing I ate were those cookies."

Events Leading to Illness: "None, except I ate those cookies."

Focused Physical Examination: Not indicated (award point)

Vitals: RR, 26; P, 120; BP, 90/60

POISONING/OVERDOSE

You arrive on the scene where a 3-year-old female is sitting on her mother's lap. The child appears very sleepy and doesn't look at you as you approach.

Initial Assessment

Chief Complaint: "I think my baby has swallowed some of my sleeping pills. Please don't let her die!"

Apparent Life Threats: Depressed central nervous system and respiratory compromise

Level of Responsiveness: Responds slowly to verbal commands

Airway: Patent

Breathing: 18 and deep

Circulation: 120 and strong

Transport Decision: Immediate

Focused History and Physical Examination

Substance: "My baby took sleeping pills. I don't know what kind they are. They just help me sleep at night."

When Ingested: "I think she must have got them about an hour ago when I was in the shower. Her older sister was supposed to be watching her."

How Much Ingested: "My prescription was almost empty. There couldn't have been more than four or five pills left. Now they're all gone. Please do something."

Effects: "She just isn't acting like herself. She's usually running around and getting into everything."

Allergies: None

Medications: None

Past Medical History: None

Last Meal: "She ate breakfast this morning."

Events Leading to Illness: "She just swallowed the pills."

Focused Physical Examination: Complete a rapid trauma assessment to rule out trauma.

Vitals: RR, 18; P, 120; BP, 90/64

ENVIRONMENTAL EMERGENCIES

You arrive on the scene as rescuers are pulling a 16-year-old female from an ice-covered creek. The teenager has been moved out of the creek onto dry land, is completely soaked, and appears drowsy.

Initial Assessment

Chief Complaint:	"I saw something in the water below the ice. When I tried to get it out, the ice broke."
Apparent Life Threats:	Generalized hypothermia
Level of Responsiveness:	Responsive, but slow to speak
Airway:	Patent
Breathing:	26 and shallow
Circulation:	No bleeding; pulse, 110 and strong; pale, wet skin still covered in wet clothing
Transport Decision:	Immediate

Focused History and Physical Examination

Source:	"I fell in the creek when the ice broke. I tried to get out, but the current was too strong."
Environment:	"The water was up to my neck. I could stand up, but I couldn't get out of the water."
Duration:	"I think I was in the water for ten minutes before they pulled me out. It felt like an hour."
Loss of Consciousness:	"I feel sick, but I never passed out."
Effects:	Lowered body temperature, slow speech patterns, "I can't stop shivering."
Allergies:	None
Medications:	None

Past Medical History:	None
Last Meal:	"I ate lunch at school three hours ago."
Events Leading to Illness:	"I thought the ice would hold me."
Focused Physical Examination:	Complete a rapid assessment to rule out trauma.
Vitals:	RR, 26; P, 110 and strong; BP, 120/80

OBSTETRICS

You arrive on the scene where a 26-year-old female is lying on the couch saying, "The baby is coming and the pain is killing me!"

Initial Assessment

Chief Complaint:	"I'm nine months pregnant and the baby is coming soon."
Apparent Life Threats:	None
Level of Responsiveness:	Awake and alert
Airway:	Patent
Breathing:	Panting, rapid breathing during contractions
Circulation:	No bleeding, pulse 120, skin is pale
Transport Decision:	Unknown

Focused History and Physical Examination

Are You Pregnant:	See chief complaint (award point if mentioned in general impression).
How Long Pregnant:	See chief complaint (award point if mentioned in general impression).

Pain or Contractions:	"My pain is every two to three minutes, and it lasts two to three minutes."	Airway:	Patent
		Breathing:	16 and effortless
		Circulation:	No bleeding, pulse 100, warm skin, and red nose
Bleeding or Discharge:	None	Transport Decision:	Delayed

Focused History and Physical Examination

Do You Feel the Need to Push:	"Yes, every time the pain begins."	How Do You Feel:	"I'm a little sick, otherwise, I just want to go to sleep."
Crowning:	Present (award point if identified in focused physical exam)	Suicidal Tendencies:	"No, I ain't going to kill myself."
Allergies:	None	Threat to Others:	"Hey man, I ain't never hurt anyone in my life."
Medications:	None	Is There a Medical Problem:	"My wife says I'm an alcoholic, but what does she know?"
Past Medical History:	"This is my third baby."		
Last Meal:	"I ate breakfast today."	Interventions:	"Yeah, I took three aspirins because I know I'm going to have one heck of a headache in the morning."
Events Leading to Illness:	"The contractions started a few hours ago and have not stopped."		
		Allergies:	None
Focused Physical Examination:	Assess for crowning, bleeding, and discharge.	Medications:	None
		Past Medical History:	"I've been in the hospital four times with those DTs."
Vitals:	RR, 40 during contractions; P, 120; BP, 140/80	Last Meal:	"Man, I haven't eaten since yesterday."

BEHAVIORAL

You arrive on the scene, where you find a 45-year-old male in the custody of the police. He is unable to stand and smells of beer. He appears to be dirty, and you notice numerous rips and tears in his clothes.

Events Leading to Illness:	"I don't care what these cops say, I didn't fall down. I was just taking a nap before going home."
Focused Physical Examination:	Complete a rapid assessment to rule out trauma.
Vitals:	RR, 16; P, 100; BP, 90/60

Initial Assessment

Chief Complaint:	"Nothing is wrong with me except these cops won't leave me alone. I only drank two beers."
Apparent Life Threats:	None
Level of Responsiveness:	Responds slowly with slurred speech to verbal questions

Cardiac Arrest Management

Instructions to the Candidate

Minimum Score: 14

This station is designed to test your ability to manage a prehospital cardiac arrest by integrating CPR skills, defibrillation, airway adjuncts, and patient/scene management skills. There will be an EMT assistant in this station. The EMT assistant will only do as you instruct him or her. As you arrive on the scene, you will encounter a patient in cardiac arrest. A first responder will be present performing single-rescuer CPR. You must immediately establish control of the scene and begin resuscitation of the patient with an AED. At the appropriate time, the patient's airway must be controlled, and you must ventilate or direct the ventilation of the patient using adjunctive equipment. You may use any of the supplies available in this room. You have ten minutes to complete this skill station. Do you have any questions?

Airway, Oxygen, Ventilation Skills/Bag Valve Mask— Apneic with Pulse

Instructions to the Candidate

Minimum Score: 13

This station is designed to test your ability to ventilate a patient using a bag valve mask. As you enter the station, you will find an apneic patient with a palpable central pulse. There are no bystanders, and artificial ventilation has not been initiated. The only patient management required is airway management and ventilatory support. You must initially ventilate the patient for a minimum of 30 seconds. You will be evaluated on the appropriateness of ventilator volumes. I will then inform you that a second rescuer has arrived and will instruct you that you must control the airway and the mask seal while the second rescuer provides ventilation. You may use only the equipment available in this room. You have five minutes to complete this station. Do you have any questions?

Spinal Immobilization— Supine Patient

Instructions to the Candidate

Minimum Score: 11

This station is designed to test your ability to provide spinal immobilization on a patient using a long spine immobilization device. You arrive on the scene with an EMT assistant. The assistant EMT has completed the scene size-up as well as the initial assessment, and no critical condition was found that would require intervention. For the purpose of this testing station, the patient's vital signs remain stable. You are required to treat the specific problem of an unstable spine using a long spine immobilization device. When moving the patient to the device, you should use the help of the assistant EMT and the evaluator. The assistant EMT should control the head and cervical spine of the patient while you and the evaluator move the patient to the immobilization device. You are responsible for the direction and subsequent action of the EMT assistant. You may use any equipment available in this room. You have ten minutes to complete this skill station. Do you have any questions?

Spinal Immobilization– Seated Patient

Instructions to the Candidate

Minimum Score: 9

This station is designed to test your ability to provide spinal immobilization of a patient using a half-spine immobilization device. You and an EMT assistant arrive on the scene of an automobile crash. The scene is safe, and there is only one patient. The assistant EMT has completed the initial assessment, and no critical condition requiring intervention was found. For the purpose of this station, the patient's vital signs remain stable. You are required to treat the specific, isolated problem of an unstable spine using a half-spine immobilization device. You are responsible for the direction and subsequent actions of the EMT assistant. Transferring and immobilizing the patient to the long spine board should be accomplished verbally. You have ten minutes to complete this skill station. Do you have any questions?

Immobilization Skills— Long Bone

Instructions to the Candidate

Minimum Score: 8

This station is designed to test your ability to properly immobilize a closed, nonangulated long bone injury. You are required to treat only the specific, isolated injury to the extremity. The scene size-up and initial assessment have been completed, and during the focused assessment, a closed, nonangulated injury of the _____ (radius, ulna, tibia, fibula) was detected. Ongoing assessment of the patient's airway, breathing, and central circulation is not necessary. You may use any equipment available in this room. You have five minutes to complete this skill station. Do you have any questions?

Immobilization Skills— Joint Injury

Instructions to the Candidate

Minimum Score: 7

This station is designed to test your ability to properly immobilize a noncomplicated shoulder injury. You are required to treat only the specific, isolated injury to the shoulder. The scene size-up and initial assessment have been accomplished on the victim, and during the focused assessment, a shoulder injury was detected. Ongoing assessment of the patient's airway, breathing, and central circulation is not necessary. You may use any equipment available in this room. You have five minutes to complete this skill station. Do you have any questions?

Bleeding Control/Shock Management

Instructions to the Candidate

Minimum Score: 5

This station is designed to test your ability to control hemorrhage. This is a scenario-based testing station. As you progress throughout the scenario, you will be given various signs and symptoms appropriate for the patient's condition. You will be required to manage the patient based on these signs and symptoms. A scenario will be read aloud to you, and you will be given an opportunity to ask clarifying questions about the scenario; however, you will not receive answers to any questions about the actual steps of the procedures to be performed. You may use any of the supplies and equipment available in this room. You have ten minutes to complete this skill station. Do you have any questions?

Scenario (Sample) Bleeding Control/ Shock Management

You respond to a stabbing and find a 25-year-old male victim. Upon examination, you find a two-inch stab wound to the inside of the right arm at the anterior elbow crease (antecubital fascia). Bright-red blood is spurting from the wound. The scene is safe, and the patient is responsive and alert. His airway is open, and he is breathing adequately. Do you have any questions?

Airway, Oxygen, Ventilation Skills/Supplemental Oxygen Administration

Instructions to the Candidate

Minimum Score: 8

This station is designed to test your ability to correctly assemble the equipment needed to administer supplemental oxygen in the prehospital setting. This is an isolated skills test. You will be required to assemble an oxygen tank and a regulator and administer oxygen to a patient using a nonrebreather mask. You may use only the equipment available in this room. You have five minutes to complete this station. Do you have any questions?

STATE CERTIFICATION REQUIREMENTS

CHAPTER SUMMARY

This chapter outlines EMT certification requirements for all 50 states, the District of Columbia, Puerto Rico, and the U.S. Virgin Islands. It also lists state EMS agencies you can contact for more information about certification requirements.

The table on pages 296–298 shows some of the minimum requirements you must meet to be certified as an EMT in the 50 states, the District of Columbia, Puerto Rico, and the U.S. Virgin Islands. The next few paragraphs explain the entries on the table.

You should know that some minimum requirements are standard and so are not listed on the table. For instance, you must be physically, mentally, and emotionally able to perform all the tasks of an EMT. Usually, you are required to have a high school diploma or GED before you begin training. You must have a clean criminal record. And, of course, you must successfully complete an EMT training program that meets the standards set by the U.S. Department of Transportation.

The minimum age for most states and territories is 18 years old; however, you should check age specifications with your local EMS agency. Some states allow you to begin a training program before you reach this minimum age, often requiring a parent or guardian's permission.

The first entry, Minimum Hours of Training, lists the number of hours this state considers sufficient for EMT training. Courses that meet the requirements will typically cover both the DOT/NHTSA-National EMS Education Standards and locality-specific protocols. Be sure to check with the licensing agency in the area where you intend to work to make sure your course meets the requirements. Note that in some states, such as California, the locality-specific requirements are just that: The requirements for EMT certification in Los Angeles differ from the requirements in San Diego and Santa Clara. You should also check with your licensing agency to see how much time you have between finishing your training course and fulfilling all the other requirements for certification—including passing the written and practical exams.

States use their own written and practical skills exams, exams from the National Registry of EMTs, or a combination of both. The entry under Training Accepted will be "State," meaning the state has its own exam; "NREMT" for National Registry; or "state and NREMT" indicating a combination of both exams. Even when the state has its own exam, you'll find it's pretty similar to the National Registry exam, and therefore to the exams in this book (except for state- or locality-specific scopes of practice and protocols). After all, the federal government mandates the curriculum of EMT courses nationwide. You can expect exams based on the same curriculum to be similar.

Some states' exams will require you to go through *their* certification processes; others will accept the National Registry Exams, if you are already certified by the NREMT. Similarly, some states will accept your certification from out of state, some will accept it if you take their exam, and some will require that you be certified through the National Registry if you are transfer-

ring from another state. In most cases, a state that accepts out-of-state certification will insist that your training program and your exam meet or exceed its standards. Some states have additional certification requirements for transferring EMTs, such as background investigation, being a state resident, being employed with an EMS agency in that state, or taking a refresher course. If you are certified in another state, you will need to show proof of certification when applying in a different state. Some states have what is known as "legal recognition," which means they will recognize and accept your training for a limited time period, often one year. This is similar to a temporary certification. During this period of legal recognition, you apply for official certification and fulfill the necessary requirements. Once the process is complete, your certification will be good for as long as that state allows. You should check with the appropriate state's EMS office for more detail.

The last column, Recertification, indicates the number of years from your initial certification to the time when you will have to be recertified. Recertification usually requires a given number of hours of continuing education, demonstration of your continuing ability to perform the necessary skills, or both—but you'll find out all about that once you're certified in the first place.

STATE	MINIMUM HOURS OF TRAINING	TRAINING ACCEPTED	RECERTIFICATION
Alabama	180	NREMT	2 years
Alaska	120	State	2 years
Arizona	130	State and NREMT	2 years
Arkansas	120	NREMT	2 years
California	160	NREMT	2 years
Colorado	250	NREMT	3 years
Connecticut	150	NREMT	2 years

STATE	MINIMUM HOURS OF TRAINING	TRAINING ACCEPTED	RECERTIFICATION
Delaware	150	NREMT	2 years
District of Columbia	NEMSES[1]	NREMT	2 years
Florida	250	NREMT	2 years
Georgia	NEMSES[1]	NREMT	2 years
Hawaii	315	NREMT	2 years
Idaho	NEMSES[1]	NREMT	3 years
Illinois	NEMSES[1]	State and NREMT	4 years
Indiana	160	State and NREMT	2 years
Iowa	NEMSES[1]	NREMT	2 years
Kansas	NEMSES[1]	NREMT	2 years
Kentucky	NEMSES[1]	NREMT	2 years
Louisiana	NEMSES[1]	NREMT	2 years
Maine	NEMSES[1]	NREMT	3 years
Maryland	165	State	3 years
Massachusetts	110	NREMT	2 years
Michigan	194	NREMT	3 years
Minnesota	NEMSIS[1]	NREMT	2 years[2]
Mississippi	183	NREMT	2 years
Missouri	110	NREMT	5 years
Montana	NEMSIS[1]	State and NREMT	2 years
Nebraska	NEMSIS[1]	NREMT	2 years
Nevada	NEMSIS[1]	NREMT	2 years
New Hampshire	NEMSIS[1]	NREMT	2 years
New Jersey	NREMT	NREMT	3 years
New Mexico	160	NREMT	2 years
New York	NEMSIS[1]	State	3 years
North Carolina	169	State	4 years
North Dakota	150	NREMT	2 years

STATE	MINIMUM HOURS OF TRAINING	TRAINING ACCEPTED	RECERTIFICATION
Ohio	150	NREMT	3 years
Oklahoma	NEMSIS[1]	NREMT	2 years
Oregon	NEMSIS[1]	NREMT	2 years
Pennsylvania	NEMSIS[1]	NREMT	3 years
Rhode Island	130	NREMT	2 years[3]
South Carolina	200	NREMT	3 years
South Dakota	NEMSES[1]	NREMT	2 years
Tennessee	NEMSES[1]	NREMT	2 years
Texas	140	State	4 years
Utah	NEMSES[1]	State	3 years
Vermont	NEMSES[1]	State and NREMT	2 years
Virginia	154	State	4 years
Washington	NEMSES[1]	State	3 years
Wisconsin	NEMSES[1]	NREMT	2 years
Wyoming	200	State	2 years
Puerto Rico			
U.S. Virgin Islands	NEMSES[1]	NREMT	2 years
N. Marianna Islands	110[4]	State and NREMT	2 years
American Samoa	300	State[5]	2 years
Guam	180	NREMT	2 years

[1] The state mandates the initial EMT course follow the National EMS Education Standards (NEMSES), but does not mandate a minimum course length. The National Education Standards recommend a course length of between 150 and 190 hours including didactic, laboratory, clinical, and field instruction.

[2] Minnesota certifications run from 27 months to 33 months depending on the date of initial certification.

[3] Rhode Island allows EMTs certified as EMT-Bs prior to January 2012 to maintain a 3-year certification period. All EMTs certified after January 2012 must maintain National Registry certification, so the renewal is every 2 years.

[4] The Northern Marianna Islands currently require 110 hours, but will be transitioning to NEMSES in the near future.

[5] Currently a local exam, but will be transitioning to the NREMT exam in the near future.

ADDITIONAL ONLINE PRACTICE

Using the codes below, you'll be able to log in and access additional online materials!

Your free online practice access code is:
FVE4WO36E2ME0N6PXE11
FVEO7Q2I3EDW5G13MJJ5

Follow these simple steps to redeem your codes:

- Go to **www.learningexpresshub.com/affiliate** and have your access codes handy.

If you're a new user:

- Click the **New user? Register here** button and complete the registration form to create your account and access your products.
- Be sure to enter your unique access codes only once. If you have multiple acess codes, you can enter them all—just use a comma to separate each code.
- The next time you visit, simply click the **Returning user? Sign in** button and enter your username and password.
- Do not re-enter previously redeemed access codes. Any products you previously accessed are saved in the **My Account** section on the site. Entering a previously redeemed access code will result in an error message.

If you're a returning user:

- Click the **Returning user? Sign in** button, enter your username and password, and click **Sign In**.
- You will automatically be brought to the **My Account** page to access your products.
- Do not re-enter previously redeemed access codes. Any products you previously accessed are saved in the **My Account** section on the site. Entering a previously redeemed access code will result in an error message.

If you're a returning user with new access codes:

- Click the **Returning user? Sign in** button, enter your username, password, and new access codes, and click **Sign In**.
- If you have multiple access codes, you can enter them all—just use a comma to separate each code.
- Do not re-enter previously redeemed access codes. Any products you previously accessed are saved in the **My Account** section on the site. Entering a previously redeemed access code will result in an error message.

If you have any questions, please contact LearningExpress Customer Support at LXHub@Learning ExpressHub.com. All inquiries will be responded to within a 24-hour period during our normal business hours: 9:00 A.M.–5:00 P.M. Eastern Time. Thank you!

NOTES